TWELVE YEARS OF NIGHT

ZWÖLF JAHRE NACHT

TWELVE YEARS OF NIGHT

ZWÖLF JAHRE NACHT

My way of life through the "Thousand-Year Reich"

Heinrich Lienau

(1883–1968)
(PRISONER #15735)

INTERPRETER IN THE POLITICAL SECTION OF CONCENTRATION CAMP SACHSENHAUSEN-ORANIENBURG

English Translation by Ingeborg Simonsen

Word Processing by Theodore Simonsen and Timothy Martin

Twelve Years of Night
Copyright © 2024 by Theodore H. Simonsen.

All rights reserved. No part of this publication may be reproduced, stored in a retrieval system, or transmitted, in any form or by any means, electronic, mechanical, photocopying, recording, or otherwise, without the prior written permission of the copyright owner.

Front Cover: German author Heinrich Lienau, prisoner #15735, in his zebra uniform. Image by Theodore H. Simonsen.
Back Cover: Lienau family picture in much better times. Image by Theodore H. Simonsen.
All interior images by Theodore H. Simonsen.

English translation from the original German by his daughter, Ingeborg Simonsen (1909–2004).
Book layout by his grandson, Theodore H. Simonsen.
Edited by Timothy A. Martin

Book design by The Troy Book Makers
Printed in the United States of America
The Troy Book Makers ♦ Troy, New York ♦ thetroybookmakers.com

ISBN: 978-1-61468-887-7

Zwölf Jahre Nacht

Mein Weg durch das „Tausendjährige Reich"

von

HEINRICH LIENAU

Dolmetscher in der politischen Abteilung des
Konzentrations-Lagers Sachsenhausen-Oranienburg
(Häftling 15 735)

VERLAG E. H. NIELSEN — FLENSBURG

Inside cover of the original German book *Zwölf Jahre Nacht*.

Contents

List of Figures viii

Forward xi

Preface 1

Introduction 5

Chapter 1: Resistance Movements Along the Border 9

Chapter 2: Hitler's Escape to Flensburg During the Röhm Affair ... 14

Chapter 3: Open Letter to Reichs-President Von Hindenburg 19

Chapter 4: The So-Called Four-Year Plan 27

Chapter 5: Göring's Fiasco In Iceland 33

Chapter 6: Hitler's Pirate Fleet 37

Chapter 7: Moving toward War 42

Chapter 8: Hitler's Inferno 48

Chapter 9: Weeks in Kiel 51

Chapter 10: Reception for New Arrivals 57

Chapter 11: Reasons for Being Brought Into Custody 70

Chapter 12: Tower A—Nothing New at This Station 95

Chapter 13: Sachsenhausen Living Conditions 105

Chapter 14: Potemkin Revisited 124

Chapter 15: The Brown Inquisition 140

Chapter 16: The Angel of Death Walks Through Sachsenhausen 156

Chapter 17: Swastika Pharaohs 177

Chapter 18: Resistance and Sabotage at Camp 194

Chapter 19: The Master Race Without Its Mask 210

Chapter 20: Talk Between the Barracks 233

Chapter 21: Dance of the Dead 255

Chapter 22: Chaos 268

Chapter 23: Hunger March on the Streets of Adolf Hitler 291

Chapter 24: Flensburg—The End of the Thousand-Year Reich . . . 307

Epilog 325

About the Author's Grandson 326

List of Figures

Inside cover of the original German book *Zwölf Jahre Nacht*..... v

German author Heinrich Lienau, prisoner #15735............. x

Figs. 1 & 2. Ingeborg Lienau's Weimar Republic Passport....... xii

Fig. 3. George and Ingeborg Simonsen's wedding picture....... xiii

Fig. 4. German author Heinrich Lienau, prisoner #15735...... xiv

Fig. 5. Danish 10 Øre pass................................... 10

Fig. 6. Göring's letterhead................................... 30

Fig. 7. Hitler's yacht *Grille* at Flensburg-Mürwik.............. 41

Fig. 8. Map of Nazi concentration camps..................... 47

Fig. 9. Heinrich Christian Lienau as inmate #15735........... 50

Fig. 10. Prisoner identity record............................. 75

Fig. 11. Petersen, who was supposed to be confined for the rest of his life, died of pneumonia....................82

Fig. 12. Nickolas Cordsen made the statement "Hitler is unfit to take care of the government," which was very unhealthy for him................................ 119

Fig. 13. Ticket for a good time. Girls were promised freedom after serving three to six months, but promises were never kept............................ 123

Fig. 14. Notes of a Russian melody.......................... 163

Fig. 15. My friend Emil Büge, the Spanish interpreter.......... 208

Fig. 16. Three powers flags. Label of the declaration made by the leaders of the three Allied nations: United States, Great Britain, and Soviet Russia. 283

Fig. 17. Himmler's last stop in Ausacker-Hüholz, Kreis, Flensburg. 311

Fig. 18. *The Last Chance* caricature (in Danish). 312

Fig. 19. *Patria*, the last place for the Dönitz Government (Reichsregierung) in Flensburg-Mürwik. Dönitz was arrested here. 314

Fig. 20. Lienau after the war, somewhat recovered. 325

German author Heinrich Lienau, prisoner #15735.

FORWARD

This book was originally written in German in 1946 by my grandfather (my Opa), Heinrich Lienau, a German citizen, when he was recuperating from his years of imprisonment in Sachsenhausen concentration camp near Berlin, Germany. Before WWII started there were several important matters that he did, which are not mentioned in the original German book, but in getting his only daughter and my future mother out of Germany. He put an ad in the Flensburg, Germany, newspaper that he wanted to give his daughter in marriage to an American of German heritage and having a Flensburg family. My other future grandfather read the advertisement and then the future grandfathers got together to set up a party where both of my future parents would "accidentally" meet and see what happens.

A birthday party for a relative was the official reason, the place was in a Mürwik restaurant party garden and the time was summer in 1933. Fortunately, for me, the young couple accidentally met, liked each other, and decided to get married in the United States. Attached is my future mother's Weimar Republic passport photo before Naziism took over Germany (Fig. 1, Fig. 2). She left Germany in 1934, George and Ingeborg were married in the United States, and I was born in 1936 (Fig. 3). Had this evacuation maneuver not been successful then I would not have been conceived and born. Curiously, Mürwik is the location of the German Naval Academy and where Nazi Germany surrendered in 1945. And so in conclusion my grandfather (Opa Lienau) is so strategically as well as biologically. My other grandfather (Opa Simonsen) came by ship to the United States in 1937 to see me and my parents. He returned to Germany and died the same year.

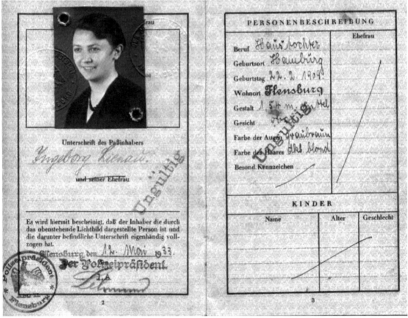

Figs. 1 & 2. Ingeborg Lienau's Weimar Republic Passport.

Fig. 3. George and Ingeborg Simonsen's wedding picture.

As a Social Democrat, journalist, and enemy of Nazism, Heinrich Lienau was already warning others through clandestine pamphlets and discreet conversations about the lies, crimes, and danger of the Nazis. In 1935 my grandfather (Opa Lienau) was arrested (Fig. 4). Once the war started in 1939, my mother had no contact at all with her parents because there was no longer any normal mail service between the United States and Germany. During those years of the Second World War, she anxiously waited for some word from her parents. Had she known how bad it really was at the time, she could not have rationally hoped for her father's survival. Although her mother Minna Lienau was not arrested, she had to endure those times as a second-class citizen. In 1945 my mother received a letter from Denmark from her father. It was from then on that she learned of his years in captivity.

My mother translated the book into English over the next 20 years on an intermittent basis. Her objective in doing this was to let the younger generation of her family and others know what those

Fig. 4. German author Heinrich Lienau, prisoner #15735.

terrible times were like from the perspective of her father. For many years my mother's manuscript consisted of a stack of typewritten onion-skinned sheets of paper waiting to be sent to a publisher. In the early 90s, I had the original translated manuscript processed into WordPerfect and several copies were passed around and read by family and friends. As a legacy of my grandfather's terrible experiences and my mother's desire to write a book, I have taken on the mission of completing this book and getting it published. Another reason for publishing this book is to remind the public of how bad the Nazi times were for people of many faiths and ethnicities. Also, it is sometimes said that those who forget the past are liable to repeat it.

One of the main objectives of the original book was to bring Sachsenhausen criminals to justice and to let the families of victims know what happened to their loved ones. That is why he named names and through a network of friends and acquaintances kept looking for former tormentors and victims. It goes without saying that with the passage of time all of the people mentioned in this book are no longer alive. I have a copy of the book Zwölf Jahre Nacht published by Verlag

E. H. Nielsen in 1949 in Flensburg, Germany to serve as a reference for questionable translated sentences. My grandfather died in 1968 at the age of 85. Sadly, many of his fellow prisoners never survived their time in Sachsenhausen concentration camp.

My mother completed the book's translation in 1992 and died in 2004 at the age of 94 with the hope that her work would eventually be published. The reader should be reminded that the time of these experiences is over 80 years ago when Germany was a Nazi terror state and speaking your mind could be your own death warrant. How he and his most trusted fellow inmates were able to do this will be revealed in the book. In 1956 my mother visited her parents again for the first time since her departure 23 years previously.

The reader of this book must wonder why does it have four authors named and why has it taken 78 years to come out in the English language. Whereas my mother, Ingeborg Simonsen, did a German to English translation by 1966 and I had completed a WordPerfect version by 1992, in the years since this job was stalled out. It took my friend, Timothy Martin, about a month to do the remaining work to prepare it for publishing. He did this using AI (artificial intelligence) skills not available years ago. I believe that it is a much more readable book with the last step. From here on the personal pronoun "I" is for Heinrich Christian Lienau.

Theodore H. Simonsen
Panama City, Florida
January 4, 2024

PREFACE

This book all started with little beginnings, a collection of memos, information, and documents that at first had been kept in a folder. Finally these notes became so numerous that it seemed worthwhile to convert it all into a book form. I think I can call it a book now, although in the beginning, I had in mind to write only a little booklet.

When Hitler appeared for the first time, in 1932, at the northern border of Germany to preach his Nazi Gospel at the Flensburg Stadium, I noticed the deception of the so-called National Socialism. His empty phrases and promises induced one of his Nazi writers to make the statement "Hurray, on this day the idea above all and everything has been victorious." Nazi Mayor Dr. Dr. Kracht (who insisted on both titles since he had two doctorates) wrote in his essay: "A new page in the city's history has been turned over; someday our grandsons are going to read it: May they do so with pride in their hearts." It turned out otherwise. The year 1945 saw the "Thousand-Year Reich" disappear into nothing at the street car terminal in Flensburg-Mürwik. After the overthrow of the Weimar Republic, the Gestapo took opponents of the Nazi regime to prisons and concentration camps by the thousands. I, myself, had not been overlooked and so I got my share of everything they had to offer. Many of the KZ (Konzentrationslager) inmates made their own notes; however, each one wrote only of his own experiences and saw only part of what really happened behind its walls. Not quite as many people were able to write down their experiences afterward or even withstand and survive these long years of terror. For the inmates, it was not only difficult to make any notes but merely to hide them, since an examination of personal belongings and clothing could be expected at any time. Anything that looked suspicious to the guards could be the doom of the inmate in whose possession it had been found. There was the constant danger of being killed on the spot or to be hung at the gallows after the evening roll call. Information about something a prisoner was not supposed to know could eventually mean a death sentence for him. Smuggling notes and letters out of the camp, even harmless ones, could be punished by having the victim tied to a post to then receive 25 lashes with a steel whip.

Beside, that there was a chance of being transferred to the penal colony, a fearsome place of torture within the camp. Not only were the S.S. (Schutzstaffel) guards constantly watching the inmates; even some of the inmates became double-crossers, and for the promise of some privilege they might inform on their own comrades and cause punishment or death at the gallows or in the gas chamber. One couldn't trust anybody without knowing him quite well for a long time. After a long and careful survey, the honest political enemies of the Nazi regime would make contact within the camp—very carefully, of course— before they would exchange their opinions and form illegal groups of opposition. In time, these activities became an underground movement within the camp. The ring of the old-fashioned political prisoners had to be kept quite close, and only a few of those men had a chance to get into a position that made it possible to get insight into some of the happenings which only members of the S.S. were supposed to know. As a rule, an inmate couldn't stay in a prominent position for very long, and without reason, he would be exchanged with someone else or taken to a different camp to prevent him from becoming too friendly or familiar with his surroundings. Among the "prominents" happened to be, for instance, employees in the registration offices, as well as in the bureaus for vital statistics, the employment offices, and also the Department for Political Prisoners. Here there were generally people employed who could speak several languages.

But before these political inmates were put into service as interpreters, they had to pass some examinations to test their general knowledge. They were also "sifted" by the camp's commandant and his assisting officers. Only after they had been regarded as reliable and trustworthy could these inmates be admitted into places that gave them some insight into what was really going on in a concentration camp. It was hot territory all right; the S.S. men were constantly spying and searching through the belongings of the inmates, confiscating anything that looked suspicious. After the first prisoners from Norway were admitted as newcomers, I was called into the political bureau to act as an interpreter. It was here where I met the consultant for Spanish-speaking inmates, Emil Büge. It didn't take long before we found confidence in each other. Since we soon recognized what an important place for getting information our new job was, we decided to keep track of everything—in writing, if possible—although we were aware of the fact that any written notes found among our belongings could mean the death sentence for us.

Nevertheless, our illegal activities had an uncertain future, since nobody knew how long the "protective custody" could last, and if we would eventually be free men again. Our most important question was, "What was the safest way to get our written notes out of this camp and where could we hide them?" Fate seemed to be with us. In this case, intelligence was stronger than the brutal force of the S.S.

Of course, we had to gamble with our lives, but we did win the battle. For the sake of human rights, we took the chance and, therefore, we were able to show the world what the name "Schutzhaftlager" really meant from our experience.

Besides being successful in smuggling important news and documents through the S.S. control, we also had a small group of our own people who understood the transmitting and receiving of messages by ham radio. We were sending and receiving. It never occurred to the camp commander or his men in charge that some of the inmates could build their own radios and secretly operate them.

The Nazi terror turned out to last for twelve years for the inmates in concentration camps, the German people as a nation, as well as for all the other countries which were overrun by Nazi hordes and stripped of their possessions. It appears that this long time, as well as the circumstances under which the opposition had to live and fight against Nazi oppression, was necessary for their accomplishment. Under the cover of darkness, which these twelve years meant to them, the enemies of the Nazi regime had a better chance to work for the common cause: Undermining the Nazi regime with all its terror.

After twelve gruesome years, it began to dawn rather slowly. And, while these early rays started to shine upon a new era, the remnants of the Hitler government, under the command of Admiral Dönitz, had not yet noticed that the government under the hooked cross, which had been established in 1933 in Hotel "Kaiserhof" in Berlin, had met now its untimely end on the ship *Patria* when it was lying at the pier in Flensburg-Mürwik. They thought they were now in power as the "Dönitz" government, giving their orders over the radio network until the occupied forces of the Allies put a stop to it.

Then it was Dönitz, Rosenberg, Himmler, and the rest of the Nazis that followed them to Flensburg who heard the bad news: Twelve years of orgies and imaginary heroism for them as compared to oppression, slavery, martyrdom, and wholesale murder for their adversaries was over. I lived through those years, survived sickness and injuries, and, above all, I have been fortunate enough to retain the notes and memos I needed for this book. After a medical operation, and some time for recuperation, which some of my Danish KZ friends provided for me in their homeland, I was finally able to complete this book.

Heinrich Lienau
Flensburg, Germany
July 1949

INTRODUCTION

"The German people have no idea of how many of them must be fooled if one wants to obtain the support of the masses."
                                                                    Hitler: *Mein Kampf*

It all started in the "Bürgerbräu Keller" in Munich where the first seven members of the Hitler gang met with the "Führer" to organize their political party under the name of "NSDAP" (National-Socialist Deutsche Arbeits Partei). The petty cash fund consisted of an old cigar box containing a rubber stamp as well as some bills and coins which had been collected, somehow, and were now guarded by a treasurer, because nobody trusted the other fellow. Hitler, the wandering crusader, was full of promises because in times of poverty and economic misery, there are always a great many people with no judgement of their own who would always listen hopefully to anyone who would promise them a better future. It was no different with Hitler when he started with his slogans like the exorbitant interest rates or "Give me four year of time" and similar phrases. First of all, he held the Jewish people responsible for all kinds of misery in the world, thereby instigating racial conflict. In the Nazi's opinion, the Jews were the most detestable people on earth as compared to the Germans whom they considered the "Master Race." Since the Germanic people used to live in northern countries, one would also hear the expression "Nordic Man" indicating a member of the ideal race.

Hitler, the borderline German, as well as Josef Goebbels, the runt among the Germans, worshipped the north as well as its people. So far, they had been about everywhere else except the northern part of Germany. Therefore, the "Führer" (leader) after being invited to pay a visit to this part of Germany, decided to undertake an election campaign or crusade. Heinrich Lose, the former peasant from Mühlenbarbek, who later became Gauleiter (district leader), acted as the campaign manager for Hitler and his underlings.

It was on April 23, 1932, when an assembly meeting took place at the stadium in Mürwik near Flensburg. Most of the people present had seen better days, were out of a job, or looking for new opportunities. Among them happened to be the former, and now unemployed, officer of the Kriegsmarine, Reinhold Heydrich, who not only on account of his many debts, but for other reasons as well, had been discharged. Hitler took him in because; after all, he belonged to the kind of people he was looking for. It was in the "Bürgerbräu" Tavern in Munich where he laid the cornerstone to the so-called Nationalist Socialist German Labor Party with a handful of individuals that were no longer suitable for a better educated society. It did not matter at all that most of them were kind of shy as far as work was concerned and, therefore, Heydrich, who later became chief of the Security Police and Acting Protector of Bohemia and Moravia, was an excellent choice for a charlatan like Hitler.

An airplane took Hitler to a little airport near Flensburg. From there, he was taken by limousine through the streets of the city that were lined with curious onlookers. The trip ended at the stadium from where one could overlook the fjord with the Danish coastline in the background. The fact that Josef Goebbels had a great opinion of himself and did not move from his master's side, should also be mentioned here because it was all too obvious to the most casual observer. He certainly had every reason to stay as close as possible to his führer since he had heard "through the grape vine" that maybe this way he could get some benefits.

After Hitler had rubbed it into the heads of his politically, not too well-oriented followers, what he meant by 14 years of misgovernment and the "rotten" Weimar republic, he introduced his own "program" by asking for higher prices for farm animals, thus offering the rural population a better way to prosperity. This brought him great applause from the owners of pork and cattle. Mr. H., a master butcher, in Flensburg, was so overwhelmed with joy that he picked out the best of his smoked hams, had it decorated with ribbons, engraved with the hooked cross (swastika) and delivered by his own wife as head of the women's brigade and with the help of some assistants in her group.

Of course, the "Führer" was surprised and very happy to receive such a wonderful gift, but unfortunately, since he happened to be a vegetarian he could not enjoy it, he told his benefactor and, therefore, he would like to take it along for his sister. At this moment, Josef Goebbels, who stood aside greedy-eyed, offered his help by taking the ham out of Adolf's hands, explaining he had a large family to support. And so, Goebbels became the proud owner of the special ham that was supposed to be the reward for Adolf's speech. Well, anyway, both of them were convinced that the people in this part of the country must have enough to eat. Later on the same Heinrich Lose suggested that behind the northern border happened to be the real paradise, a land that would overflow with milk and honey, Adolf's, as well as Josef's, interest for the north became very strong.

Hitler remained at the stadium for a while yet, staring longingly over to Denmark, the "promised" land. Not before the noise from the cheering and shouting mob had brought him back to reality, and while he was on his way back to the airport, did it dawn on him that there was plenty "to do" for him in this northern country, thinking of future conquests.

CHAPTER 1

RESISTANCE MOVEMENTS ALONG THE BORDER

"The German people are the freest in the world.—Our critics are feeble, degenerate, democratic individuals. — Some of them even claim that the Jew is a human being."
                                                    Goebbels

It finally happened. On January 30, 1933, Hitler took over by force; it was his coup d'état against the government, as he called his forceful movement. It is hard to understand how in this frontier region he could win so many followers among these rather stubborn people. But, here like almost everywhere else, it happened to be the less able and efficient individuals, like the farmers with run-down farms and small businessmen and craftsmen in debt who didn't mind at all seeing another inflation coming. People with more foresight, of course, could not be persuaded to join the Hitler party; they kept quiet meanwhile waiting to see what would happen next. Since freedom of the press no longer existed in Flensburg, one was obliged to get information about the news, as far as Germany was concerned, from Danish and other foreign newspapers sold in Denmark. However, taking these newspapers across the border, like smuggling, and into German territory, was very risky since they were bringing the facts about the ruthless ways the Nazis were treating and arresting people who happened to be active members of other political parties.

Already, after a few days, the first victims of the Nazi persecution, people from north and central Germany, among them leading members of other political parties, as well as religious organizations, arrived at the Danish border to cross over to Denmark.

As long as they had the required Danish 10 Øre pass with them, they would be taken over the border by special agents who would turn them over to their political partners. Quite a few of these refugees were known to me, maybe not personally, but I knew they happened to be determined enemies of the Nazi regime. All these emigrants entered Denmark without interference and many of them continued their journey into foreign countries. It is not always possible to record every trick used for smuggling human cargo, but it can be said that the Danish 10 Øre pass, issued for a three-day visit, did a great deal of service (Fig. 5).

Fig. 5. Danish 10 Øre pass.

It was not unusual when on these escape trips some 50-odd people, whose lives were already in jeopardy, were taken on a single 20-minute steamship trip to nearby Kollund, a little resort town on the Flensburg fjord. After all, Hitler's program: "Keep the heads rolling," as mentioned in *Mein Kampf* was already well underway. The Danish country border, itself, contained many open spaces through which mostly single pedestrians could be led to safety. Besides that, it was no secret that there were many helping hands available among the Danish people, especially the inspectors at the border, who would overlook and ignore these trespassing incidents if a human life was at stake. Besides being relied upon for the safe transfer of people out of Germany, these friendly Danish agents would also do their best to smuggle illegal political literature across the border from Denmark to Germany. In some cases, these illegal newspapers were taken by wheelbarrow, covered with hay or potatoes, or whatever was available at the time of the year. But since the border is leading for a distance through the swamp of Jardelund where also peat moss is taken from the ground, these bundles of papers were also taken by wagon covered with peat moss—always by night time, of course—and, finally, delivered to a certain safe place in Flensburg and other border towns on the German side. The green-uniformed German customs officials seemed to be, in their political orientation, leaning more toward a neutral color, instead of brown, the Nazi color. Not a single case came to light about sabotage. Quite a few truckloads with tree trunks came across the border, escorted by a customs officer who was sitting on a canvas bag containing the illegal newspapers.

It was not enough to look out for Gestapo spies on the German side of the border only; no, because the Danish territory was infiltrated with German spies as well. Besides that, they were exchanged frequently. It has happened that these spies, at least some of them, were bold enough to intercept Danish mail, searching for letters written by or sent to people who were under suspicion for political reasons.

Also, so-called "German Nationals" of Danish parentage could be put into service as spies for the Gestapo, as will be shown here, for example.

A ship laying at Sønderborg harbor in Denmark had among its cargo two bundles of anti-Nazi newspapers, most likely *Der Neue Vorwärts* or *Die Sozialistische Aktion*, printed in Prague, both of which had already made a long journey through Poland. These 100 kg bales were supposed to be taken by ship to Flensburg from where a truck from Hamburg was to pick them up for further transportation. A dealer in old papers, whom I happened to know personally, had purchased a load of some hundred bales of Danish old paper which were supposed to be taken by motor ship to Flensburg. The bales of illegal papers had been carefully stacked among them, looking the same as the others, and could have made the trip without being noticed; they looked exactly like the rest. Soon, some rumors spread concerning this shipment. In a restaurant near the harbor, I found out from a Danish longshoreman, that a phone call came through concerning the ship loaded with the bale of papers. After some inquiry on my side, I was sure that this phone call was made to the Gestapo in Flensburg. This meant prompt action. First of all, the ship had to be delayed, pretending engine trouble or such, and, by now, it was getting dark. The ship sailed through the night and arrived in Flensburg in the early morning hours, where the Gestapo with some hired workers were waiting. By 6 a.m., the workers started unloading the ship and opened every bale of papers despite the protest of the old paper dealer.

When by noon time nothing suspicious had been found, the paper dealer had everything repacked and presented the bill for this kind of work to the Gestapo who actually paid it, not without some protests, of course. And the spy from Sønderburg who made that phone call was dismissed for making false statements. Actually, his message was correct, but he had no idea that some longshoremen, who spoke both German and Danish, had heard his phone conversation. And what happened with the bales containing the illegal papers? Well, they did arrive early in the morning in Hamburg. They had been picked up by a fisherman who was notified just in time. He took them on board during the night near the lightship *Kalkgrund* and brought them over to the German coast at a rather deserted place, where a truck and driver had been waiting so he could take them to Hamburg.

Paper smugglers have not always been successful in their undertakings. A casual remark of what was going on, too much confidence in people whose political background or orientation was not too well-known, drinking parties with a conversation that usually goes with it; all this could bring disaster, resulting in arrest, that mostly ended in jail terms.

It all depended on circumstances and when the best time for transporting illegal reading material could be. The chances were sometimes good during the daylight hours. A transport car, in this case a model Adler, equipped with a loudspeaker, had to be smuggled over to Denmark. It came from Berlin. One had to change license plates so I borrowed my own and drove this car over the border during the day at a very busy traffic hour and delivered it to my political friends who were already waiting for it. Any parts needed for repair I would smuggle over later. It should be acknowledged that the Danish border policemen, as well as the customs inspectors, gave us a helping hand with these transfers. It gave them satisfaction and maybe some fun, too, knowing that they played their part in undermining the Nazis. Until my arrest in May 1935, I kept on bringing anti-Nazi papers and letters both ways across the border and also helped people I knew well enough to get across and away from possible Nazi persecution. I considered it more or less my obligation to help people who had a hard time, on account of their persecution by the Nazis.

CHAPTER 2

HITLER'S ESCAPE TO FLENSBURG DURING THE RÖHM AFFAIR

In order to thank you, my dear Ernest Röhm for the unforgettable services rendered by you on behalf of the National-Socialist movement and the German people, and to show you how thankful I am for my destiny to call a man like you a friend and comrade in arms. In cordial friendship and thankful devotion.
   Your Adolf Hitler,
(Taken from a birthday letter written a short time before Hitler had Röhm shot to death on June 30, 1934.)

During the summer months, the people of Flensburg used to take little steamships for their daily pleasure trips around the fjord, and it seemed that most of these vacationers preferred the landing places on the Danish coast, with their beautiful surroundings, like, for instance, Kollund, Søderhaff, or Grafenstein and many others. Especially on Sundays when the sun was shining, the traffic was quite heavy. One of these beautiful Sundays happened to be July 1, 1934, when I took my family down to the harbor to get the first boat bound for the Danish coast. I also took along the Sunday issue of the *Flensburg Avis* to read on board. A bulletin from Berlin caught my interest as it was on the front page. There in Berlin, something out of the ordinary must have happened, but it was impossible to find out from the paper what really was at stake. Since quite a few passengers were reading the

Avis too, this article soon became the general topic of conversation on board. Everyone was waiting for the ship to land in Kollund, the first stop on the Danish coast, in order to get hold of a Danish paper or to listen to the Kalundborg-Copenhagen broadcast for further news. We were not disappointed; extra bulletins in print were already for sale on the dock, and over the radio, we heard further details regarding an incident that soon became known as the "Röhm Affair." Not until the return trip in the evening, would one get more information through the Danish news broadcast of what was going on. However, for safety's sake, the newspapers were not taken along to Flensburg as it could have been disastrous being caught with them while passing through the German customs control booth. The streets that used to be so quiet on Sunday evenings were now alive with black-uniformed S.S. troopers from Berlin, as could be seen by a great number of cars carrying Berlin IA license numbers. However, the people of Flensburg did not yet find out what was going on. Not before the next morning did I get some information that was rather important to me.

A druggist, living nearby in the center of the city and, who on the sideline, happened to be a Nazi block warden, came to my door asking for a personal interview, apparently taking me for a Nazi sympathizer. I asked him to come in, of course.

"Herr Lienau," he said, "I have to fulfill a very important task for the party (Nazi, of course). I am coming to you because I am sure you are going to give me your assistance." Well, of course, I wanted to hear first what kind of a secret mission he had in store for me. "What I have to do is, I have to find two rooms for a high-ranking government official for a few days and, therefore, I am asking you to reserve your two front rooms towards the street for this purpose. These gentlemen are holding a secret conference at the "Bahnhof Hotel" nearby and would like to stay with private people."

Upon my inquiry as to which of these gentlemen one had in mind to board in my apartment, the block warden confided to me that it was very important for me to take care of either the Führer himself, Minister Hess, or Minister Goebbels. Since I didn't change my expression nor the color of my face nor gave the impression that could be taken for refusal, he continued: "The news of this meeting as well as the names of the participants must not be made public in this city. I am counting on your utmost secrecy." I assured him he had it. "We are pretty sure," the druggist continued, "that the Führer may get a few rooms from Mr. Prien, the owner of the Bahnhof Hotel, and that means we only have to find rooms for Minister Hess and Minister Goebbels. I would prefer it if you could take care of Mr. Goebbels since I already have a room for his chauffeur in the apartment of the owner who has the fruit and vegetable store across the street."

Now it was up to me to choose among these three, but I thought it was advisable to tell him that we already had some guests and were expecting more visitors for these days. And beside the point, I told him, it has always been up to my wife to make these decisions. And so I asked him, since my wife was not home at this time, to please come again in the afternoon to talk things over with her. The block warden agreed and left. After I did recover somewhat, I called my wife who had stayed in the rear of the apartment and not, as I pretended, someplace else. I told her about the conversation I just had and whom one had in mind to board with us. My wife, and more so, my daughter, who happened to be home on a visit from the United States, were sorry that they could not be of any help but were willing, in case the quartermaster should return in the afternoon, to explain the reasons for being unable to accommodate such distinguished gentlemen. We just didn't have the space available at this time.

The druggist did not come back in the afternoon, and so my wife and daughter were spared the trouble of explaining the reason for refusal. As soon as my visitor left, I took this excellent opportunity, since I had quite a bit of information already, to find out some more about this meeting and when it would take place. I got in touch with a friend of mine who lived in the hotel in order to decide what should be done next. My friend M. managed to get himself a gold Nazi party badge and so equipped he pretended to be an usher or doorman at the entrance of the assembly hall. In fact, he played his part so well that most of the

Nazi officials took him for a well-trained and hand-picked guard. He had a chance to remain unobserved between drapes and the locked door of the assembly room during Hitler's speech concerning justification of the murders committed against Röhm and his followers.

Hitler tried to vindicate himself against the assassination of his former friend Röhm, and his followers, with these words: *"One murder case is a crime—thousands of murders is world history."* In Hitler's not-too-long speech with explanations, it was revealed in a shaky, nervous voice that he had been forced to do what just had happened. For reasons of security, his own, of course, the members of his regime and party had been transferred to Flensburg to continue with their administration of government until the revolt would have been abolished. For a while, one had to wait and see what kind of move the followers of Röhm may possibly undertake within the Reich. No one had any knowledge of his (Hitler's) presence here at the border. It was prohibited, under penalty of death, to talk about Hitler's trip—flight, of course—to Flensburg, nor its purpose. After that, some recommendations of a private nature were dealt out: Nobody is to be seen on the streets or in public places.

One guy who stuck completely to this command was Dr Ley. He was sitting in a quiet corner of the hotel, enjoying himself, as usual, with glasses of hard liquor, as I was told later, confidentially, by the hotel owner. It also became known that Hess wanted to find out for himself what kind of a drink "Flensburger Grog" was, and so he had it served to him in all kinds of strengths and brands in a saloon with the nickname, "Hotel Ehebruch" or, as we would say, "Hotel Adultery." Hitler's remaining accomplices had themselves driven in their cars through the streets of Flensburg, evidently to gain enough knowledge of the surrounding territory, just in case an escape should become necessary. These rides stretched all the way to Kupfermühle, a little resort town close to the Danish border. The fact that the whole Hitler mob wore nothing but civilian clothes, can also be pointed out here because in their regular uniforms, they would have been recognized by the public right away.

Precautions had already been taken in the event Hitler and his clique were forced to flee across the border. At the pier of the resort town of Glücksburg, located 10 km east of Flensburg, on the German side of the fjord, a ship's tender was kept under steady steam, right in front of the "Kurhaus Hotel." The name of this ship had been covered up very carefully with planks and tarpaulins, and it was impossible to find out from one of the crew members what the name of this ship was, or its mission, nor the reason for being anchored here at this particular landing pier.

When, after two more days of waiting, Hitler didn't get any disturbing news from Berlin, Munich, and other "danger points," the whole mob disappeared overnight, without fanfare, and moved back to Berlin. The tender left Glücksburg, too, and rumors were spread among the people that this could have been a smuggling vessel. Thus, the Hitler spook went by without being noticed by the people; not even members of his own party could find out what kind of so-called "high-ranking" visitors had been in Flensburg nor for what reason.

A few days after this meeting in Flensburg, Hitler called his puppet show together in his so-called "Reichstag" and had a new law, consisting of only one paragraph, proclaimed; according to which the committed mass murders were sanctioned as being necessary for the security of the Reich. In the chronicles of the city of Flensburg mentioned before, Burgermeister Kracht, one can read the following article: "In July 1934, the city of Flensburg saw the Reich's—and county leaders within its walls—at which opportunity Reichminister Hess and Dr. Goebbels received a welcome ovation." The fact that Hitler and his whole gang moved to Flensburg to escape possible harm by members of the Röhm party was shamefully omitted.

CHAPTER 3

OPEN LETTER TO REICHS-PRESIDENT VON HINDENBURG

"Europe and the whole world may go up in flames. What do we care! Germany has to live, in order to be free."
Röhm; in his autobiography

The unsuccessful Röhm plot still kept the minds busy and, especially at the Danish border, one could be well-informed through the foreign press as to the details of this incident and also the reasons behind it. Even the Gestapo became aware that something extraordinary had happened. Since smuggling of a few papers by a few commuters did not seem advisable, one could see the citizens of Flensburg crossing the border, more or less in mass movements, to visit the little resort towns like Krusau, Kollund, and Padberg, where they would sit down in cafes, lunch rooms, taverns, with a cup of coffee and maybe something else and read the latest news about the current events in the "Third Reich." These picked-up news stories became the topic of conversation later during the evening among the relatives, friends and neighbors at the home front.

Several weeks after the Röhm plot, a meeting of the Danish democratic movement took place on "Die kleine Ochseninsel" (a little island in the fjord not-too-far from Kollund) at which I, too, was present and later joined in the discussions. The latest edition of their newspaper had just arrived, was read by the public and later became subject to further conversation. This edition contained a copy of the open letter to President von Hindenburg, written by an S.A. man, named Kruse, in which he described in great detail the fire of the Reichstag's Building as being instigated by and also the arguments between Hitler and Röhm just before the arson took place. Kruse belonged to a ten man group, picked out and ordered by Göring to set the Reichstag building on fire. While nine of these S.A. men were eliminated one by one by the S.S. soon afterward, and most likely shot in order to remove witnesses against Göring, S.A. man Kruse, being an aide to Röhm, succeeded to escape from Bad Wiessee where Röhm had been assassinated and get to Switzerland, taking the diary of Röhm along with him. At that time the English language broadcast announced this incident in more details. A few copies of this "Kruse letter" also found their way to Flensburg where they were mimeographed and handed out to trustworthy people. Already, after a few days, it could be noticed that the number of Kruse letters had greatly increased because more and more copies of them were given out to friends and neighbors or whoever wanted them. Wherever I happened to be on my business trips, the conversation was generally about the Kruse letter. Meanwhile, the Gestapo made frantic efforts to locate the sender, printer, reproducer or whoever had anything to do with these letters. Since it was a well-known fact that the Gestapo had very seldom been able to find things out for themselves, but instead had to rely on the cooperation of spies and double-crossers, so in this case they, too, hired the help of informers.

When, in the fall of 1934, I happened to be on a business trip to Lübeck on behalf of our firm, "Biovis Werke GmbH" of which I was a part owner, I met our agent, Ficke, and I soon found out that he, too, had something to say about the Kruse letter and so we kept talking about it for a while. Not long after that, I had one search party after another in our apartment, all without results. Every typewriter of our company was thoroughly inspected by the Gestapo and their helpers and the letters carefully compared with the letters on any kind of Kruse letter they just got hold of. Nothing could be found to incriminate me. The informer, Ficke, together with his father and brother-in-law now tried to blackmail me also without success. After that Ficke swore under oath that he had received a copy of the Kruse letters from me. The efforts of the Gestapo to get hold of one copy of the newspaper, *Socialistic Action*, must have been in vain. Even I had been unable, later on, to obtain a copy of the Kruse letter from friends of mine or acquaintances. They seemed to have disappeared. Only shortly before this book was ready for printing, did I finally get hold of one copy, actually only a cut-out from this newspaper containing the Kruse letter. Some friends in Sweden gave it to me; the date was early August 1934. It reads as follows:

A Reichstag arsonist announces himself

S.A. man Ernest Kruse, #134522, wrote a letter from Switzerland to President von Hindenburg. Kruse belonged to the Röhm staff. A copy of this letter was sent simultaneously to the editor of the newspaper Deutsche Freiheit. In this letter Kruse introduced himself as the last arsonist who was involved in the Reichstag fire. He claims to have Röhm's personal papers in his possession which he intends to hand over to the British government for information and publication. Here is the letter:

"On February 10, 1933, Röhm, Heines, and Ernst selected a ten man group, including me, to take part in a secret meeting. The plan on how to set the Reichstag building on fire was discussed thoroughly, and each man was asked if he was willing to participate, then pledged under oath to keep silent and wait for further commands. A man by the name of Lobike refused to play any part in this plot; his conscience would not permit him to commit such a crime. He had been taken away without being allowed to make any statements. We never saw him again. However, the rest of us were suspecting to where he had been taken; but we kept quiet, we knew too well that otherwise we too would never see the sun again.

Someone else by the name of Van der Lubbe was ordered to take part in the Reichstag's fire. He was also under Röhm's staff and was very devoted to him besides being a crazy hunter who wanted to show off also. He was not told about us, however. Instead he was ordered to enter the building alone with torches that were handed to him and to set the side rooms on fire in a specific order while we at the same time had to set fire with explosives to the big assembly room. We had a drill practice twice at night and had to run from the president's palace through a cellarway and back again. I didn't want to go into any more details, only name the people that were directly involved: Heines and Ernst as leaders, each of whom had a group of five men, namely: Brähm, Stettmann, Nagel, Sirop, Kummelsbach, Dieriger, Bratschke, Lehmann, Schmitz, and Kruse. Now, today, I cannot state the exact time anymore as to the minute when the order came during the night of February 27, while we were assembled in the cellar of the president's palace with Göring. We were also told that Van der Lubbe had already arrived at the building. Every one of us had a cellophane bag containing some light powder and a roll of cellophane tape. What kind of powder it was they did not tell us. Each of us was ordered to put these cellophane bags into specific places and to connect each bag with a tape to the next one in line and then to tape toward the cellar exit. Here Ernst and Heines were standing, both of them holding a bunch of tapes, and after we had moved through the cellar entrance, these two men ignited the tapes upon Röhm's command. Röhm also made sure that Van der Lubbe was still jumping around in the vestibule while the fire was set. Snakes of fire moved in all directions. Whenever a bag of powder was hit, it sounded like a detonation; the explosive powder flew through the air like burning flour, and in no time everything was enveloped in a fiery cloud. We ran away for cover. The job had been accomplished. Van der Lubbe was caught in the inferno as planned; but it had to be that way. One had promised him previously that after a possible jail term of some duration which couldn't be avoided in order to show the people that justice had been done, that he might be set free secretly and shipped to America with a lot of money. Here he could live like a rich man, enjoy life; and therefore it should not be too bad spending a few months behind bars where one would provide him with as much comfort as possible under these circumstances. How well did these men keep their promise! I am shuddering in terror whenever I think about it; I am trembling while thinking about my comrades who had been forced to commit this crime under penalty of death for refusal and who disappeared afterward, one after another. Only Röhm, Heines, Ernst, and Nagel were still alive at this time. However, Nagel and Heines were shot to death on June 30, 1933. (Röhm was shot on June 6, 1934.)"

Although this letter as written by Kruse had been published in many prominent foreign newspapers, Hitler, Göring, and Goebbels did not dare to protest. This indeed would have been very difficult for them. Especially in those points which the Supreme Court tried to avoid and which would have thrown suspicion on the Nazis themselves for having caused the Reichstag fire. Here the representation of the S.A. man, Kruse, furnishes credible evidence. He who keeps silent incriminates himself.

In a special session of the Hanseatic Court, I, the author, was accused of violating the law about malicious gossip. Before the first trial a hearing took place for Ficke in the courthouse of Schwartau where he denied his accusations against me. My court appointed lawyer, Dr. Reuss of Hamburg, had his testimony put under oath and declared that Ficke had committed perjury. During the main trial that took place on May 15, 1935, Ficke swore that he had, contrary to his previous statement, received a copy of the Kruse letter from me. However, the exhibit that was included in the trial papers had been obtained from another source, as the judge stated in his speech.

But despite the fact that Ficke had been found guilty of perjury, I was arrested in the courtroom. After four days of trial, during which my defense lawyer convincingly pleaded for my acquittal, and by demonstrating how this trial would defeat the law—for which he received notice that his right to practice law would be suspended—I was convicted on June 14, 1935 by Judge von Bargen of the Hanseatic Special Court in Hamburg and sentenced to two years in jail. On account of my stubborn denial—and this was emphasized loudly and clearly—the time I had spent in detention prior to the trial was not to be deducted from my jail term.

Before the last day in court, I had to undergo several hearings by a prosecutor with the name of Jauch, a rather nasty fellow, as became evident through several other political trials. He wanted to get confessions by extortions and threatened me that if I didn't give any testimony the way the court wanted to hear it, he would see to it that my head would be laid down on my feet!! At the last trial I had to spend the night before in the cellar next to the cell of a communist prisoner, named Fiete Schulze, who was executed the next morning on the chopping block. Jauch said: "I let you stay in the cellar during the night so that you could spend the last hours next to your cell neighbor, the political convict Fiete Schulze who had just been executed." "You better confess now, no more denials, the game is over. If you are not going to admit now that you had these pamphlets mimeographed and distributed, you may understand that you will meet the same fate as Fiete Schulze." Since I did not have anything to admit but persisted in arguing that nobody could force me to take the blame for any unlawful activities I had not been involved in, I was taken back into custody. On the day before the final session in court a repeat performance took place with the same negative result for Jauch. A few days later I was transferred to the jail in Fuhlsbüttel near Hamburg, and in September 1935, I was taken to the penitentiary at Lübeck-Lauerhof. Over here one had hardly any reason to complain about the food, lodging or treatment: After all most of the wardens were still from the old crew. Only one Nazi supervisor by the name of August Kosegarten joined the crowd, but he was a harmless fellow, just like his name.

Through my employment in the office, I had the opportunity to look into many branches of the administration. I also came in contact with the prison for women where all the laundry was done and repaired. Here I took the opportunity to talk briefly to the women. I found out that anyone who was due to be released within a month had his name marked down in a special office file. However, the prisoners themselves were looking forward to their day of dismissal only with mixed feelings, because for many of them it did not mean being released but transferred into a concentration camp instead. It also happened that while members of the family were waiting to take their relative home, a Gestapo man cut in between them, seized the released prisoner, to have him shipped off to a concentration camp. As I had been sentenced to two years in jail, I too had to take it for granted that at the end of this term I would be transferred to a concentration camp. This thought had always been on my mind and so I tried to figure out ways and means by which I might be able to escape the Gestapo.

The year was 1936. The coming war was already casting its shadow ahead: for instance the rationing of butter and other food items went down to 80%. Soon after that one could read about the lack of raw material in this or that category. One could read about self-sufficiency and finally about Göring's four-year plan. New raw materials had to be found and new articles that were much in demand had to be invented so that the Third Reich was no longer dependent on other countries. All this I found out during my time as a prisoner, from newspapers that were lying around. The day of my release came closer. A few days before that, Director Leonard asked me to come to his office where he told me that I would be a free man and not scheduled for further confinement in a concentration camp. I was allowed to notify my wife to let her know the time of my release so she could really accompany me home. After two years and one month I was free again. Of course, the Nazis wouldn't let me get out one hour sooner, only the director of the jail gave me permission to let me go before noon time instead of in the evening, as he had the authority to do.

CHAPTER 4

THE SO-CALLED FOUR-YEAR PLAN

"Too much fat will increase the waist line. I myself did eat less butter and have lost already 20 lbs. in weight."

Göring

As has been mentioned before, the four-year plan had to become a reality, the sooner the better. Hermann Göring wanted the Third Reich to become an economically independent nation. At first, we read about his plans for the economy in the jail paper which had the nickname *"Light Tower,"* as this local rag was called. Everyone was asked to cooperate to make something useful out of all kinds of things that were just lying around unnoticed. It was a challenge for the so-called inventor and other contemporaries who hoped to be resourceful. As it has already been possible to turn wood into wood pulp, then into cellulose, from which finally suits and dresses could be made, there was a chance to use other raw materials and, by refining them, maybe new products could be made out of them, maybe something nobody thought of before.

The raw material I had in mind to offer was older than the hills; it was seaweed, only in Germany it had hardly been touched. There were several kinds of seaweed, a raw material I was familiar with for decades, and also with its use in industry, and I certainly could prove it. A businessman from Lübeck whom I happened to meet among the political inmates and who also spent some time with me here but was released shortly before me, already made some connections with the head office of the Four-Year Plan in Berlin.

In a few days, the contact was made. By telegram, I was asked to come to Berlin, and on one of the first days of October 1937, I entered the "holy sanctum" of the Four-Year Plan which was located in a building at 68–70 Behrenstrasse. An S.S. man was sitting at the entrance, asking for identification and writing down the names of the visitors into a register. Besides this, or maybe it was more important, he was selling tickets that would entitle the visitors to go to all kinds of Nazi party events. But due to lack of interest, most people wouldn't go anyway, I suppose. However, in order to be taken care of faster, I sacrificed a couple of Marks for some tickets. These inspections, including ticket sales, took place on almost every staircase and corner of a corridor. When I finally reached the waiting room leading to the office of the big chief, I counted seven tickets in my pocket for which I had spent about 20 Marks. While leaving the building afterward, I returned all of these tickets to the S.S. canvassers for resale. This way I could avoid further questioning as well as buying more of these unwanted tickets.

The waiting room was filled with so-called inventors and people who thought they had good ideas that could be turned into cash as well as those who were hoping to make a profit somehow or somewhere. The telegram made it comparatively easy for me to get through the hallways and stairways of this building; it also secured me preference above many others in the waiting line. Soon I was standing in the doorway of the big reception room, welcomed with a handshake by the big chief himself. It was not Hermann Göring but either his right-hand or left-hand man who introduced himself as Oberst (Colonel) V. Loeb. Then I explained to Oberst Loeb my ideas whereby I could notice already, in a few moments, that this officer was not burdened with too much technical or material knowledge. He also was honest enough to admit it. He turned to a messenger who was standing nearby and had him show me the way through a maze of hallways to the office of the technical expert in this matter. This gentleman, a

Luftwaffe (Air Force) officer, also received me very politely by telling me how glad and honored he felt to be introduced into a field of science that was, up to now, completely unknown to him. If he happened to be an army or naval officer, then most likely he would have had some knowledge on this matter, but as a Luftwaffe officer—well, one could perhaps understand.

Sure, I could understand and took this for granted, whereupon I gave him a detailed explanation for about an hour so he could acquire some knowledge in this field which he might have picked up some years ago. Meanwhile, some other Luftwaffe officers joined us, listening carefully and asking questions which left no doubt in my mind that none of these officers were acquainted with this field: Seaweed from the ocean. The total staff of the Four-Year Plan office consisted exclusively of Luftwaffe officers who had been compelled, due to lack of some other kind of occupation, to make themselves familiar and useful in other fields of trade and industry, science or technology.

During my discussion I came to speak about the existence of useful seaweed, hereby describing the coastal waters of Iceland and Norway as particularly rich in these plants, the officers became very alert and even more interested when I could tell them that I happened to be familiar with these shorelines. They promised me a promotion for my enterprise in every way, and I was also asked to keep this office well-informed about further developments in this specific field, either by phone or in writing. As I did not like to leave empty-handed, I asked for a letter of confirmation stating what kind of a mission I would have to perform for the Four-Year Plan. Upon my return to Flensburg, I confronted the Gestapo with this letter as they had taken my passport away and were also threatening me with confinement in a concentration camp in case I should be found guilty of anti-Nazi activities which would make me an enemy of the Reich. Now they could read it in black and white that I had been entrusted with a politically worthwhile position for the Third Reich. And so, for a while, I had peace anyway. However, I soon noticed that my rather abundant correspondence with this office in Berlin had been opened and inspected frequently. But through this kind of control system, it could only be assured that I had nothing to do with any kind of illegal activities.

When I reported to Berlin that I would need foreign currency for a trip abroad as well as a new passport, I received the following letter on Göring's letterhead (Fig. 6):

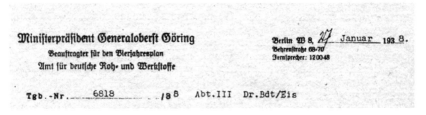

Fig. 6. Göring's letterhead.

> *Ministerpräsident Generaloberst Göring*
> *Beauftragter für den Vierjahrsplan*
> *Amt für deutsche Roh-und-Werkstoffe*
>   *Berlin W 8, 27. Januar 1938*
>   *Behrenstr. 68/70*
>   *Fernsprecher: 12 00 48*
>   *Tgb.Nr. 6818/38 Abt. III Dr. Bdt/Eis*
>   *Bei Rückfragen unbedingt anzugeben*
>   *Bezug: Ihr Schreiben vom 30. 1. 1938*
>   *Betr. Vithormin, Kraftfuttermittel*

Translated it would be:

> *In case of inquiry refer to this number on behalf of: Your letter, dated Jan. 30, 1938*
>   *Re: Vithormin, foodstuff for animals*
> *Mr. Heinrich Lienau*
>   *Flensburg*
>   *With regard to furthering your enterprise by permitting you to inspect equipment for the drying of plants commercially in foreign countries and also to locate coastlines with abundant growth of seaweeds, a petition has*

been sent to the minister of finance in Kiel according to the enclosed copy.

A special request to the police department regarding the issue of a passport has officially not been considered necessary.
End copy.   Authorized signature: Beschmidt.

While the correspondence with the office for the Four-Year Plan was running in full gear, I also had made, in the meantime, contact with people in Denmark and Iceland. I happened to know that with the cooperation of the government, a corporation had been founded on Iceland with the purpose to utilize seaweeds. At first I had written discussions with the Icelandic ambassador, Mr. Sveinn Björnsson, who later became president of Iceland. In September I made a trip there for a personal interview.

This journey had its drawbacks as the Gestapo did not want to issue a passport for me, on account of the threatening danger of another conflict; in this case, a meeting between Hitler, Mussolini, Chamberlain, and Daladier in Munich. Through the Swedish Trade Union Press I had been informed that, in the event of a war, Hitler intended to put about 40,000 political enemies into concentration camps. Since I might as well include myself in these 40,000, I thought it advisable to spend the next few days on the opposite side of the German border and see what would happen.

On that day, which happened to be September 28, 1938, the day on which the decision, if war or peace, was supposed to be made in Munich, I took a walk across the border, unconcerned, in bright sunshine, and without a passport. The traffic happened to be rather heavy during the hours before noon. Quite a few foreigners happened to be among the travelers as one could hear. They, too, tried to get into such a nice and quiet country like Denmark. While near the border at Kupfermühle, a little resort town near the Baltic, a mass exodus by cars and busses took place. The border railroad station at Padborg became swamped with train passengers who came from Hamburg via Flensburg, sometimes all the way by express from Paris and other places. My wife who was bringing me my suitcase was also on one of these trains. Already on my trip to Copenhagen, I heard that, so far, war has been avoided. After consultation with the Icelandic ambassador and taking care of business matters that were necessary for a trip to Iceland, I had to leave Denmark within the next fourteen days. To prevent being captured by the Gestapo while crossing the border into Germany, I waited until nighttime to make this trip. Hardly ever did I "sweat so much blood" while crossing illegally than on this particular night while the border on the German side was swarming with Gestapo spies. Nobody knew the location of my trail through the woods and so I made it home safely, despite all the obstacles around me; after all, it was a very dark night with some fog covering the landscape.

The political situation went back to normal; and therefore, the police department gave me back my passport which entitled me to stay abroad for several months. Early in 1939, I sailed with the Icelandic steamship *Dettifos* for Iceland, where I joined the newly founded company for research on seaweeds as a participating member.

After my arrival, I contacted some political friends who were staying in Iceland, more or less as immigrants. They numbered about fifty. However, the number of German people could be estimated at around more than one hundred; most of them were living in Reykjavik, the capital. I moved in with an Icelandic family and tried to avoid contact with any German people I didn't know much about since I had been forewarned at my arrival that some spies for the Nazis could be among them.

CHAPTER 5

GÖRING'S FIASCO IN ICELAND

"I am a philanthropist; there is no doubt about it. I am really sociable. I would rather shoot a few times too close or a few times too far, but I am going to shoot by all means."
Göring

During the last days of March 1939, news arrived in Reykjavik that some German delegates from Berlin were on their way to this country on the steamship *Dronning Alexandrine*. The purpose was to get permission from the Icelandic government for the erection of a base on this island for their "Lufthansa" airline. The Icelandic press protested right away against this proposition. When the delegation, consisting mostly of members of the Luftwaffe and the foreign ministry, arrived at the parliament building in Reykjavik, they were told in plain language that the Icelandic government would not permit any foreign company or enterprise to use their island as an air base. About four or five of these gentlemen left immediately after this decision and sailed home.

The following afternoon, I had a phone call from the German consul, Dr. Timmermann, inviting me to a little party at the consulate building. I accepted, and when I arrived at the reception room at around 8:00 o'clock, I was introduced to three gentlemen: Dr. Best of the Foreign Ministry and two meteorologists, Drs. Junge and Merz. It can be mentioned here that Dr. Best, together with Dr. Bovensiepen, Panke, and V. Hanneken turned out to be codefendants in the so-called "little Nuremberg trial" that began June 16, 1948, in Copenhagen. Despite an ample supply of stimulating drinks and delicious food, the conversation didn't seem to get off to a good start, due to the disappointment of Dr. Best, who couldn't get over the fact that members of his delegation had to return to Berlin empty-handed. He held Dr. Timmermann, in a rather reproachful manner, responsible for the failure to obtain an air base in Iceland for such an important German enterprise. Dr. Timmermann pointed out that, in this case, only the Icelandic government had the authority to grant this permission. Thereupon, Dr. Best indicated that refusal of the German petition could have an unpleasant aftereffect on his position.

This concealed threat, however, failed to make a big impression on Dr. Timmermann; on the contrary, he came out with some funny jokes about Hitler, Goebbels, Göring, as well as other members of the Nazi gang, and the present government, which gave me a chance to contribute some of my own supply of anti-Nazi jokes. During this conversation, an article in a German newspaper was mentioned, according to which Himmler stated that the S.S. were descendants of the Vikings, and that he had in mind to prove his theory by carrying out an exhumation program on Icelandic graves.

We did not overlook in pointing out to Dr. Best, that in the event a skull with a Goebbels' type jaw bone or a club foot or maybe another skull with a small cavity for the brain should be discovered, proof of origin would have been already partly established. The atrocious assaults upon peace-loving people by the Vikings did have a remarkable resemblance with the transgressions of the Nazi S.S. so that, therefore, one could conclude that a relationship does exist. Annoyed by these wisecracks, Dr. Best stopped this discussion and gazed into a corner of the room, hoping to find another topic of conversation. When, by a casual glance, Dr. Best noticed the books of the German poet, Heinrich Heine, (who happened to be Jewish) on one of the front shelves of the consul's library, and besides that, had to hear from Dr. Timmermann how much he admired the writings of this poet, Dr. Best lost his patience. Not even *Mein Kampf* or *The Mythos of the 20th Century* were among his book collections. It was about time for

Dr. Best to undertake a thorough investigation of this northern part of the world as well as of his world-forgotten representative, who evidently had been left on the job since the damned days of the Weimar Republic.

The fact that Dr. Best became very angry for not getting an outpost on this island can easily be understood by realizing that Göring had tried already in the previous year, 1938, to gain favors from the Icelandic people by handing them an expensive present. He gave them an amphibious plane which was flying mostly between Reykjavik and Akureyri. The fact that Göring had put out some bait in vain must have been very depressing for Dr. Best. He was confirmed by the old saying that ingratitude was the world's reward; it was the same here in Iceland.

Therefore, Dr. Best left this ungracious country with the next ship; only the two meteorologists stayed on, evidently to make weather forecasts. A few days later, Dr. Timmermann received a letter informing him that he was no longer consul and had to return to Berlin. I never heard of him again. The consulate was without a consul and any business matter was being taken care of by Mr. Haubold, the secretary.

A few days later, rumors spread that a new diplomatic representative had been appointed, this time a consul general. Well, after all, Great Britain, Denmark, Sweden, and Norway had their consul general and France had the same in mind. It stands to reason that, therefore, Hitler with such an important nation as the "Great German Reich" after it had swallowed up Austria, certainly could not stand behind those countries. However, Hitler had trouble with the Austrian consul in Iceland because he didn't recognize "Adolf" as his master and commander-in-chief, and, for that very reason; he would not let him have any important papers or documents. So, if Adolf wanted something then, he would have to look for it himself.

Finally, the name of the new German consul general was announced; he was soon to arrive and his name was Professor Gerlach, from Jena. After some investigating, it became evident that Professor Gerlach happened to be a very close friend of William Gustloff of

Switzerland. After Gustloff's violent death, Switzerland had Professor Gerlach deported, and now this man was supposed to be in charge of the German consulate in Iceland! On April 18, this new diplomat arrived in Reykjavik, together with his wife, two daughters, and a maid. They had traveled by ship; the *Dronning Alexandrine* which must have gone through some mighty rough weather. Possibly, Professor Gerlach was also disturbed by dark clouds on the political horizon, as it looked in some countries very much like some entanglements in various parts of the world, according to the broadcasting station in Reykjavik.

After presenting his credentials to the Icelandic government, the new consul general went to work at once, arranging Hitler's birthday party for April 20th. But the ceremony had to be placed a day ahead so it would not collide with the Icelandic holiday of "*Sumardagurinn fyrsyi*," meaning the beginning of summer. Although the consul general did send me his personal invitation to this party, I replied that I was very sorry for not being able to attend, on account of some very important forthcoming business deals. I certainly had my fill of these Nazi speech givers; and besides that, I did not yet get over the "Heldengedenktag" (Day of Commemoration of Heroes)—for the Germans, of course,—which took place in March. I left the "Wauttemplerhaus," where this event took place already during the welcome speech because by then I had enough. The fact that the Nazis from the far north sent their Führer congratulations on his birthday via telegram was announced over the radio in "Hotel Borg" where I stayed. I also heard that the political outlook had become very serious. Everything indicated that Hitler wanted to start a war. Sure, while staying in this northern part of the world, I happened to be in a safe place for the time being, even though my own fate was of no importance. Then again, according to another interpretation, things didn't seem to be quite so bad because my wife did get her passport for Iceland without difficulties. In fact, I was expecting her with the next steamship, the *Gullfoss*.

CHAPTER 6

HITLER'S PIRATE FLEET

"We do not suffer from any kind of inferiority complexes – not in the least."

Hitler.

The sea around Iceland is of great importance for the fishing industry, not only for the Icelanders, themselves, but also for many other nations that are using these waters in search of herring and codfish too. As a protection for their own fishing vessels, each nation had its own patrol boats cruising nearby. These patrol boats had a warlike appearance, but one didn't have to think war was imminent just because a French warship and the British training ship *Vindictive* were lying at anchor outside the harbor. A Danish patrol boat was also cruising in these waters, as was the Icelandic patrol boat *Thor*. This ship had only one cannon on board. In fact, that happened to be the only cannon Iceland possessed, since this country was, unlike others, not interested in guns. It may also be said here that Iceland did not have any military forces or army. The only uniformed forces were members of the police department stationed in the capital of Reykjavik, but they carried no weapons. They were hand-picked husky fellows, resembling the old Vikings in appearance, who were able to take care of anybody creating a disturbance, and they did it with their bare hands.

As a protection for the German fishing fleet, the *Emden* was expected to arrive. It was the same ship that had already been in service the previous year. However, the Icelanders had a very unpleasant recollection of the *Emden* on account of the improper conduct of its crew members in the streets of Reykjavik. The supply ship for food and liquid fuel for the *Emden* arrived during the middle of May and stayed somewhat outside the harbor. Its name was MHS *Samland* as I found out from the harbor department. Around noon time, the Norwegian mail ship, *Lyra*, from Bergen, Norway, steered into the inner harbor while I was talking to some Icelanders on the dock. Two German-speaking civilians standing nearby were wondering what kind of a ship this could possibly be. I thought I might as well give these foreigners the information. They thanked me in German and introduced themselves as Captain Bartels of the *Samland* and the other gentleman was the engineer of the same ship.

After talking for a while, I was invited to a sightseeing tour of the ship, which I accepted for the next afternoon. A tender picked me up from the pier. At first, I was entertained in the dining room where I also got some information as to the tonnage of the ship as well as its destination. It was supposed to supply warships at sea with food and liquid fuel.

While walking through the ship, I found out that it had a crew of 90 men whose uniform resembled neither that of the Kriegsmarine nor the Merchant Marine. The deep-laying foredeck was covered with miles of pipelines and floats, and the starboard side was stocked with oil tanks. While passing by the cargo quarters, I noticed that these were empty, but I saw large quantities of empty bags piled high, as well as barrels and boxes in large numbers, all empty. A big refrigerated room with nothing but empty meat hooks hanging from the ceiling was there too, and so I really had no idea with what kind of goods this ship was supposed to supply the *Emden*.

Upon further questioning, I understood that this ship had a sister ship by the name of *Altmark* and that, in the event of a war, both of these ships had to follow the submarines. During World War I, the U-boats torpedoed merchant vessels which, subsequently, would sink to the bottom with its full cargo. In the war to come, a ship's valuable content had to be salvaged, and the *Samland* and *Altmark* were put into service to take over the supply. Well, this kind of explanation was enough to convince me that Hitler had created a new kind of seagoing vessel for the next war, which looked to me more like pirate ships or something like sea robbery on a modern scale. For the next day, I made myself available as a guide for the crew to visit the hot springs near Hveragerdi, where the installations for the drying process of seaweeds were located and which was also the place I was working, mostly as a supervisor. During the trip which took place in several busses, I got quite some more information as to the anticipated take-overs of the ships' cargoes which they hoped to accomplish, like piecework, in the event of a war.

Quite by chance, I happened to meet the ship's engineer of the *Vindictive* who seemed to be unable to communicate with the crew of a Danish motor ship. After I had made the translation and the Danes had left the ship, the ship's engineer invited me to see him in the Hotel "Island" where we soon got involved in a stimulating conversation. This way, my British host heard about my political viewpoint, as well as the prison term I had to endure, as an opponent of the Nazi regime. With the agreement to another visit on one of the next evenings, we departed with a "Good night."

Meanwhile, the new German consul, General Gerlach, received his household goods by freighter via Hamburg and moved into his new residence. Also taken along were two PKW (Personenkraftwagen) automobiles which he used for trips in and around Reykjavik to show the inhabitants that he was there. Then he thought about gathering the German colony, at some time, around him. And so on May 19, 1938, a notice appeared in the Thursday edition (Fimmtudagur) of the Reykjavik newspaper *Morgundbladid* among the Icelandic printing the following notice in German:

> *The Consul General and Mrs. Gerlach would be very glad to see the men and women members of the German colony at a tea party in Hotel "Borg" on May 20th between 4 and 6 o'clock in the afternoon.*

The consul called, but not everybody came. Even though the immigrants stayed away, they were still anxious to find out what the new diplomatic representative of the Third Reich had to say. It so happened that I was appointed to be a reporter at the 5 o'clock tea party. Around fifty guests arrived and among them were Icelandics married to Germans. Behind Mr. Gerlach's seat was the familiar big flag with the swastika covering most of the wall. The salutation consisted of shouting "Heil Hitler" with the right arm stretched out like on a fly-catching mission, a form of greeting which I always avoided: Rheumatism in the right arm. Of course, I used this excuse wherever and whenever the Nazi salute took place. After all visitors had taken their seats in the big hall, Mr. Gerlach made his salute to Mr. Vohle, the chief of the foreign organization, hereby adding in his speech the remark that the German people here in the far north, had a special duty and that it was his own ambition to convert every German into a National-Socialist. He certainly had great ideas: The wife of the consul was elected to be director of the women's organization, in accordance with the Nazi rules and regulations, and his 16-year-old daughter was supposed to bring some shine and glory to the youth organization. The best-liked of all was a little girl, maybe 8 years old, who went from table to table with a friendly smile, while presenting Bremer cigars and cigarettes to the guests.

Meanwhile, the consul general pointed out in detail what had to be done to make Iceland a cornerstone of the Great German Empire, so that even Hitler, himself, would find his pleasure on this Nazi-converted island. It was, indeed, regrettable not to have gained an air base on this island, despite Hermann's giving an aircraft to the country. Now that Gerlach was here as consul general, a second attempt would be made to achieve this goal.

He also had in mind to buy a big house that was currently still occupied by the British consul general. Next to it, a big meeting hall was supposed to be built in which the supporters of the Nazi regime would have a chance to listen to many more propaganda speeches for the Third Reich. And so he went on and on. When, finally, the guests went up from their seats, and topped with another Hitler salute, I took the opportunity to make my way to the coat room, from where I disappeared outdoors.

It was almost 6 o'clock and, according to schedule, the tender of the *Vindictive* was lying at the pier waiting to pick me up. Meanwhile, the German Nazis were unaware that I had left; they had no intention to break up the party and, therefore, remained at the Hotel "Borg" enjoying themselves at the banquet with tea, liqueur, and some delicacies while listening to promises and grand new ideas of which the Nazis seemed to have a never-ending supply. I remained on board the *Vindictive* for about an hour and found it very entertaining. In the evening, I was again among my friends, the immigrants, because they, too, wanted to hear something about the consul's tea party during the afternoon. Not only that, they also had to find out about the *Samland*. This ship had a displacement of 9,000 tons and was able to make the trip from Iceland to its home port in Wilhelmshaven in less than three days and, therefore, happened to be a fast-moving ship. Its crew would get a very short shore leave at its base under strict measures of security. The crew was also pledged not to reveal anything that had been seen or heard while on board.

Personally, I don't think that the name *Samland* became known to many people. Also, I have not been able to find out if she met with the same fate as her sister ship the *Altmark*, which went down near the Norwegian coast. Hitler's delight in Kriegsmarine maneuvers was quite absurd and proved how ignorant he really was in the field of strategy. This fact became evident as soon as the war started. It was important to him to put himself into the foreground as a "strategist at sea." On his "Führer yacht," the *Grille*, he acted like a snob during those days in 1938 before the meeting in Munich with Chamberlin. The *Grille*, which was laying at anchor in front of the Naval Academy in Flensburg-Mürwik, will be mentioned again (Fig. 7).

Fig. 7. Hitler's yacht *Grille* at Flensburg-Mürwik.

CHAPTER 7

MOVING TOWARD WAR

"Poland has to have her lesson. She has to creep to the cross and get a beating. I can prove by my actions that I love the peace."

Hitler (At the invasion of Poland)

The pursuit of the establishment that I had been managing in Iceland encountered some difficulties since the necessary machinery had to be brought over from the European mainland. I had in mind to take a vacation for a few months and bring my wife on a trip to the USA since I had the opportunity to board the Icelandic freighter *Katla* which could accommodate a few passengers and cross the Atlantic in about 16 days. The route was nearly the same that the Vikings under Leif Ericson took when they first sailed for North America and named it Vineland.

Fatefully, we changed our minds and decided to return to Flensburg instead because some business and private matters had to be taken care of. The political situation didn't seem to be too threatening in any way, and we were hoping to pack all our furniture and have it shipped to Iceland by the fall. In the middle of June 1938, we left Reykjavik with the Icelandic steamship *Gullfoss*, made a stopover at Edinburgh, and arrived in Copenhagen by the end of the month. There we stayed for a few days with some friends. Any newspaper clippings or written material of suspicious nature that could be held against us by the Nazis were left behind in Copenhagen as a precaution, hoping that on some latter-day, we might get it over the border. After a thorough examination of our baggage and clothing by the Gestapo, while the customs officials left us alone, we were able to cross the Danish border at Padborg and finally arrived at Flensburg. A few days after my return, I received a postcard with an order to come at once to the office of the Kriegsmarine command station, located at Flensburg-Mürwik. Since I was much too old for military service, the only reason for being asked to appear, I figured, would be in connection with my trip to Iceland.

My guess that they were curious and anxious to find out about my affairs in that country was correct. The reception was very friendly and polite; I walked from one room into the next, because everyone around wanted to listen to me. I gave a courteous talk but evaded replies and would rather talk about the landscape, waterfalls, hot springs or geysers, anything one could read about in travel literature. Finally, I was asked to travel to Kiel and report at the residence of a Kriegsmarine lieutenant by the name of Lemke who happened to reside with his staff in a mansion in Kiel-Düsternbrook. Here, too, I had a very friendly reception, and the questions were about the same that I was asked before in Flensburg-Mürwik. Sure, they knew I had been on the Icelandic coast on a business trip, but they wanted to know something about possible military installations or storage depots or docks for foreign ships, how the reception of the radio was, if the northern lights would cause any kind of disturbance and, of course, what kind of news could be heard mostly over the radio broadcast. I answered all their questions, but these Kriegsmarine officers still didn't seem to be satisfied.

Later on, a car drove by and an officer took me to the headquarters of the Naval High Command "Ostsee" (the Baltic) where I was introduced to a group of Kriegsmarine officers. Here they wanted to know if I could understand Danish, Norwegian, and Icelandic news programs. If so, they wanted to bring me to the broadcasting station right away. With this task, I would have to cut off all connections with the outside world. All I could do would be to write under censorship and receive visitors under conditions comparable to those of a voluntary prison term.

At this point, I thought it advisable to intervene by mentioning that my hearing had been impaired, due to an ear ailment which did handicap me quite a bit in understanding correctly what had been said. Thereupon, I was offered first-class treatment by an ear specialist. In this case, I would have to make my decision within a week whether I would be willing to accept this first-rate confidential position or not, that is, after treatment. At the same time, I was handed a piece of paper with the request to read and sign it, after which I had to mail it to a given address. This would automatically take care of everything. Nodding, I left the office and took the next street car to the railroad station.

On the way I read the paper: It was a form for new membership to be filled out by me in order to become a member of a district department for Nazi propaganda. I also had to prove that I had never been under indictment for political reasons (criminal offenses apparently were no hindrance) and that I stood fully behind the ideals of National Socialism. Since I was unable to answer either of these questions truthfully and with a clean conscience, I didn't reply at all. About two weeks later, I received a short notice from the Kriegsmarine High Command "Ostsee," stating that I was no longer considered a candidate for their employment. Evidently, the Nazi High Command, in collaboration with the headquarters for Nazi propaganda and the Gestapo in Flensburg, had discovered in the meantime that I had already a long record, as far as political offenses were concerned.

Someone must have found something damaging or incriminating about my political past and I also became aware that my outspoken remarks in the German Consulate building had gone on Dr. Best's nerves and that while making his report about Dr. Timmermann, whose loyalty to the Nazi system could also be considered suspect, Dr. Best could have given his opinion about me also. Through some of my friends, I found out that the Gestapo kept me under surveillance and that a spy was watching me all the time. Since I didn't agree at all with what the Nazi press reported, I tried to get all the necessary information as far as possible from foreign newspapers. All I had to do was to go to the Danish library in Flensburg, which had an assortment of Danish papers and magazines on hand in the reading room for anybody to choose from. It didn't take me too long to notice that a man unknown to me would soon follow me into the reading room and take a place at a nearby table. His curiosity did concern me all right and not the contents of the foreign papers in front of him which evidently he couldn't even read. The librarians and their assistants also kept an eye on this mysterious stranger who happened to be a bookbinder's helper, as someone had found out in the meantime.

If I wanted to whisper to another visitor in the library, I used Danish on purpose only and in a low voice, of course, but never did this conversation concern anything else besides the weather so that nobody could be exposed. But then, when I didn't go to the library for a week, I was told that my shadow, the spy, hadn't been there either. In order to find out if the Gestapo had someone to follow me again, my wife and I visited a Danish family with whom we were very friendly in the little town of Padborg on the Danish border. It happened to be during the early part of the day and it was on September 3, 1939. Here, we had the opportunity to listen to the Danish broadcast from Copenhagen-Kalundborg. Every half hour, we heard the news about Germany, according to which the political situation seemed rather critical. And it sure was. It hit us like lightning out of a fair sky when we heard the bulletin about Germany's attack on Poland, and that by 5 o'clock in the afternoon, gunfire had already been returned. At the first moment, this bulletin was somewhat like a shock to me and my next thought was maybe I should stay in Denmark. And so I was thinking it over carefully, should I return or not? While crossing the border in the morning, the German passport officer let us pass through without questioning and, therefore, I concluded that the Gestapo was not—at least at that moment—looking for me; otherwise, the sergeant in charge would have received orders to have me arrested. And so we returned to Flensburg in the evening, after passing both through the Danish and German passport control, without noticing anything out of the ordinary on the German side of the border. There was no indication that the border might be closed.

The following days, too, were passing quietly for me, although I noticed again, after a while, that a "Shadow" was following me. I was granted permission to take a job, this time laying the groundwork for an airport near the township of Taro, not far from Flensburg. I happened to stay there for several weeks and did not notice that somebody might be spying on me. Meanwhile, through connections with some well-minded people, I was offered another job that was more to my liking; however, the employment office refused to let me change jobs because my working papers carried the remark by which I had to be considered unreliable for political reasons. I tried to explain it to the officer in charge who found nothing better to do than to notify the Gestapo.

The same afternoon I visited the reading room of the library again where I noticed the spy again. The following day on the 17th of October, 1939—I was arrested in our apartment and taken before Gestapo Officer Woinke, who accused me of having delivered speeches detrimental to the Nazi regime.

As it was my right to do, I denied everything. My request to confront my accusers with any witnesses to any such occasions was strictly denied. Instead, I was taken to the city jail in Flensburg where I stayed until the Gestapo had obtained an arrest warrant for me from the headquarters in Berlin, signed by Heydrich. Incidentally, Heydrich, an ex-Naval officer, indebted and with an obscure past, nevertheless, now a big shot among the Nazis had by now risen to a high-ranking position among the Nazi warlords. Several days before Christmas, I was taken for a ride with stop-overs in Altona and the infamous police jail in Berlin, nicknamed "Alex," and finally on December 21, 1939, I arrived at the concentration camp of Sachsenhausen-Oranienburg, which described itself as a camp of protective custody (Fig. 8).

Fig. 8. Map of Nazi concentration camps.

CHAPTER 8

HITLER'S INFERNO

"Let all of you who are entering here give up hope."
Dante: *Divine Comedy*

One of mankind's greatest poets, the Italian writer, Dante, described in his *Divine Comedy* the terrors of hell. It is a vision, written in many songs which he left to posterity as his best and most famous work.

If Dante had foreseen the so-called camps for protective custody of Adolf Hitler, he would have been compelled to increase the songs about hell a hundredfold, provided his hand had not failed him in writing it down on paper, hereby giving a real account of Hitler's cruelties. Dante's visions have been overshadowed by far by Hitler's actual brutalities because, in the inferno of the National-Socialists, the weirdest fantasies became a cruel reality.

"Let all of you who are entering here give up every hope."

This inscription above the entrance gate of hell in Dante's *Divine Comedy* could have been engraved with unconditional justification above every gate to those more than a hundred concentration camps—falsely and erroneously called "camps for protective custody." Nearly everyone behind whom the gate to such a camp closed had good reason to part with the outside world forever; he wouldn't see freedom again. Those few who eventually did return alive but broken in body and spirit disappeared like raindrops in the sea; as a general rule, the last step for the majority of inmates was through the chimneys of the crematories.

Three big H's were hovering like a bad omen from the beginning to the end over these Nazi infernos: Hitler, Himmler, and Heydrich. As a substitute in the background, Dr. Werner Best, who was also involved in bringing the so-called Sicherheitsdienst (SD) (Safety Service), into existence, as well as the summons for protective custody which was about equivalent to a death sentence. These were the men who founded the extermination camps for people, thereby earning themselves the infamous glory of being mankind's most notorious criminals of all time. Of course, they had their prototypes like Nero or Attila, the king of the Huns, and perhaps, the greatest of all the Asiatic despots, Genghis Khan, overshadowed by far. The principle of this barbarian was to never show mercy but to destroy fertile countries and beautiful cities and to rob all attainable treasures and works of art, as well as to stamp out human lives. All of this became the guideline for Hitler and his cohorts. While historical records about Genghis Khan show an estimated 5 million human lives lost, the Hitler War has cost at least 30 million lives, of which some 11 million were murdered in concentration camps.

The concentration camp, Sachsenhausen, belonged to the city district of Oranienburg, 30 km north of Berlin, connected with the northern railroad. It was built on the cleared ground of the Sachsenhausen Forest during 1934–1938. Inmates under enforced labor and under the watchful eyes of the S.S. had to do the work. Besides Dachau and Buchenwald, Sachsenhausen was one of the main concentration camps. Being in the vicinity of Berlin, Sachsenhausen became a sample concentration camp that was visited frequently by leading Nazi officials, military personnel, as well as agents from foreign nations. Prominent prisoners were transferred from the city jail in Berlin to this concentration camp. They were taken into a cellblock without name or identification, but only a short time after that they succumbed to the S.S. bullets or the gas chamber. The roll call record would only give in its conclusion the number of victims "bumped off," so to speak, with the remark, "Removed from the list of inmates…." Those inmates that had been killed already in the RSHA, the so-called safety control office for the Third Reich in Berlin, located at Prinz Albrecht St. 8, would be taken directly in sealed wooden boxes to the crematories, but it was impossible to keep a record of how many former prisoners died this way.

Compared with Dachau and Buchenwald, concentration camp Sachsenhausen did not stand much behind in the way of atrocities and murders that took place here in large numbers. The following chapters may give the reader some insight into the dungeons, filled with terror and despair. The training methods to kill, which were taught in special classes, had been put into practical use by the S.S. in these concentration camps. The torturers and executioners who had to carry out the verdicts of the criminal courts in the Middle Ages were blunderers compared to the S.S. crew members in the concentration camps. The thirst for blood by the Nazi vampires increased more and more the faster the Third Reich went towards its doom. The big extermination camps like Belsen and Auschwitz have shown the cultured world in an undisguised way how degenerate the followers of the so-called "Master Race" really were.

Mankind tends to forget easily, even after having endured terrible times. Among those who were friendly toward the Nazi system, and they are still around today, some people are eagerly trying to deny that these atrocities ever took place or, at least, they try to minimize any kind of wrongdoing. Anyone who has read pages like these can hardly forget everything. He is more likely to become an ardent enemy of any fascist or Nazi regime as well as any kind of militarism related to this kind of government. In fact, he could become a crusader in protecting human rights, which the Hitler regime had tried to destroy forever in a merciless way (Fig. 9).

Fig. 9. Heinrich Christian Lienau as inmate #15735.

CHAPTER 9

WEEKS IN KIEL

"Upon whom did we inflict even a single insult...or whose property did we take?"

Hitler, 1938

On May 8, 1940, after I had the first months in the concentration camp behind me, I was ordered to go to the storage department for clothes. "Getting dressed," I was told. Besides that, I heard rumors that I might be released. After receiving some sandwiches to take along on a trip I was taken by an S.S. guard to the commandant. On the way, I became aware that no release was in sight for me because two Gestapo men said that I was to be transferred to Kiel. It was also pointed out to me that these guards were well-armed, just in case I should try to escape. Shaking my head, I pointed out that they really couldn't expect me to do some running; indeed I was glad to be still able to stand on my own legs, thanks to the concentration camp diet I had been living on until now. As a precaution, they put handcuffs on me while taking me to the railroad station. Later in the train compartment, a guard removed the cuffs so I could eat my sandwiches. Maybe with other passengers sitting around in the same train compartment, he didn't want to attract any special attention. In the evening we arrived in Kiel where I took up residence in the "Flower," nickname for police jail.

Already during the trip I kept on wondering for what reason I was being transferred to Kiel. I couldn't get away from the thought that after Denmark had been occupied by German troops for about a month, that the Gestapo might have possibly found something incriminating on me. I was unable to guess what kind of an offense it could have been since I had been involved in quite a few political things. In my mind I went over every possible transgression, as well as a plausible or best explanation in case I needed an alibi. The hearing by the Gestapo which took place the next morning confirmed my suspicions. The accusation was betraying the country to the enemy and high treason due to some incriminating evidence. Alternately, Dr. Schmidt and Herr Orsin of the Gestapo, both of them experts in administering mental cruelty, went to work on me in order to force me into admitting the charges read to me. As cool and relaxed as I could be, I firmly denied any involvement in the unlawful acts they tried to charge me with. I only admitted knowing the names of some Danish citizens they called out, like Jens Dons-Kolding, Hans Lytzen-Bredebro, and Emil Fries from Götterup, who were accused also. With a determination as strong as possible, I denied their alleged damaging testimonies and demanded that my accusers show me the transcripts complete with their signatures.

After some delay, they tried to explain that these documents were forthcoming. The only alleged offense I was shown was that of Jens Dons who was supposed to have been working for the Secret Service. Some written records had been found at Dons' residence with a register of names. Quite a few arrests had been made from the disclosed names. Sure enough, Dons had written down some information I had given him confidentially with my name next to it. However, when it came to the exact time of our meetings, he had made an error of two years as I could see in the written statement.

It was a big surprise for them when I told the Gestapo agents that I couldn't possibly have been at this time with Dons in Tondern, Mjolden, or any other Danish border town because at that time I happened to be a prisoner in the Lübeck jail. Besides that, I didn't get any furlough for a trip to Denmark in order to commit any illegal or treasonous acts with Dons. An inquiry by phone to the director of the penitentiary in Lübeck confirmed my statements. Therefore, I vigorously refused to sign the lengthy confession they held in front of me, especially then, when they purposely set the date ahead. I had won a victory and gotten off the hook on which the Gestapo had tried to hang me; however, they held out the prospect of another hearing. Meanwhile, I was taken to the Kiel city jail at "Faeschstrasse" in strict solitary confinement, where I had to wait for several weeks for the next session in court. The food in this place was good and plentiful. There are no prison walls or doors that can prevent the spread of news or other communications. Already, the next morning, I found out that another concentration camp inmate by the name of Richard Normann had landed in this "fortress," and his name was also mentioned in the Dons case. Within a few hours, we had made contact, despite the so-called "solitary confinement" in which Normann was also held. On the next walk around the prison yard, we explained the rest to each other. Meanwhile, we waited for the hearings to take place.

This time it was not the Gestapo who conducted the hearing, but a judge of the district court named Jessen, a very pleasant gentleman and lawmaker to whom I was known since years as a journalist in Platt-German literature. He informed me that no incriminating material could be held against me and that the alleged statements of the codefendants were nothing but falsifications prepared by the Gestapo. Now I got all the privileges a judge was able to grant me, like permission to write, to go shopping (within the jail), to receive visitors, to read papers, and I was even allowed to shave. This way I hardly noticed any restraint. Besides that, I was put in charge of getting the library books in order, on recommendation of the chief of the guards. During my stay in the jail at Kiel, I had time to write a novel about our homeland, a part of another story about Hamburg, as well as another little novel. The last one was confiscated by the Gestapo while, thanks to the cooperation of the judge of the court of inquiry, I was able to hand the two other manuscripts to my wife on visiting days.

After a short time, I also had the opportunity of being employed as an assistant clerk in the registry and this way, I had a chance to meet more of my former political friends, people who also had been brought to jail for similar "offenses" as the ones I had been accused of.

Among them happened to be a Mr. Svend Johannsen, the inspector of the Danish school in Schleswig, a Mr. Lassen, a locomotive engineer from Padborg, as well as some others. It didn't take long until the whole jail became filled with more and more Danish citizens who had been found guilty of committing "work sabotage."

The German employment agency "Die Arbeitsfront" had made an agreement with the similar Danish agency "Fagforbund," and, accordingly, to these the hourly wages were set at 85 pfennigs (0.85 Reichsmark). When payday came and the Danish workers were only paid 0.55 RM (equivalent to 85 Øre in Danish money) they quit their jobs whereupon the Gestapo brought these "work saboteurs" to jail. Therefore, it didn't take too long until this place became rather overpopulated. Soon after, some Norwegians also joined the crowd, among them some girls who had their hair cut off by the Gestapo. Maybe they had been too friendly or helpful or whatever. Since there was no one around who could speak Norwegian, I offered my services and advanced to the position of interpreter. This way it was also my duty to censor all the incoming and outgoing letters of the Danish and Norwegian prisoners. Nobody seemed to notice that I turned out to be a "bull in a china closet." I merely glanced through the ingoing and outgoing mail, put the censor stamp of approval on it, and then the chief of the guards would sign the mail.

Meanwhile, it became quite uncomfortable on the outside. Kiel had felt its first heavy bombing attacks that caused a lot of damage, and some lives had been lost too. Although the German press tried to conceal the news concerning these attacks as much as possible, I got the news straight from the returning labor commandos while helping at the tables in the mess hall at suppertime. This way I found out about a German fleet that met with disaster trying to invade England. All kinds of available and navigable vessels from rubber rafts to fishing boots on upwards in size had been collected for this invasion fleet; Hitler's armada of floating coffins, one could say, in order to bring England down to her knees. The British fleet, however, didn't even have to go into action for their defense because a big storm out of the southwest worked over this rather unsuitable collection of floating derelicts. Only a few surviving ships were able to save themselves and make their way back to Wilhelmshaven and Cuxhaven from where some men made the journey back to Kiel. The German North Sea coastline was littered with wreckage and drowned victims of Hitler's criminal undertaking. Neither the German press nor the radio gave an account of this incident; only those who were lucky enough to be among the rescued were able to give some details of this event.

Some time ago there used to be a song: "We were marching against England" which they may have recited in a mournful voice instead of singing it. A pretty well-known proverb could also have been applied to Hitler as the commander-in-chief of this ill-fated invasion attempt: *"The young man is sailing out with a thousand masts, but as an old man he is drifting homewards into the harbor in a lifeboat."* At one of the shipyards in Kiel, an aircraft carrier was being launched and was ready for its first shakedown cruise, although the last coat of paint was not dry yet. The trial run was a short one: It went from the surface of the Kiel harbor right down to the bottom. A direct hit by a bomb did the whole job. At that time nobody ever heard of the only aircraft carrier *Hindenburg*. Everything had to be kept quiet, and silence was not difficult to maintain as the ship was lying out of sight on the harbor bottom, causing no reason for further discussion. As far as food and treatment were concerned I had nothing to complain about, but I was still waiting for whatever the Gestapo might next do to me. The increasing number of bombing attacks made the stay in jail rather uncomfortable because in the vicinity there had been some direct hits, and according to rumors, one part of the jail at the Ringstrasse had already been destroyed. And so the summer went by, giving me the impression or maybe hope that I would have to stay in jail for good, rather than being shifted back to the concentration camp. The only trouble was we had to face these bombing attacks.

On one of the last days in November, during the early afternoon, one of the guards came to my cell, all excited, telling me I had to get ready for a release; the order would soon be here in writing. While packing my belongings together, I had certain doubts as to the validity of the news. Finally, a letter came with the message that the arrest warrant against me, dated August 28, 1940, had been repealed on request of the chief justice of the People's Court. Well, here I had it in black and white.

Holding my bundle, I was now waiting for the cell door to be unlocked so that I could get my freedom. Sure, the cell door was opened; but this time the guard looked rather worried, telling me that it might take some time yet because the Gestapo had given the order by phone that I had to stay here for a little longer. And so I unpacked my bag again, waiting for the next move of the Gestapo, who had a new arrest warrant ready for me a few days later.

By now it was Christmas time again when I moved back into Hitler's inferno for the second time as a "returnee." The intermission in Kiel seemed almost forgotten when a letter from the chief justice of the People's Court, dated April 4, 1941, arrived with the news that the investigation against me had been suspended. Several months later the other codefendants, Nic Ehlers and Rich Normann, both from Kiel, also returned in order to take up residence in Sachsenhausen again, since they also were under suspended sentences because I had previously established some dates as being correct. This way it was in favor for all of us. In fact, this little error may have saved our lives, which could have come to an end with a death sentence from the People's Court.

CHAPTER 10

RECEPTION FOR NEW ARRIVALS

"There has been more culture in Germany during the last six years than for England during the last hundred years."

Hitler

It was an icy cold winter morning. Busses filled to the seams with prisoners rattled over the uneven pavement of the streets of Berlin towards their destination in a northerly direction: Concentration Camp Sachsenhausen. This living cargo had spent several nights at the "Alex," the police jail of Berlin, in the company of criminals of all kinds, in fact with the so-called scum of humanity. All passengers were glad to get out of these louse-infested, stinking boxes, although it was still very dark and early in the morning. Sachsenhausen! What did these passengers who came out of the buses know about this place? It couldn't be worse here than it had been at the "Alex." A cold wind blew through the cracks between frames and windows of these vehicles. The last cigarette went around: everyone was allowed two draws. We should be at our destination pretty soon, one of these returned inmates had just mentioned casually.

After a few more turns, the busses came to a stop. "Everyone outside! Step forward, five in a line!" was the command. Somewhat scared, the prisoners followed the order. "Aren't you pig son of a bitch going to take off your hat," and by that, an old man who could be in his seventies and was rather shaky on his legs could feel the kick of an iron-clad boot at the seat of his pants with such an impact that he was thrown on the concrete where he broke his nose. "Maybe you think we are going to pick you up and carry you inside? Go on, you fellows, get this old faker on his feet and drag him through the gate." Bareheaded, the long column of men went forward, carrying the crippled old man between them through the gate, on top of which one could read the inscription: "*Camp for Protective Custody.*"

Well, "protective" custody couldn't be so bad after all. A concentration camp was much worse. At least this was the general opinion of the new arrivals. Now they were standing here, five in a row, inside the gate, but they had to keep their hats in their hands, despite the icy cold wind. Now they were standing here, facing the great gray wall. In front of them, they saw a sign almost covered with snow, but it had the warning sign on it: the familiar skull and crossbones, the symbol usually seen on labels with poisonous contents, such as on medicine bottles. Then there was the live wire on top of the barbed fence which carried the figures of Spanish horsemen, suggesting electrocution; that is in case someone touched this wire.

As an introduction, a returned inmate or (returnee) would whisper to newcomers that talking was strictly forbidden. Also, stomping with the feet, due to the bitter cold temperature had to stop at once. For more than two hours these new arrivals, who were almost frozen to an icicle, had to stand outside beside the gate. By now the hands of the clock at the tower had moved to twelve, noon time.

"Must be time to eat," some men whispered to each other. But the hands of the clock kept on moving while nobody gave the signal for lunchtime. Instead, three uniformed S.S. men approached the column of waiting prisoners. The "returnee" started to cough, obviously trying to call the sight of these S.S. men to the attention of the newcomers. "Careful: "Iron Gustav," Schubert, and Bugdalla are on their way. Don't move!" Nobody had any idea of what was in store for them at the hands of these merciless and brutal S.S. men. "Why are you here?" Iron Gustav asked the last man in line on the left side. Gloating over the victim's malfortune for being asked, the other two S.S. men stood there with a grin on their faces, waiting to hear the answer which happened to be in this case: "Political indictment."

A slap in the face with the fist convinced him that the explanation was insufficient. "What kind of crime did you commit? I want to know, you bum, before you wipe the blood from your trap." "I have been framed, why and by whom, I don't know," was the answer, after which he wiped over his mouth and put the blood-soaked handkerchief back into his coat pocket. "Sure, you innocent angel, what party did you belong to?" the Iron Gustav wanted to know. When he replied "Social Democrat," he got a kick in his chin that made him stumble backward, upsetting momentarily the man behind him in his upright position. "Are you SOBs going to stand quiet?" And, by that, this fellow who admitted being a Communist after being asked got a kick with an ironclad boot in his stomach, causing him to bend forward in pain and to land on his knees. Meanwhile, the other two S.S. men and another one by the name of Saathof were gloating with pleasure while watching these incidents before picking out their own victims. A criminal, marked in the concentration camp as a habitual offender with the letters BV ("Berufs Verbrecher," meaning a criminal by occupation) as well as the man next to him were the first to get hit on the head and elsewhere.

"Why don't you stand up straight?" Saathof asked an old invalid with hearing difficulties. "Officer, may I go to the toilet? I have a serious stomach ailment," was the answer. Strangely enough, he didn't get another kick, only an answer he really didn't expect. "Go ahead and shit in your pants, you wouldn't have to live much longer anyway. What kind of wishes do tramps like these still have? It's amazing. Maybe they think I came here to wipe their asses." Not far from here Blockleader Schubert, kept his eye on a Catholic priest named Untermann who had been brought here in his vestments. Apparently, he didn't have much to say while being questioned and after a while, he got away with only a few kicks in his stomach.

Somewhat more excitement occurred in another section where Iron Gustav got hold of a Jew whom he asked why and for what reason he was here. He used to be a merchant, one could understand after a few words. Iron Gustav had just one piece of advice for him: "I am going to give you a rope on which you can hang yourself within 36 hours, if not; I will give you my personal assistance."

However, the Jew didn't follow instructions during these 36 hours. Even after four weeks, one could still see him standing in line in the Jewish section during roll call. How and when the S.S. got rid of him has never been found out for sure because the dying of the Jewish people during a long and severe cold spell took on epidemic proportions. They were made to stand outside for half a day at the time with an empty stomach, while only dressed in scanty clothes that would not withstand the bitter cold.

A Protestant minister from one of the East Frisian Islands, by the name of Bokelo, also had the misfortune of landing in Iron Gustav's clutches. The mere fact that he was preaching and while delivering his sermon made some subversive remarks against the "Führer," was one of the greatest crimes under the Nazi law. Foaming with rage he yelled at the young minister: "And then the parish didn't pull you down from the pulpit in order to beat you to death?" "No," was the precise answer, "the parish was in full agreement with me."

This made Iron Gustav stunned and speechless at first. Then again, one could almost get the impression he had in mind to have this brave man of the gospel stoned to death with the help of the other two blockleaders or maybe buried under a pile of ice where he could freeze to death. Right now pieces of ice were lying around in big quantities. But nothing like this happened. After a hard kick in the face, this courageous minister got off the hook, for this time anyway. By now it was way past lunchtime, but the new arrivals still had not anything to eat. Well, maybe they had lost their appetite already. "Lay down on the ground, all of you!" was Schubert's command after Iron Gustav had left. Some of the people were already in the snow, overpowered by the cold as well as the low resistance they had under these circumstances.

The next order was: "Get rolling, all across the place," and the whole company rolled over the ice and snow towards the reception booth. Not everyone could make it. Some just lay still on the icy ground and had to be carried away later by other inmates. Only one was carted away:

the old man with the bad stomach ailment. The push-cart for the dead took him to the morgue. According to the death certificate, the cause of death was described as: Disturbance of the circulatory system. Well, after all, every life comes eventually to an end through some kind of a disturbance, like freezing, starving, being beaten to death, hanging from the gallows, or breathing in the gas chamber; however, the cause of death reads always: Disturbance of the circulatory system.

Meanwhile, the prisoners arrived after their trip through snow and ice at the reception center, Barrack B. They got up somewhat clumsily, but with the "help" of some club-wielding S.S. men, they were driven through a narrow door. First, they went to the political department for the registration of names, occupations, and addresses. Anyone who couldn't answer and say why he was sentenced to this camp got punches in the nose from Schubert or sometimes kicks with the boots. Iron Gustav had left for a while, leaving his helpers to "take care" of the new arrivals.

"Get over here, you bastards, take all your belongings, clothes, and what have you to this department over here." Armed with his identification card with his number on it, as well as the statement as to what kind of crime he had been accused of, the new inmate was hurried over to the bathhouse. Thank goodness the water was warm and, under the influence of a warm room, the new arrivals felt more alive again, at least for a little while. And now get dried up again. An old rag that was supposed to be a towel a long time ago was thrown around their necks. And, hurry up! Get into the dressing room. A worn-out shirt with part of a sleeve missing had to do, same with the underpants that were almost reaching down to the knees, a pair of torn and patched-up socks, shoes with holes, a pair of pants made of wood fiber with a hat that would almost fit, and the outfit for the newcomer was completed, with a jacket striped in blue and white.

"Stand in line, five in a row," was Schubert's command. Casually, he glanced at the line-up, and then disappeared through the door. Everyone was breathing much easier now. One inmate who had been there a while already took the newcomers to the section for new arrivals where they had to be shown their seat in the mess hall, their cot, and locker for their clothes. That was Egon Nickel, a political inmate. He also took special care of the new people by giving them some hot turnip soup. He knew these new ones must be starved and frozen from what they had been through. Some comrades sacrificed a piece of dry bread from their own meager ration to give it to the new ones. After that followed a short lecture to get everyone who was new acquainted with these surroundings as well as some warning messages concerning possible surprise visits by the S.S.; after that bedtime—try to get some sleep on the ice-cold cots.

And so time moved on, and it was springtime again. However, it was a rather unpleasant day in April. According to the calendar, it was April 16, 1940. Blockleader Baierle, better known under the nickname "Little Pork Face" took a group of newly arrived prisoners to Block B. Following his command, all of them had to roll on the ground across the exercise yard to the place of destination. A rather big and somewhat heavy man didn't seem to be able to keep pace. Seeing this, Baierle kept this struggling and moaning individual rolling across the place by kicking him with his boots. Finally, as the last one in line, this unfortunate victim of the S.S. sadists arrived at Block B. Once inside he got special treatment. While bending his knees he had to hold a wooden stool in his outstretched arm, but as soon as his arm started to shake under the strain, Baierle tortured him with more kicks in his sides. It was obvious that this man, already in his sixties, was suffering from heart disease and maybe a hernia as well. At last, he dropped over and fainted. Baierle kept on hitting him until he could see it was useless. Then the political prisoners took care of him first with first aid treatments and then they had to check his personal papers which were needed for registration.

Well, this happened to be Dr. William Hammer, born June 18, 1879, the holder of five degrees in medicine and related sciences, author of articles in medical journals, and a constant coworker for the popular weekly magazine *Volkswohl* in Berlin, in which he would publish articles on how to keep well and what kind of foods to eat for a healthy nutrition. He made, however, a grave mistake as a physician by recommending how the sick and disabled could be kept alive instead of weeding these "unnecessary eaters" out, once and for all before they could become a burden and a liability to the Reich. Well, a physician of this kind simply had to be eliminated. His arrest warrant also contained an order for special treatment which meant, in concentration camp language, getting rid of him, the sooner the better. Baierle had already given it a good start. The other S.S. sadists, like Bugdalla, Van Deezen, Flickert, Juhren, Knittler, Meierhofer, and several more, continued to practice all kinds of torture on him. They also took Dr. Hammer to the great brick factory "Klinker"—more about his place in another chapter—with the result that he succumbed at the end of these maltreatments on May 16, 1940, about a month after he had been taken to this concentration camp. A pushcart took his body back to camp for the evening roll call. Among the death notices the simple facts: "18594 deceased," and so he was taken to the morgue.

Shortly after World War II broke out, all persons whose political orientation was somewhat questionable, among them intellectuals, members of the armed forces, scientists, lawmakers, and others were taken into this concentration camp. From Vienna, came the prosecutor of the "Dollfuss murder trial." He had recommended the death penalty for both defendants who were accused of the assassination of the Austrian, Chancellor Dollfuss. By the time this brave prosecutor reached the gate to the exercise yard, the S.S. vultures jumped upon him and kept on beating him with clubs while others kicked him with their boots until, finally, his terrible mutilated body had to be carried away.

A World War I German officer, Dr. Lothar Erdmann, had the misfortune of being beaten by an S.S. trooper right upon his arrival at this concentration camp. He objected to this kind of treatment with the remark that he happened to be an officer of World War I and that both his sons were now serving in similar positions in World War II. The result—more maltreatment until this victim, too, had to be carried out to the infirmary. He died two days later. Cause of death (as usual) circulatory disorders.

One day an elegant limousine driven by a private chauffeur rolled through the gate over the yard toward Barrack #56, which later was occupied by political prisoners. Inside the limo was an old gentleman wrapped in blankets and sitting next to him an S.S. man. Well, since when are newcomers taken here by private car, especially in such an expensive one? This surely must be a very important guest, or maybe a very good friend of Adolf himself. This was no holiday. It happened to be November 23, 1942. However, it could be said that the weather was rather unpleasant and cold; even the barracks had the heat on already. The chauffeur brought the neatly dressed old gentleman, about 70 years of age, to the registration desk. According to his own doctor's certificate, he was suffering from heart disease, combined with dropsy and other ailments. His badly swollen feet were clad in felt slippers. He had to sit down. It was quite an effort for the comrades in the registration office to hear what he had to say and to find out who he was. The arrest warrant he carried with him indicated his name was Councilor of Commerce Mr. Adolf Pochwadt, owner of the Kaolin plant, located at 90 Cologne Street, Cologne-Godesberg, who had been in solitary confinement since May 1940. Due to his ailments, he had to be taken to the camp's hospital, it said on his warrant. Pochwadt got inmate number #53572 and was taken by stretcher to sick bay. After the evening roll call, I had a chance to visit Pochwadt in the infirmary where the orderlies had put him in a special bed in an isolated corner. From him, who could feel that the end was near, I found out about his case history which is as follows: Pochwadt had sent a letter of complaint to Funk, minister of the Reich's economy. His complaint was about member #17 of the NSDAP, by the name of Ludwig von Freien-Seipoldsdorf, who had cheated him out of 1.8 million Marks. Following an order by the Nazi party, he had to sell one of his plants to member #17, who was considered to be a member of the Nazi party for a long time, a so-called old fighter, and who, therefore, didn't have to pay nearly as much as Pochwadt had been asking for.

In his grievance to Funk, he had used some rather strong expressions, something like "lousy pig" and maybe some other four-letter words. Even though these terms might have been the right kind of words under these circumstances, they nevertheless caused his arrest by the Gestapo. Pochwadt's total assets of some 18 million Marks were confiscated by the Nazi party. On top of that, they threatened him with more accusations of treason and other subversive activities for which he could be indicted. All this must have caused a lot of worry to the old and very sick man. During my visits, I also found out from him that the Nazis had tried to get some special formulas from him, which he had used in the manufacture of weather-resistant paints, a material that was far superior to oil paints. Unfortunately, Pochwadt was never released; he died on December 12, 1942, in the concentration camp infirmary.

After Hitler declared he had conquered Poland completely, it didn't take long until the Polish people, men and women, young and old, were taken into custody and locked up in some of these concentration camps. Even schoolchildren were no exception. Hitler had in mind to get rid of all Polish intelligentsia. To make it possible to have large numbers of "prisoners of war" and guerillas brought into captivity, he had students arrested right in their classrooms. Patrons of the theaters and movie houses were also taken into custody while on their way home. This way, Hitler was able to proclaim, through the press and over the radio, about how many prisoners had been taken, thereby trying to make the world believe how successful the German Army had been.

During the first days of April 1940, a troop of Polish captives, about 600 men, arrived at Sachsenhausen concentration camp. They had been arrested in Bromberg and other cities, Polish and German people mixed together. All of them were well-dressed and carried with them an ample supply of currency and other valuables. These people happened to be mostly merchants, manufacturers, and land owners; well anyway, they belonged to the so-called upper class. There had been no reason at all for any of these arrests. The Nazis merely had in mind to get hold of their possessions, such as jewelry, watches, and cash, all of which they confiscated right away. The reception of this transport took place in what we called the "Little Camp," consisting of Barracks #15 through 18.

In this transport were also several Catholic priests who became the targets of special atrocities at the hands of blockleaders Baierle, Knittle, Maienhofer, Schubert, Fickert, and others. All of these newcomers were taken to Wing A of Block 17 for registration. From there, they were herded to Wing B, where they had to leave their personal possessions, such as valuables, jewelry, and cash. After that, Baierle, Schubert, and their fellow henchmen looked their new victims over and mistreated them whenever they felt like it.

In the middle of the barracks, stood one of those lockers for clothes; they had three doors. These lockers were just about big enough so that one slender person could squeeze through its doors. In this case, however, a rather heavyset or stout person was forced into each locker compartment. After all three lockers were occupied, the whole closet was tipped over in such a way that the people inside would fall on their faces. After that, the S.S. thugs turned the closet over so it was standing upside down, whereupon they would tip it over so that the people inside would land on their backs. The final move was to get it back into its normal position.

After the doors were opened the victims would fall out. They had quite some injuries, with the blood running from the mouth and the noses broken quite often, and some had broken bones and skull fractures. These men had to be taken to the infirmary. In case the comrades didn't carry them away fast enough, first to the dressing room, then to the room for treatment, then the S.S. guards went after them by beating upon them with ironclad sticks, so that the blood would squirt out of their open wounds. Anybody who was still able to stand on his own feet, after being undressed, was chased outside stark naked, where he had to wait his turn to get into the washroom in order to clean his wounds. This was in Barrack #18. There were no bathtubs or showers, only little pans with some warm water to put their feet in. As there were no water pipes, the water had to be brought in by the truckload; that is wagons containing barrels full of water which, of course, didn't stay warm for too long. It could also be mentioned here that these maltreated new arrivals had to hand over to the guards any edible material, such as sandwiches, smoked ham, sausages, butter, and cheese which they may have had on them when they arrived. In fact, there were some receptacles standing around to put everything in. What happened to it later? Of course, the S.S. men helped themselves to it before somebody else would pick it out again.

A somewhat later arriving troop of Polish people—about 1000 men—didn't get a reception that could be called humane. By the way they were dressed, they seemed to be working people, many of them from the country. As usual, old and young were together. With sticks and cat o'nine tails, they were driven through the gate of hell, as it was called, where they were greeted with words like, "We are going to teach you Polacks our culture, as you will see." After that, they were marched into the reception room, known also as the infamous "Little Camp."

An old man in his seventies was given a helping hand by his son after he couldn't walk anymore unassisted. They were the last ones to arrive at the entrance door, where the old man collapsed, unable to take another step. He was lying there, possibly close to death, which did not hinder Schubert in the least from kicking him in the face with his stormtrooper boots while yelling at him, "Will you Polish pig get up and get moving!?" Begging for mercy, his son only asked, please not to mistreat his dying father. In answer, Schubert hit him in the face with something resembling a baseball bat. Then, with a kick in the rear, the son was thrown towards the nearest S.S. man. Meanwhile, the body of the father was thrown on a push-cart and taken to the crematory. But just before that, Schubert took the watch and the wallet from the old man. Then, nonchalantly, he lit himself a cigarette, of which he had an ample supply, all pilfered from the merchandise these prisoners had with them upon their arrival.

On an earlier transport, which arrived at the camp on December 20, 1939, an elderly landowner from Westphalia landed at this camp. His name was August Klosterschulte. According to his arrest warrant he was to get special treatment, with the result of a fast disappearance.

His undoing was letting soldiers whom he had to board at his estate, sleep only on straw, instead of giving them beds. Klosterschulte, an ardent Catholic, was also a determined Nazi foe, which explains the reason behind the order for special maltreatment. So, in this case, the blockleader, Saathof, together with his colleague Hoess, took over from here by beating the old man daily with an ironclad club at the roll calls and whenever they saw him inside the building.

When I met Klosterschulte several days later in the bathhouse, I noticed how his body was covered with bruises and open wounds. Soon after that, he was transferred to the "Klinker," a brick factory, in order to get from Bugdalla, another Nazi henchman, the last treatment. On the evening of January 13, 1940, Klosterschulte, who was, by now, completely helpless, was brought back to camp in a truck. Here he had to stand in line for the roll call in the ice-cold temperature. He soon collapsed and lay on the ground where Saathof kicked him with his boots all over. When Klosterschulte didn't move, Saathof jumped upon him with all his weight so that the blood squirted out of his mouth like a fountain. Four comrades carried the dying man into the infirmary. An autopsy revealed torn lungs and liver with several broken ribs piercing through his lungs and liver. Now his family was notified, "Death due to double pneumonia." After that followed a letter that read somewhat like this:

> *"Several days ago your father called in sick whereupon he was transferred to the hospital for medical treatment. We can assure you that he was given the best possible care as far as doctors and nurses are concerned. Despite all the efforts of our surgeons and medical staff, it was impossible to keep his ailments under control. We are expressing our deepest sympathy to the great loss of your father. The deceased did not have any wishes."* —signed:
> "Heil Hitler"
> *Loritz*
> *Commanding Officer.*

At that time it was still permissible to let the family of the deceased have the body for burial. However, before it was returned, the body was laid out instead in a coffin in an automobile garage that was temporarily converted into a funeral parlor. During the ceremonies, a sergeant would speak a few words of condolence at the coffin to the relatives that happened to be present. After that, the body was taken out of the coffin, which was only a showcase, and placed into a wooden crate, which was then sealed and labeled with the address of the home cemetery. A strict order was given not to open the crate upon arrival but to bury it immediately.

Among the newcomers of another transport, dated May 9, 1942, happened to be a rather sickly man named Arno Kubig, 62 years of age, and a waiter by trade. He could not endure the bending exercises on his knees nor the rolling all across the exercise lot. "That's the way we all may have to go," were his last words before he died, even before his name could be registered. His arrest warrant was the only clue to his identity with no reason why he had been arrested.

On another occasion, which happened in April 1941, a Frenchman by the name of Arman Faure, who didn't understand any German, had been beaten terribly, right upon his arrival, and without any reason at all. When camp officer Suhren, asked him why he was bleeding, he could only say: "I'm beaten." "What, you have been beaten? That's a lie and an accusation against a commanding officer." Then he and his accomplice, another S.S. man by the name of Hecht, jumped down on him, thereby letting their anger out on him with more bestialities.

These are only a few examples to give the reader some idea of what did happen to some unfortunate newcomers. However, what they had to endure after being made "residents" in this camp—will be revealed in the following chapters.

CHAPTER 11

REASONS FOR BEING BROUGHT INTO CUSTODY
(Heydrich's Passports to Hell)

"While living on earth I only believe in Adolf Hitler. Sometimes I am afraid God could become jealous on account of the overwhelming events that a single humble human being is able to achieve."

Dr. Robert Ley

Göring is supposed to have said that the inmates of concentration camps represent the scum of humanity and that he didn't want to be held responsible for throwing out the pails with the garbage. Well, if Göring was comparing the concentration camps with garbage dumps, one shouldn't be surprised when, in the uninformed portions of the population, (and how few found out the truth about concentration camps and their captives) the general impression persisted that the Nazis were separating the worst criminals, the scum, from the Master Race, thus proving to the people there so benevolent influence upon mankind.

Well, who were these inmates and why have they been taken here? Who called for their imprisonment and what were the reasons for their arrest and subsequent incarceration in these camps? And to top it all off, why were they called "prisoners in protective custody?" In plain language, this was supposed to mean that, under these circumstances, a person had to be protected from his fellow men. An arrest warrant would read something like this:

> District Governor The city and the date
> In this case: Flensburg, July 9, 1934 –
> 103/2 Warrant for the farmer Nikolaus Cordsen, Grossenwiehe/ Kreis Flensburg
> State
> Following an order by the Police Headquarters in Altona, I impose upon you, in accordance with article #83, paragraph #1 as decreed by our president for the protection of the people and the state, dated February 28, 1933, by the Superior Court and in connection with paragraph #2 of the Prussian Justice Department, dated March 2, 1933, as decreed in code 33, section 41 of the Police Administration, dated June 1, 1931, page 77, the arrest warrant. You will be held in protective custody. You are accused of causing unrest among the people in your hometown of Grossenwiehe by using phrases in your speeches which you did compare with some quotations of the Bible. It must be expected that the uproar on account of you will lead to far more serious consequences. The safety of your own person seems to be enough endangered to warrant the arrest and keep you in protective custody for the duration of four days.
> Signed as a substitute
> by Carstensen.

The four days in custody didn't change Herr Cordsen into an obedient Nazi follower. And that is why, after a prolonged stay in jail, he was taken to this concentration camp. More about Cordsen's case will be brought to light in a later chapter.

As a rule, the induction into a concentration camp was done by an arrest warrant from RSHA Headquarters in Berlin, printed on red paper, signed by a stamp machine with the name of the officer in charge, originally Heydrich and later Kaltenbrunner. This kind of arrest warrant could almost be compared with a death sentence; it surely was a passport to hell, the hell of the Third Reich. In many cases, a return to normal life was impossible. Upon induction into a concentration camp, a separation was made between those who were supposed to be in protective custody and others who were kept there as a precaution. Political prisoners, as well as those who were quoting the Bible, belonged to the first group, while antisocials and criminally inclined persons belonged to the second. As a visible sign, the political inmates had to wear red triangles made of cloth above their registration number as well as on the right leg of their pants. Jehovah's Witnesses had to wear the same markings in purple; the criminals wore green, and the antisocials, brown. However, after the Nazis decided that brown was supposed to be the color for the Nazi system, it could no longer be worn by this group; therefore, these triangles were painted over with some kind of black ink.

The wearers of the red sign were by no means only politicals, no, it could happen that the majority were regular, ordinary criminals who had been placed there by the Gestapo, with one purpose in mind: To serve as informants for the Nazis. They figured if they wore green markings, they might not be able to make contact with the politicals in order to spy on them.

It didn't take long for the interpreters and clerks in the political department to spot the infiltration of red-marked spies. Therefore, they saw to it that all the politicals were promptly informed about the camouflaged newcomers. But, despite all precautions, it could happen that these elements were successful in their dirty work by causing quite some hardship among the politicals, which could lead to special punishment, even death, as a result. After the establishment of concentration camps back in 1933, the first occupants were more or less the leaders and prominent figures in the Communist and Socialist parties, since the Nazis had to expect these persons to be the real enemies of the Nazi regime. Little by little, they would also imprison groups of people belonging to Jehovah's Witnesses, as well as ordinary criminals and antisocials.

During the summer of 1936, a drastic action against the so-called antisocials took place of "cleaning the streets," by taking anyone into custody who could be a hobo, tramp, a vagrant, peddler, wandering showman or musician, or even a gypsy. According to the Nazi doctrine, these elements were nothing but superfluous or unnecessary populace, not even real people. It may be said; however, that most of these people were earning their living and paying taxes even though some had a somewhat unsteady existence. Those few who went around begging, as well as some half-wits or funny characters that could be found anywhere, didn't matter to the Nazi regime.

Well, this "clean-up action" brought an end to the carefree life of young and wandering tradesmen and some homeless fellows who like to spend most of their time outdoors. From then on, any soliciting had to be done by the Nazis only. They started "organizing" the raising of funds on a rather large scale by using extortion in their methods while collecting from people who really didn't like to make any donations or contributions toward the Nazi cause. Just the same, the Nazis never seemed to have a large cash fund. So they kept on collecting under all kinds of names and for any kind of purpose. Yes, they had quite a few organizations working and collecting for them. Everyone had a different name and was supposed to have a different purpose. They had one thing in common: Every one of these organizations had the letters "NS" (National Socialism, Nationalsozialismus) in front of them. This collection took place from house to house, in public, on street corners, wherever many people could be met. The purpose for all these collections was always the same, for the benefit of the people and to raise the standard of living.

Meanwhile, the commitment of political prisoners continued without interruption since the Nazis recognized among the readers of newspapers and magazines, with subversive content, a threat to the Nazi cause. Therefore, these people could no longer be permitted to circulate among the others and had to be taken to one of these concentration camps. When in September 1939, the war against Poland became a reality, it didn't take long until mass arrests of prominent, but anti-Nazi-oriented people, took place. In seemingly endless caravans, they were marched into the concentration camps. Reason for commitment? Endangering the security of the Third Reich. In any event, this was the excuse. If it was not the security of the state that was presumably at stake, grounds for being arrested could also be an implication that the newly arrested might cause some unrest or dissatisfaction among the rest of the people, just by spreading anti-fascist ideas around. Next came any damaging, disdainful, or contemptible remarks a person could have made against the Nazi regime, which would give him a passport to a concentration camp. Sometimes, only some criticism or a scornful word to the wrong listener could cause an arrest. In quite a few cases, no reason for being arrested was available, for instance, if the arrested persons were foreigners. The mere fact of not being a German citizen was enough to make one's commitment to a concentration camp necessary. It was standard procedure to take Jewish people and Jehovah's Witnesses, on account of their beliefs, right away into custody. Gypsies were considered antisocials and, therefore, had to be removed from the public.

Due to the ever-increasing demands for skilled labor for the Nazi War Machine, all kinds of trained craftsmen were next to be dumped into concentration camps. Here no distinction, if German or foreign, was made. And if, for instance, the demand for cobblers or tailors could not be filled from among the imprisoned people, another survey among society's free enterprises took place, with the intent to pick out some likely candidates. From here on the concentration camps became more like something resembling an employment agency. Nazi-friendly business firms and manufacturers could now obtain cheap labor from the concentration camps. Of course, these firms had to pay more than regular wages, not to the workers, but to the concentration camp administrators. Room and board for an inmate was rather insignificant on a large scale. It happened to be about one Mark per day for one worker, while the wages came to about six Marks for skilled labor a day and three Marks for the unskilled. After all, this was quite some extra income for the concentration camps.

The personal papers of Rupert Mayer #16397, a Catholic priest who had been committed on December 22, 1939, indicated that he would rather be shot to death than reveal confessions. It happened that in August 1939, about a hundred party members who presumably believed in a monarchy had been arrested in Southern Germany. This Catholic priest who knew about the circumstances was supposed to testify, which he refused.

Two other Catholic priests, Joseph Schulz #28620 and Joseph Zillikin, both from little villages near Andernach am Rhine, were taken into for purposely turning their backs when Hermann Göring and his party entered a restaurant. "Ignoring the Reich's field marshal" was the notation on the arrest warrant. As a special penalty, both of them had to do some rigorous exercises for two hours daily, like holding their hands behind the neck while bending the knees up and down. Furthermore, some extra dirty jobs were assigned to them. All prisoners had a prisoner identity record, such as the one for Joseph Zillikin (Fig. 10).

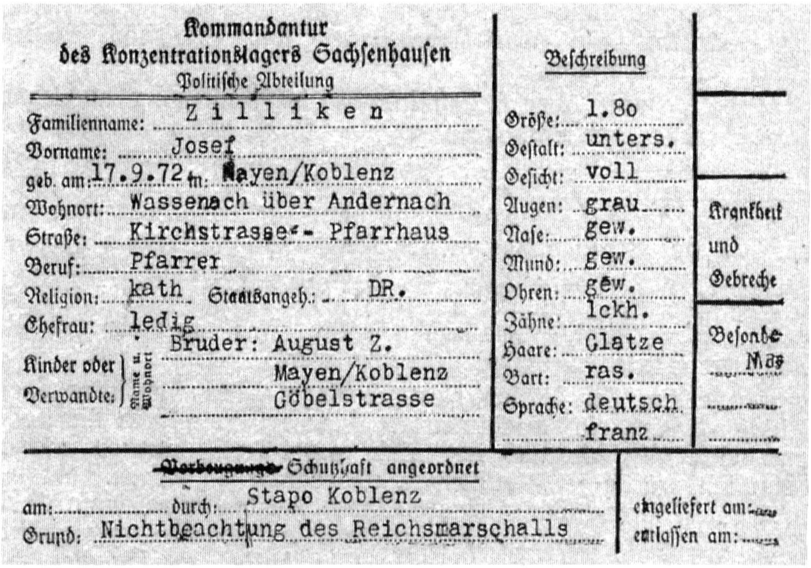

Kommandantur
des Konzentrationslagers Sachsenhausen
Politische Abteilung

Familienname: Z i l l i k e n
Vorname: Josef
geb. am: 17.9.72 in: Mayen/Koblenz
Wohnort: Wassenach über Andernach
Straße: Kirchstrasse - Pfarrhaus
Beruf: Pfarrer
Religion: kath Staatsangeh.: DR.
Ehefrau: ledig
Kinder oder Verwandte: Name Wohnort: Bruder: August Z. Mayen/Koblenz Göbelstrasse

Beschreibung
Größe: 1.80
Gestalt: unters.
Gesicht: voll
Augen: grau
Nase: gew.
Mund: gew.
Ohren: gew.
Zähne: lckh.
Haare: Glatze
Bart: ras.
Sprache: deutsch franz

Krankheit und Gebrechen
Besonde- Mas

~~Vorbeugungs~~ Schutzhaft angeordnet
am: durch: Stapo Koblenz
Grund: Nichtbeachtung des Reichsmarschalls
eingeliefert am:
entlassen am:

Fig. 10. Prisoner identity record.

A short time later, it seemed as if the ghost of the Almighty of Karin Hall (Göring) was floating around in again, this time in the person of a certain art connoisseur and caretaker who was brought into custody. His name was Emil Weber and he got his ticket with #42239 on it. The Gestapo had him detained for ten days since he had made some critical remarks. The landowners around Karin Hall and its vicinity had complained to him about Göring's extravagant hunting parties that took place in their fields and woodlands, causing considerable crop damage for which they couldn't get any kind of compensation.

With such a disorderly government, one shouldn't be surprised that the prices went way up and that inflation was on its way. One didn't even have any control over their own children who were taken away by the so-called H. J. (Hitler Jugend). The fact that Weber agreed with the complaining landowners soon became known to members of the Gestapo, and it didn't take long before he was arrested. After serving ten days, he was released and put to work at Karin Hall again. Polishing Göring's medals and art collections, which could have gotten tarnished during his absence, was enough of an excuse to have him set free again.

The appearance of fortune tellers, individuals who could predict the future or read it from cards, had always bothered the Nazis. The number of fortune tellers decreased considerably since the war began, especially those claiming that they could read the future out of discarded coffee grounds. After all, there was hardly any more coffee left in the stores, or whatever they called coffee, mostly it was some kind of roasted barley or other grain. Next, came the clairvoyants because they were regarded to be very dangerous. For instance, a well-known seer by the name of Hannussen was removed already before the war for his allegedly disturbing the peace of mind of government officials including the superstitious Adolf himself. The immediate arrests of all persons known to be seers or clairvoyants became a new law; they all were taken to concentration camps. For that reason, a man by the name of Wilhelm Steinert #61300, wasn't surprised to be taken out of circulation when he had already predicted in 1939 that after more than four years the Nazis would lose the war. And so he became an inmate in this concentration camp, where every evening on the exercise yard, he could listen to Goebbels broadcast about the absolute and even "final victory" for the Nazis, which would become certain in only a matter of time.

The group of people calling themselves clairvoyants happened to be quite large, and Adolf must have feared yet believed them. Right after Mussolini's arrest by his own people in July 1943, every person who claimed to be able to predict the future or to be a clairvoyant had to appear at the nearest Gestapo headquarters to show proof of their ability. Hitler wanted to know where the Italian revolutionaries had taken his old friend "Il Duce." Apparently, a clue from one seer did bring some light into the darkness surrounding the whereabouts of Mussolini. Understandably, clairvoyants had to be careful about predicting the downfall of the Third Reich. Needless to say, the majority of the inmates were, by now, under the impression that the Nazis would sooner or later lose this war. They could figure that out without being able to read a crystal ball.

Among some newcomers who had been taken to Sachsenhausen concentration camp, happened to be two pupils, sons of a clergyman from Stettin, Klaus Reichmuth #41650, and Klaus Rendtorff #4162, who were kept in confinement for three months, then sent home on probation by the camp director. Their crime: they had been accused of publishing a certain anti-Nazi circular, written by Bishop von Galen of Muenster.

These are just a few examples to demonstrate for what reason people were brought to this concentration camp. Here is another case in which the Nazis insisted on an arrest. Involved was Cornelius Arnold #36245, a Dutchman from Rotterdam, who was taken into custody for having fought for the leftists in the Spanish Civil War, a fact that was of no concern to the Nazis. Then there was the 14-year-old Polish boy Zygmund Grzywinsky, #37602, who was accused of sabotage. He was not strong enough to do the hard labor of a regular farm hand. Park and recreation director, Oskar Alexander #40732, of Bad Bramstedt-Holstein, got an order not to leave his hometown. Because he took a train to Hamburg to attend funeral services for a member of his family, he was arrested and taken to this concentration camp, which he didn't leave alive again.

Ridiculing the Nazi salute was another way to get into trouble, as Ferdinand Klement #40983 found out. What he had done could only be handled more like an atonement which meant a stay and that would include "special education." Let's hear his case. At the occasion of a Nazi congregation, everyone saluted "Heil Hitler" with his right arm raised, and this man, Klement, had the nerve to lay a real loud fart instead!!

Misdemeanors like these were not the only incidents that could inflict some damage to the prestige of the Nazi system, there were a thousand and one things nobody thought of that could inflict some damage to the structure of the Nazi system. The Nazis were suspicious. Any questionable behavior gave reason for further investigation. One of the characters under strong suspicion was a man from Tyrol by the name of Kajetan Schörghofer #41461, whom another inmate had to carry on his back to the political department because he happened to be an amputee. In his homeland of Tyrol, this unfortunate cripple was using a cart he could only move with his hands while distributing anti-Nazi pamphlets. He never left the concentration camp alive. A so-called sick transport took him to the "herb garden," the nickname for the gas chamber.

Being helpful to the Jews, sometimes only a "hello" on the street could be all that was necessary to be put under arrest and into a concentration camp. A man by the name of Heinrich Gerlach #53802 found that out because he had helped a Jew to get his shoes resoled. Carrying trunks belonging to Jewish travelers caused one porter to be arrested and taken to this concentration camp. Also sitting next to Jewish people in public places, as well as drinking coffee together in a cafeteria, was an offense and reason for arrest and commitment. It was really bad for people accused of causing "defamation" of the Nazi race. Anyone who would degrade the structure of the Nazi system was considered a criminal like, for instance, the half-invalid, Theodore Strasser, age 56, who occasionally would help a 65-year-old Jewish woman with her grocery shopping and some work around the house because she was partly paralyzed. For 16 years, he had helped her until the Nuremberg law declared this kind of help a crime. Because he didn't pay any attention to this law he was taken into custody after he had already spent several weeks at Labor Camp Wühlheide, where he had time to think about the "defamation of the Master Race."

Spreading so-called horror tales about the Nazis, as well as debasing the reputation of the Nazi party itself was always a crime that called for imprisonment. Telling others what he had witnessed, as an inmate in a concentration camp, was criticized as slander and denied as being only horror tales; therefore, punishable with concentration camp confinement. One of the people who found that out was Max Bandush #37602 who, after his release, had given a true account of the activities in a concentration camp crematory. He was taken into custody as a "repeater" and got a terrible beating from the S.S. guards upon his arrival.

Another inmate was held captive in Sachsenhausen for still another reason. An order came from Berlin and was sent to Prague where they wanted a man by the name of Anton Schreiber, and according to a report he had to be taken into custody for a hearing to take place on December 1, 1941. The documentation for his arrest is as follows:

> *"As he has in his capacity as a faith healer caused unfavorable and detrimental influence, leading to considerable unrest among large segments of the population, and as he has, given the war, been trying to undermine the unity of the interior front, A. Schreiber is to be transferred to a concentration camp. Commitment papers, an arrest warrant, and a short report had to be prepared upon his arrival at this concentration camp."*
> Signed:
> *RSHA Röhm 4 C 2 H #10130, Heydrich/Ne*

The doors and windows, so to speak, were wide open to any foes of the Nazi system; there was always room in these concentration camps. Anyone who liked to get rid of a neighbor he disliked, a stubborn creditor, or just a person he had a grudge against, all he had to do was to make an unfavorable report at the nearest Nazi information center, saying that so and so could be an enemy of the state. As a rule, without investigating these accusations, the Gestapo took care of the arrest, had the "passport to hell" (nickname for protective custody), issued and delivered, and the informer got rid of the person he disliked or who was somehow or somewhere in his way.

Following is an outstanding case, revealing in all detail how a Nazi, with the mind of a criminal, had brought his political enemy into a concentration camp that finally caused his death:

> *The Police Department: Viöl, August 26, 1939.*
> *District magistrate in Husum*
> Re: <u>Denunciation and arrest warrant for Bakermeister Hans Petersen</u>
> *In reference to the enclosed report, I urge your administrator to have the baker Hans Petersen in Viöl arrested with the request to have him taken to the nearest Gestapo Headquarters. Evidently, Petersen had the intention to spread unrest among the people, as well as to ridicule the German news broadcast and to change this news into untruthful slander. Already last year he had made questionable remarks about the crisis in the Sudetenland. Here he went from house to house to sell his bakery products, thereby making it possible to make similar unfavorable remarks to his customers. This way, he could have caused ill feelings or moods of depression, especially among our women. He is well-known as a strong adversary to the Nazi cause since long ago, and during the last few years, he became more and more of a criticizer and defeatist. He still refused the Hitler salute. The general unrest in*

this part of the country is rather strong. Therefore, I consider it absolutely necessary to make it impossible for him to keep on going from house to house spreading bad news. This is especially important nowadays when all our people have to keep their nerves quiet and their minds undisturbed. Therefore, I regard it as being very important to have him taken into police custody and order his arrest on account of his undesirable comments which are causing strong reactions in our town. I further request to have this case presented to the Gestapo.
The County Clerk
Signed: Carstensen/Hermann.

As could not be expected otherwise, this denunciation was successful. Petersen was at first taken to the city jail in Kiel until the so-called passport to hell, issued by the RSHA in Berlin arrived. It looked like this:

Geheime Staatspolizei (Gestapo)
Berlin SW 11, Sept. 20, 1939
B # 11 D Haft #3417
    Warrant for protective custody
First and second name: Hans Petersen
    Birthday and location: April 20, 1892: Sörupholz
Occupation: Baker/Owner of Store
    Family: Married
Nationality: RD (Reichsdeutsch) German
    Religion: Ev (Evangelisch, Lutheran)
    Race: Explain, if not Aryan
    Address: Viöl
is to be taken into custody.
Reasons:
    "According to the result of the police investigation, Petersen is, through his behavior, endangering the stability and security of the people and the nation and is

causing unrest through his agitating and defeat-inspiring speeches."
signed: Heydrich
notarized: Pieper, recording secretary.

The statement of the accusing county clerk that the agitation and unrest in the township had been widespread was nothing but a lie because Petersen enjoyed the friendship and confidence of the people in his hometown. He was one of them, the friends for peace, especially in those days when the agitation for a war against Poland reached a high point, which finally resulted in an attack against this nation.

The year was 1939. However, Petersen was taken to Concentration Camp Sachsenhausen. Here, he suffered the cruelties, atrocities, and torments inflicted by the Nazis until he died on January 25, 1942. A telegram advised his wife that her husband died of pneumonia and that she would have to wait for further news from the Gestapo. All preceding efforts by his wife to have him released from the concentration camp had been in vain. According to the request of Carstensen, the county clerk, who was his political enemy, Petersen was supposed to be confined for the rest of his life. I found out about this through the documents on file for Petersen (Fig. 11). But still, when later after the war, the so-called De Nazification trials took place; Carstensen had the nerve to admit only being a follower of the Nazi system. This trial took place in Husum on February 1, 1949, where the county clerk, Carstensen, was placed in Group III with a fine of DM 4000.00 and the cost of the trial. After that, this case was taken to the prosecutor's office, this time to be tried as a crime against humanity.

Fig. 11. Petersen, who was supposed to be confined for the rest of his life, died of pneumonia.

One should really be under the impression that the Nazi government with a membership of presumably 99% followers, could not have been shaken to its very foundation by the remaining 1% of disgruntled people, or those that still held on to the previous government. However, the mass arrests gave us another picture. Journalists, poets, musicians, painters, in fact, all kinds of artists besides the intellectuals, caused Hitler's power to tremble, and, therefore, it was of utmost importance to have these persons taken out of circulation and shipped to concentration camps. The Frisian poet and linguist, Jens Mungaard of Keitum/Sylt, had been accused of endangering the unity of the German language through his activity as a writer and lecturer on this subject. That is why he was taken to this concentration camp. On February 15, 1940, he died there following a severe case of pneumonia. The commanding officer denied admittance of this very sick man to the infirmary, and so Mungaard succumbed on a bag of straw in Barrack #27.

Contrary to the general opinion that Göring was honored by jokes made about him must be disregarded as fairy tales. Anybody who tried to make jokes or wisecracks about the government or the men around Hitler was threatened with a stay in a concentration camp while a repeat performance would bring him behind barbed wires for sure. At no time did so many jokes and funny stories about the Nazis originate as during the Nazi regime.

Being made fun of could have a depressing effect on that person, but if it should have happened to one of the Nazis, then the offender had to disappear from the surface, at least for the time being. As a rule, they were taken to a concentration camp. There was a time when almost every day well-known entertainers were taken into custody for having given some rather amusing performances consisting mostly of a variety of jokes about the Nazi system.

It was, therefore, no surprise when one of the best performers in a Berlin nightclub, a man known mostly by his first name, Werner, found himself one day among the inmates in the political department of a concentration camp. Reason for his confinement: making fun of leading personalities. Now let's hear what Werner had to say about the Nazi bigwigs while on stage in front of an audience. "I didn't say anything, but I had to perform, because that's what I am getting paid for and so I only remarked that the Germans seem to be a peculiar kind of people because they are using the plural form while speaking. Already, with William II, it became obvious as he constantly spoke of "We, William in the grace of God" instead of I, William, etc. And now, for instance, the proverb: "Lies have short legs." Why don't we say: "The liar has one short leg." That's all I said, further comments came from the audience by repeating the name "Goebbels" over and over again. And there was absolutely nothing that I could do to prevent it or even stop it. That was Werner's explanation. The result was a warning from the Gestapo, who called him "an instigator for the general public." (Josef Goebbels, the Minister for Propaganda, did have a club foot and walked with a limp.)

At his next performance, Werner was more cautious. He didn't say anything, he couldn't say anything, because he wore a huge dog's muzzle over his head while walking across the stage. The public got a kick out of it and started laughing but finally stamped with their feet and urged Werner to say at least a few words. After all, they had paid for their ticket to see and hear the show too.

Well, finally, as he could see the audience wouldn't give him any peace, he took off the muzzle and made this comment, "Ladies and gentlemen, the political part is over, now I am starting." But he didn't even have a chance to do anything else because, by then, some Gestapo men took hold of him and led him away for a private audience and lecture as well. Werner insisted that he didn't intend to say anything against leading personalities or make fun of them. He even promised to say absolutely nothing at his next performance, although he was really under contract to do some acting.

When at the next performance in front of a big audience he crept around the stage floor on his hands and knees, like in a circus without saying anything, the people were wondering. Finally, the public got sick and tired of this kind of acting and asked, "Why are you creeping around like that?" Thereupon, Werner got up to his full height of more than 6 ft. and remarked, "There is no reason for asking this question because nowadays everybody is creeping." That was too much for the Gestapo. At a time when the general public was standing enthusiastically behind a common unity for all the German people where they cheered and applauded Hitler, Göring, Goebbels, and the other bigwigs of the Nazi empire, there was no time or reason to talk about creeps. Result: final warning. Now, what else could he do? Lose his engagement or try to give a performance that could not be interpreted as some kind of mockery about the Nazi system.

While standing again in front of the auditorium that was filled almost to the last seat, he was considering if he should say anything or if only some kind of mimic would be sufficient. This time it seemed as if he didn't come to any conclusion because, all of a sudden, the lights went out and Werner took a flashlight out of his pocket. At least this way he could show the people that he was still there. Holding his flashlight, he came down from the stage, walked through the aisles and rows where the people were sitting, as if trying to find something on the floor. Thereupon, roaring laughter and shouts of encouragement from the public. So, finally, he went back up on the stage saying, "Ladies and gentlemen, I believe I can assure you this has nothing to do with the conduct of the people in charge, but rather with the conduction (of electrical power) meaning in a sense: leadership of the government." After that, the Gestapo lost their patience because, obviously, any fault in the electrical wire system was not the reason for criticism, but the wrongdoings within the government itself were. Therefore, the court in charge of the security and safety of the Reich had him arrested and convicted as a mockerer with a sentence to go to a concentration camp.

If every single reason for being shipped to a concentration camp had been listed, a few extra books would have been needed. But here, for instance, is another incident that should not be overlooked about a man by the name of Anton Kloucek #39485. All he did was ask the bartender of a saloon to please turn off the radio when the OKW news, with all the alleged victories for the Nazis, was being broadcast. Then there was the chauffeur, Kurt Toepfer #40680. He had been charged with overtaking the car in front of him which belonged to a high-ranking Nazi official. This happened on a super highway. This was certainly reason enough to give an overtaker an overhauling in a concentration camp. Being a vegetarian made no exception. A lawyer by the name of Otto Rauth #42872, had to find out for himself. While living in Mexico, he became interested in a certain diet by the name of Mazdaznan, which was teaching a vegetarian way of eating and a natural way of living.

Any efforts by the working people to gain better working conditions or high-paying jobs by changing their place of employment was regarded a work sabotage or refusal to work. Punishment: a stay in one of the concentration camps where they were grouped together with the so-called antisocials. The Gestapo worked rather inconsiderately; sometimes they took refusal to work as a political offense, which had to be punished accordingly. The commitment of criminals took place more or less at random. In quite a few instances, people who followed a trade were taken for regular criminals, although they had never been convicted or even charged with a crime before. Being labeled a criminal was for these people an unjustified punishment. All Gypsies were registered as antisocials, regardless, even though the majority of them had their own permanent living quarters and were working in some kind of trade, and they even paid taxes. Among the work brigade of the concentration camps, the Gypsies proved themselves as helpful and willing coworkers; there was no reason to treat them like antisocials. However, the general treatment of Gypsies was not nearly as cruel or severe as that meted out to the Jewish people who had to endure most of the atrocities.

It may also be mentioned here that a so-called Aryan was incarcerated just because he had been living together with a Gypsy woman for about 15 years. His name was Willy Schröder #53827, and he was the father of her two children. However, he was forced to abandon his family, as this union was considered contrary to the so-called purity of the race (Aryan in this case). The Gestapo seemed to enjoy digging into intimate love and family affairs. Anybody of the Slavic or Romanic race, who was involved in personal relations with a German woman, sometimes only in a friendly way, would run the risk of being put into a concentration camp. The same held for Germans who had a love affair with foreign girls. This is why so many people who were romantically involved with someone of the wrong race were put behind bars, although they never had committed any crimes. It can also be mentioned that the love partners, too, received the "blessing" of the concentration camps. Reasons for being taken into custody were put into writing like this: he or she has violated the wholesome and rightful opinion toward the German nation to the fullest extent. For instance, it was considered an immoral act for Bronislaw Ganeass #52735, a 12-year-old Polish school boy, to walk hand in hand with an 11-year-old German girl as they went to school together.

The commitment of cripples, invalids, blind people, and those who were no longer able to work on account of old age, seemed to have only one purpose: that of getting rid of these unfortunate ones. Already the change to worn-out, insufficient clothes, the way they had to live in these barracks, the poorly selected food rations, and the lack of heat; all were contributing factors to lower their resistance which, in some cases, led to an early death, especially if they were brought in during the winter months. A few weeks of cruel treatment by inhuman blockleaders caused the death of many old and helpless people. Therefore, it didn't take long until these unfortunates finally left the concentration camps, oftentimes via the chimneys of the crematories.

From all parts of the country, the S.S. and Gestapo collected these unfortunate victims with mainly one thought in mind, to eliminate these unnecessary eaters. Why did they bring in the blind 80-year-old Idriz Musie #39143, from Serbia, who had to be helped along by his comrades all the way? It was unbelievable; he had been classified as a dangerous criminal. The number of different reasons for being shipped to a concentration camp could be increased a hundredfold, according to statistics kept on file.

A special chapter can be allocated for homosexuals also known as "175ers" who had to wear a pink triangle on their prison uniforms. It is none of my business to act in their defense or to turn against them for their preferred lifestyle. People like these were held captive in concentration camps, without any proof of their wrongdoing. They could have been head of a family who may have been connected with a gay partner during their youth and, therefore, they were registered like the worst criminals, treated accordingly with the intent to dispose of them. The extermination of homosexuals was another task for which the S.S. had a high priority. Kept in isolation, they had to do the dirtiest work, regardless of their physical condition. When, by nightfall, several of them had succumbed to their misery, the S.S. didn't mind at all. Only when, by January 1943, the death toll among them had reached 24, on a single day, the commanding officer became a little concerned. Then came a temporary intermission and the remaining homosexuals felt a little more like human beings again. However, any of them who survived the capitulation was, indeed, a very lucky fellow.

Besides these more or less conventional reasons for being arrested, there were others. For instance, being under suspicion for printing illegal pamphlets and the congregation of people with the same anti-Nazi political orientation. This was mostly the case with former members of the leftist parties, as well as followers of the witnesses in the so-called "Scheringer Lynch murder trial." The identification tickets these prisoners had to wear during their transport were very informative in their description as to the "general danger" these people would present, for instance: "Escaped criminal, handcuffs absolutely necessary; under suspicion of being a dangerous fugitive from justice; inclination to commit suicide, must also be handcuffed in train compartments for prisoners."

The inhumane treatment the Gestapo used in order to bring more prisoners to the concentration camps, may be described with the ordeal some of the professors at the University of Krakow, Poland, had to endure. After Poland's defeat the professors, deans, and students were ordered to assemble in the university's auditorium to get some new instructions. After this large room was almost filled to capacity, the doors were locked and everyone inside declared a prisoner. Soon after that, they were transported to concentration camp Sachsenhausen, where they arrived in the beginning of December 1939. The first of these transports consisted of 60 persons who received inmate numbers #13995–14054. Their numbers increased with more transports arriving in January 1940. The mortality rate of these professors who were mostly older gentlemen of advanced years, among them a few Ph.Ds. of the University of Leipzig and other German institutions of higher learning, was very high. Approximately one-quarter of teachers who had been taken to Sachsenhausen died as the result of hunger, cold, and mistreatment by the end of 1940. The reason behind this action was the Nazi extermination program of the Polish intelligentsia. Anyone who was still alive was eventually released in February 1941, under certain conditions; however, even among these freed people the Gestapo and S.S. caused quite a few of them to die as a result of further maltreatment, cold, and starvation after their return to Poland.

Mr. Jan Navak, a professor of geology, Mr. Wilk, an astronomer, Mr. Koiaczkoski, a professor of Polish history, as well as instructor for biology and agriculture at the faculty of Wiodek, died this way, while Mr. Ottmann, the old secretary of the university, and Mr. Heydel, professor of economy, were shot to death during one of the so-called "special actions."

More people succumbed to the atrocities as for instance, the president of the Polish Academy of Sciences, Professor Thaddaeus Kowalski, who died after the war in the spring of 1948. I received the death notice from his relatives. He was one of the best comrades I met at the concentration camp. We exchanged letters after the capitulation.

Another chapter will be devoted to the extermination of the intellectuals of all nations by the "brown plague" as the Nazis are called later in this book. There was nothing they hated more than intelligence in an opponent. Even this they could understand, and history has confirmed from time to time that in the end intellectual superiority will be the victor over brutal force. But just the same, the destruction of the intelligentsia element continued. Shortly before the capture of Krakow's professors, 1100 students of the Czechoslovakian Universities, Prague and Brünn, arrived at this concentration camp. The date was November 18, 1939. They had been accused of participating in a political demonstration in Prague. Even though most of these students had been set free as time went on, there were quite a few who had been kept prisoners until the final days when the concentration camp was liberated by the Allies. It should be mentioned here that these students from Czechoslovakia were part of the finest and most helpful inmates among the whole group of prisoners. If they could possibly save a human life, one could count on them that they would do their very best. The patients in the infirmary had great praise for them; after all, a good many of them happened to be medical students and I, myself, will never forget many of them who also worked together with me as interpreters. Josef Zeman, Robert Janik, Oleg Homola, Alex Strobach, and many others work together with me in the political section.

Since the reasons for being arrested and taken to a concentration camp were seldom valid, the poor victims, likewise, were not able-bodied enough to withstand the strain of imprisonment. It was not up to a physician to decide if these victims of the S.S. or Gestapo were strong enough to be handled as prisoners. To make it look legitimate, all prospective prisoners were taken to a police physician who would fill out and sign a form saying that he or she was physically able to be taken on a transport to any concentration camp. Just in case a police physician would show concern about the condition of the victim, then the Gestapo would overrule his decision. Here are just a few examples which are kept on file for reference:

Gestapo Headquarters in Plauen, June 7, 1940

> re: medical report of Edward Prosch #25950, a tailor, "Considered able to withstand confinement in a concentration camp, despite poor health as a result of malnutrition."

Gestapo Headquarters in Karlsbad, July 4, 1940

> re: medical report of Josef Seitz #26907, "Considered able to work to some extent, jaw bone defect, therefore, unable to chew properly, result: very emaciated."
>
> re: medical report of Heinrich Wagner #26908, "Limited capacity to work, somewhat feeble-minded but able to understand."
>
> re: medical report of Adam Kudrich #26885, lawyer and attorney, transferred from Gestapo headquarters Oppeln, July 8, 1940. Here the statement said: "Severe kidney ailment, transfer to an infirmary recommended, outside that, physically able to perform some work."

The police physician in Königsberg, Prussia, had this to say about Franz Gerlach, on December 19, 1942. "He is able to stay in the concentration camp, as well as being in the workforce; however, he has a hernia as big as a man's head." The RKPA (some government officials) wanted to know if Gerlach, after recuperation, would be able to serve in the armed forces.

All inmates suffering from a hernia were operated on in the concentration camps, but anybody who could get away with it, did so because it was well-known that the mortality rate among the inmates in surgery was very high. It has been pointed out in previous cases that, besides phony reasons, suspicion alone could lead to imprisonment. It also happened that people were brought to a concentration camp after they had already been acquitted after a trial in court. For instance, Alfred Durych, inmate #48424, arrived at Sachsenhausen on September 22, 1942, after his acquittal by a special jury in Leitmeritz. He had been charged with listening to foreign radio broadcasts. He was not the only one; there were many others taken into custody and held prisoner in concentration camps for this or similar reasons.

Soon after the occupation of Norway, the manager of a large Berlin business firm, dealing in furs, found himself among the inmates in this concentration camp. What happened was that shortly before that, a wealthy-looking lady came to his establishment to have alterations done on her fur coat. After the manager had this coat brought to his office so he could look it over carefully, he refused to have any alterations done to it by his firm. Enraged to hear his refusal she asked, "Do you know who I am?" "It does not matter who you are" was the answer. "I am Frau V. Terboven, the wife of the ambassador to Norway, and if you keep on refusing to have this coat altered, you are going to find out what is going to happen to you the hard way." However, by introducing herself and threatening him, this businessman could not be persuaded to do the work she asked for. Firmly, he gave her his explanation, "This coat has been manufactured in our establishment as a limited edition only coat—no copies—because it is the coronation coat of Maud, Queen of Norway; therefore, I will not make any alterations on it." Just for refusing to make alterations to the queen's coronation coat, which somehow had been stolen and gotten into the hands of the ambassador's wife, the manager of the fur store landed in Sachsenhausen.

It has been mentioned already that criminals, dressed like political prisoners, were placed among the inmates and given positions from which they could spy and denounce their comrades. Such spying could go on for quite a while before the inmates involved were detected. In one of the next chapters, I will come back to an incident in which Dr. Pochel and I got involved and were under suspicion, thanks to the systematic spying and informing by a certain S.A. man. His name was Arthur Wirth from Saxony. It didn't take him long before he had a position as a supervisor among the inmates from which he could carry on his denunciations against the political prisoners. As a reward for his services, he soon was released by his Nazi supervisor. Another inmate who came here for "his own protection" was Albert N. #44384, a criminal who already had been convicted 16 times and sentenced to 25 years in prison, besides 6 years in jail, all for criminal offenses. Career criminal, Frederick R. #57729, with some 16 convictions to his credit and camouflaged by the red triangle on his uniform, like all political inmates, also became an informer for the Nazis.

The story of a Socialist with a sixth sense for predicting future events is as follows: Otto Schmidt, inmate #13534, was brought in for protective custody in 1939, and was taken to a cellblock. Schmidt had predicted the doomsday for the Nazis. Because of an ailment, he had been transferred to the state hospital in Berlin. While there, he wrote a letter which he gave to the Gestapo, indicating that he was a clairvoyant and that he had "seen" how an S.S. leader, named Ettlinger, had committed two murders within the cellblock and that the camp commandant, Loritz had tried his best to conceal it. The event he claimed to have "seen" proved to be real, the murders took place while Schmidt was in the hospital; everything happened as he predicted. In order to make sure that no further incidents would be "seen" and foretold by Schmidt, he was hanged, without verdict, on October 20, 1942.

A few months before that, on July 7, 1942, 244 French miners from the Pas de Calais region were taken to this camp for demonstrating against insufficient wages. During the so-called Luna action, the Gestapo had taken 1603 Frenchmen as prisoners who arrived on January 23, 1943. Political, as well as criminal, prisoners were herded together. Early in April 1943, 45 Frenchmen were taken by plane from Tunisia to Naples, but by July 6, 1943, they, also, ended up in Sachsenhausen. These were mostly intellectuals, among them several physicians. Shortly before that, Pierre Chautemps #59030, was taken to this concentration camp. He happened to be the brother of the French prime minister. The offense: he had been accused of listening to the British radio broadcast. The son of a Dutch airplane manufacturer came to Sachsenhausen after being accused of flying the royal Dutch family to England. Furthermore, he was under suspicion of having taken other prominent Dutch families there.

A special group among the Nazi prison guards consisted of so-called "drill sergeants," nicknamed among the inmates as "bone men" and the "SAT" (Special Action Trooper), otherwise known as "Outcast of the Military." Both groups had nothing to be proud of. The "bone men," earmarked by two crossed leg bones attached to their worn-out uniforms, were assigned to some easy jobs like watchman or fireman for inside duties. This way they were to be "trained" to become useful and "able-bodied" S.S. men. Actually, both types of military outcasts were sentenced to a concentration camp for stealing from their own comrades or similar offenses, like petty larceny. The Nazis thought that by keeping them in a concentration camp for some time they could be "rehabilitated." However, in both cases, the end result could only be described as negative.

I would like to close this chapter with the description of a man who came here because he might have been able to rock Adolf Hitler's position as the "Führer" to its foundation. His name was Hans Olitzka, born in 1901 as the son of a mine owner, who was working on the extraction of mercury. Oliztzka, who became #41191, had but one thing in mind, he wanted to unify not only all political parties, as Hitler had intended when he founded the NSDAP, but he also wanted to combine all creeds like, for instance, the Jews, Catholics, Protestants, Moslems, Hindus, Buddhists, and other Asiatic religions as well as Jehovah's Witnesses, all into one unified religion. He had already published a pamphlet on it with the title, *True Christianity According to Today's Interpretation*. He traveled to Berchtesgaden so he could speak to Adolf Hitler and his staff. However, he was soon brought to a stop as Hitler became worried about having a competitor, especially when this fellow asked to be made Minister of Religion, a position that, under these circumstances, would even overshadow that of the Pope. This was too much for Adolf. He pressed the button whereupon "the Pope of all Popes" was taken away and put into a guest room, where he was searched from top to bottom. His new Bible about unified religion was confiscated. After that, he was handed some sandwiches and permitted to take the next train back to Berlin. Not long after his arrival, the Gestapo visited him and took him along to police headquarters at the Alexander Platz, as a prisoner, of course. From here on, the "New Messiah," Hans Orizka, was transferred to where, after being shifted from one labor commando to another, he finally ended up in the infirmary, broken in body and spirit. In 1943 he succumbed to TB, and Adolf didn't have to worry about him anymore as a possible rival.

CHAPTER 12

TOWER A—NOTHING NEW AT THIS STATION

"Wherever I have been during these times, all I could see were people full of enthusiasm and with happy faces."
                                                    Hitler 1938.

"Without the German nation, only barbaric people would exist. That I love the peace, I don't have to mention. — The German power has to be victorious."

It was past midnight. The dim rays of the moon were shining eerily through the ice-covered window panes of the dormitory and over the hungry and haggard-looking faces of the inmates who tried to find a few hours of rest or sleep beneath their worn-out blankets. They were lying two together, which gave them a better chance to keep warm, on the straw bags that seemed to feel so damp at this time of the year. Some snoring interrupted the dead of night. To the right side of the door, a sick man was moaning. He had been refused acceptance to the infirmary, even though in the evening the doctor had already diagnosed pneumonia, with a temperature of over 40°C (104°F).

"*Let these dogs croak,*" these were the words the S.S. physician screamed at the caretaker after he had felt the pulse and read the thermometer. "*That would be something, letting these lazy dogs lay in our warm beds instead of working.*" So there was nothing else that two of his comrades could do for him, except return him to the barracks, where the block elder, Egon, did the best he could by giving him an extra blanket and some warm tea. The temperature was by now -20°C (-4°F) on the outside and likely to drop towards the morning.

In the front building where the commanding officers had their own headquarters, a pre-Christmas party was in full swing. Some of the men had been on furlough and were now "boozing it up." Alcoholic beverages seemed to be plentiful and anyone who felt he needed another drink would help himself. After a while, the party seemed to be over. The S.S. men were leaving the building. Maybe it was time to go to their own living quarters. Not so, one could hear the noise they were making, and it came nearer. Sure enough, they were stamping over the frozen snow on the exercise plaza towards the barracks where the inmates were kept. Suddenly the outside door was kicked open and in came three blockleaders, Schubert, Meierhofer, and Kittler, all quite a bit under the influence. As usual, they had their sticks with them and the first one who got a beating was Egon, the blockleader and general caretaker of the inmates. This was just the beginning. *"Why didn't you bastard get up, pay attention, and report the number of inmates?"* Schubert wanted to know. But before he had a chance to answer, the other two sadists rushed into the sleeping room to harass and create havoc among the sleeping inmates.

Egon never got a chance to report the number of inmates in his barrack because, by now, Schubert followed the others into the sleeping quarters, hereby joining them in beating upon the still sleeping inmates. It turned out to be a terrible scene for the poor helpless inmates. But this was not all because now the S.S. thugs screamed at the half-asleep inmates, *"Out with you, you lazy bums, get outside, all of you."* They were swinging their sticks behind them. Anyone unfortunate enough to stumble on the hard, frozen snow would feel a kick from a heavy military boot behind him. Not only that, the inmates had to walk bare-footed, wearing only their night shirts. In this fashion, they were chased several times around the barracks. Anyone who was not fast enough would be chased with swinging sticks the S.S. men were holding. If they fell because the frozen snow was hurting their feet they were kicked with boots or even trampled on. Now to the sick man: As he did not make a move, he was torn from his straw bag, thrown on the floor, and beaten severely by the S.S. bandits. Egon, the caretaker, tried to explain that this man was very ill with pneumonia and a high temperature. *"Looks like you are trying to save this lazy son of a bitch,"* was the answer of one of the S.S. thugs, whereupon Egon had to take another beating. When, finally, the shivering inmates found their way back through the darkness to the door of the barracks, they first made sure the S.S. terror had left before they entered the building, carefully, one by one. Then someone noticed them walking slowly and somewhat unsteady toward their own headquarters. That means that during this night only one barrack, this particular one housing the political inmates, became victim of the carriers of the brown plague, as they were called.

Egon took a final walk around the barrack, just to make sure that everyone had returned. Unfortunately, four of the men were lying on the ground, unable to get up by themselves; they had been beaten too severely by their torturers and had to be carried into the day room, which was still a little warmth from the fire in the stove. However, a closer look revealed that all of them had received extensive injuries, which made it necessary to bring them to the infirmary in the morning. Several of the comrades tried to help the sick man with the high fever as best as they could. But it was too late. The S.S. guards had done the job completely. His body was carried out into the hall where, already, another dead inmate was lying, also a victim of atrocities, hunger, and cold.

It was half past four in the morning when the alarm clock near the cot of the block elder started to ring. Still worn-out and tired, he rubbed his eyes. He hardly had three hours of sleep after this nightmare was over. Before waking the men who were in charge of him, he had to make a report in the registration office about the number of inmates left in his barracks. There were 426 men, including three in the hospital block. On his way back, passing the laundry building he glanced at the outside thermometer, it looked like -30°C (-22°F). He finally returned to his cellblock when he heard the bell ringing from the tower that it was time to get up.

Still looking drowsy, the inmates, who certainly didn't get much sleep or comfort during the last night, got up from their straw bags, picked up their belongings, and walked to the washroom to wash their faces and hands. They hardly took notice that two of their comrades were lying dead on the floor, waiting to be transported to the morgue after the morning roll call.

Inmates in charge of serving breakfast brought some pitchers filled with some brown, warm liquid, which they called coffee, and poured some of it into everyone's mug. At table #3, one man was missing; sure enough, that was the sick one from last night, whom the S.S. terrorists had finished off for good. At table #4, two seats were empty. That means the dormitory has to be checked; they were still lying on their straw bags. *"Time to get up,"* someone shouted, while someone else tried to shake them to wake them up. It didn't do any good; they too were dead, frozen to death after the ordeal outside last night on the exercise plaza. That means, so far, three dead in one night in this barrack, all victims of cold, hunger, and Nazi cruelty. A clerk from the office picked up their few pieces of clothing that were hanging in the locker. Some leftover bread with marmalade, which they had tried to save for a rainy day, had already been taken by some of their hungry comrades who had noticed, before the alarm, that their friends didn't make it through the night. Dead men do not need any food, and hunger shows no respect at times of want and despair.

By now, another harsh sound of the bell out on the exercise plaza could be heard, besides this announcement, *"Everyone outside"* is the command. In rows of five, they had to line up in front of the blocks. "Attention!" Meanwhile block elders, office workers, and others in charge, are walking through the rows, counting the men. There have to be 426, three of them in the infirmary. But that is not all. Meanwhile, four more men were dead; however, they, too, had to stand up, each of them supported on both sides by an inmate. This was the rule. Even dead inmates had to stand in line until the roll call was over. Then they were dragged, each one by two inmates, towards the cellar for the dead, located underneath the infirmary. After that, their names were taken off the register.

From Tower A three powerful spotlights were casting their rays over the plaza and the approaching columns of inmates. Into every hidden corner, the glaring light is shining, as if to search for or sweep out anybody who may be hiding in the dark. Something seems to be out of order in one of the last columns. In Block 65, one inmate is missing. He has to be found. A shot could be heard coming from Tower B; it was meant for the inmate they were looking for. He had already tried to escape underneath the barbed wire that was charged with electric voltage, but now he lost his life from a guard's bullet.

Lined up in groups of five, the whole body of inmates stood at attention on the exercise plaza, when an officer in charge collected the report sheets regarding the number of men in each column from each group leader. From Tower A above the main entrance, the guard on duty beside the machine gun announced in a monotone voice, *"Tower A, no news to report."* No, nothing new had happened. The terror scenes during the night, as well as the inmates whose lives had been rubbed out in one way or another since the last confrontation on the exercise plaza, all were happenings that could occur any day or night; therefore, nothing new had actually happened.

"Attention, labor force, get in line!" At once, men were moving around like ants in an ant hill, trying to find their labor commandos they had been assigned to, as fast as possible, in order to march from here to their specific place of work. Only a few groups of craftsmen were staying at the camp. The largest column of workers went through the gate towards the "Klinker," a brick factory, led by armed Nazi guards, as well as some police dogs. How many of these unfortunate ones will not be able to leave this murderous place as the "Klinker" at night, and return to the concentration camp, is anybody's guess. How many of them will be shot while trying to escape, and return as dead bodies on one of these push-carts that were used for moving stones and dirt?

It was about 6:30 a.m. by the time the last labor columns had marched off through the gate, but still, most of the inmates had to stay on the exercise plaza, in maybe -30°C (-22°F) cold, some in worn-out coats, some dressed very poorly, waiting for the command, *"Standing columns, move on!"* By now, the clock at the tower showed nine; it was the beginning of daylight. Freezing, starving men, looking like living skeletons, were shaking around, just to keep their ice-cold limbs from freezing altogether.

From the window of the commanding officer's suite, one could hear the sharp voice of the "Iron Gustav" all over the place, *"Stand quiet, nobody is going to move now!"* For a few moments, everyone tried to stand still. But then one man was falling over, then another and another, and so forth. All over, one could see men lying on the ground who were afterward carried into the inside quarter, each one carried by four comrades. More than 50 men had been counted already and, by the time they were taken inside, more did drop down until, at last, the camp's physician gave orders to let every inmate move inside their cellblocks in order to prevent further death due to the freezing temperature. When by the time the clock from the tower had struck ten, the still able-bodied men had moved toward their blocks, somewhere around a hundred sick people were standing in front of the gate, some of them moaning, some bending over in pain. Nevertheless, they were not allowed to get inside the infirmary. Instead, "Iron Gustav" thought of another remedy by calling on two blockleaders, Fickert and Saathoff by name, who got the order to chase the ailing men away from the building and make them roll all over the ground. The result: twelve badly injured who, soon afterward, could be carried inside by the caretakers from the morgue, dead, of course.

It may be said, however, that the inmates in the living quarters were protected against the worst effects of the cold. But those assigned to the so-called "standing commandoes" had to remain in the cold washrooms or toilets, standing squeezed together like sardines in an atmosphere bad enough to choke or even suffocate anyone who had to stay there long enough. Those who didn't belong to this rather unfortunate group had to walk over to Block 17 where these so-called "rag pickers" got their special treatment administered; by a brute named Böhm, a criminal with a red triangle on his sleeve who came from Worms. He gave the inmates a terrible time.

Behind Block 17, from the direction of Blocks 37 and 38, one could hear some loud outcries mingled with the well-known cursing words of the S.S. blockleaders. Through the partly thawed window panes of Block 17, one could see a very sad picture of martyrdom. Jewish people were driven through the piled-up snow with clubs and cat'o nine tails, beaten cruelly, and stepped upon whenever they stumbled to the ground. After the cries for help and the cursing subsided, some of the rag pickers were brave enough to go outside in order to find out what had really happened.

It was a horrible sight. About ten Jews, mostly elderly and crippled, were lying there, blood-covered, some with broken skulls with part of their brains dropping out. Some were still moaning but not a single one of these massacred people survived these brutalities. The carriers for the dead had a very hard day, picking up these casualties. One could see blood all over, even some of the intestines hanging out, and the day was not over yet.

By now it was noon time. One didn't have to watch the clock, one could feel it in the stomach. At lunchtime the labor force got their food ration, consisting of boiled turnips and potatoes that had been frozen outside in the field before cooking. That is it. Everything had to be eaten in less than 10 minutes while standing up. This way it would take less time and they could go back to work. By now a transport of newcomers is marching through the gate, pushed on from behind by S.S. men. After that they had to line up inside, next to the gate, their heads uncovered. While standing there for some time some of the older and, perhaps weaker, newcomers dropped to the ground from exhaustion after a long trip. But they soon were "encouraged" with some kicks from the S.S. boots to get up again which did not work. So they were kicked to roll over in the frozen snow all the way to Barrack B where the admission took place, handled mostly by political inmates.

In the penal colony, the unfortunate inmates had to run with their knees bent and their hands behind their heads. To make them run faster, Blockleader Bugdalla, nicknamed Brutala, wielded his club with some brutal force among them. While forced to roll over on the ground some of the tormented inmates threw up some of their last meal. Nevertheless, everyone else in line had to keep on rolling right over this slimy reddish-looking mess, so that by the time they arrived at the washroom they looked more like pigs than human beings. After cleaning off most of this mess with ice-cold water, they had to get out of the washroom again and stand in line outside. The prison garb of one of the men apparently was not clean enough, according to Bugdalla, therefore, he took the water hose himself and sprayed the ice-cold water on him. Dripping wet and shivering from the cold, he stood there in front of the barracks while the others walked into their own barracks, that is, after the roll call.

Gruesome events seem to forecast their shadows. Between the Barracks B and E, for instance, a portable gallows was erected. People were wondering who could be the next victim after the evening roll call. Nobody knows, not even the condemned man himself. He most likely may still be working quite unconcerned at his job or he may be looking with some foreboding through the bars of an isolation cell, thereby noticing the gallows. Meanwhile, some speculation had reached the camp through the grapevine that someone had escaped from the "Klinker" and that in the event the fugitive could not be caught in time for the evening roll call, standing on the exercise plaza throughout the night could be expected.

Now the bell is ringing for roll call. The men from the "Klinker" were marching through the gate. On the wagon for utensils that was pushed and pulled by about a dozen inmates were three bodies, one of them covered with gunshot wounds through the head and back; the others were victims of the freezing cold, as well as mistreatment. Someone came over with a pushcart in order to transfer the corpses to the morgue. The one who had been shot was the fugitive. His body was used as an exhibit by lying him on a stretcher, clad only in pants and in full view of all the returning inmates who had to pass this way. This was supposed to be a warning for anyone who may have an escape from this concentration camp in mind.

All groups of inmates were standing at attention for roll call. The officer in charge, and soon after that, the commander of the concentration camp, came through the gate, followed by some unknown but high-ranking officials, apparently to be witnesses at the hanging that was soon to take place. From watch Tower A, the S.S. guard on duty announced in the same monotonous voice, "*Nothing new at Station A.*" After roll call, everyone had to remain at his post in order to hear from the commanding officer that the death penalty is certain for anybody who tries to get away from the concentration camp, itself, or the place of work assigned to him on the outside. This dead inmate on the stretcher was supposed to serve as a frightening example.

Following this announcement, the group leader stated that this very day another fugitive who had been taken into custody while trying to escape will be hung at the gallows until dead. Soon after that the gate to the isolation block was opened and the victim with cuffs on his hands and feet was led to the gallows. Without hope or willpower, the poor soul walked his last mile to the place of execution. Here he was supposed to step on an elevated platform under the noose, but he refused. With brutal force, three S.S. henchmen lifted the condemned man on the board, while another one put the rope around his neck. After that, the board was kicked away with a foot, and the body of the unfortunate victim dropped down. After about 15 minutes, all the other inmates who were working at the crematory took the corpse down, put it into a wooden box that was intended for this purpose, and carried it over to the incinerator.

For today, the commanding officer had made a little change in the evening program. While the body on the gallows was still swinging in the wind, one could hear the shouting voice of the "Iron Gustav," "*Start singing!!*" But, it was not a hymn or a melody suitable for a funeral he had in mind. Instead, a messenger had to bring a stepladder and put it up in the middle of the street leading to the main building. Then, one of our comrades, a political prisoner by the name of Haller, had to step on this makeshift podium and act as the orchestra leader. The tribunal became a play, the songs were Nazi songs. What a joke. And, so the tragedy came to an end.

Several inmates fainted during the execution. "*Stand up straight!*" came the command. Then everyone had to march towards the cellblocks. The guard who blew the horn from Tower A gave the signal, the S.S. was off duty for the day and marched through the gate toward their own quarters. It wasn't really warm, just the chill was off in the living quarters of the inmates; therefore, the seats around the stove were always taken first. Only after the bread rations were distributed on the tables—300 grams per man per day—it became somewhat quiet in the room. Today, the men also got their ration of margarine—50 g—which was used by most of the inmates right away to spread on the bread. A mug of coffee-colored liquid flushed it all down. Save something for the next day? No way, hungry people finished everything, including the last crumbs. But maybe there was a chance later on to snatch a few raw potatoes from the cellar. After all, inmates had to peel them and, while cooking, maybe there were a few extras for their comrades. This would help to ease the hunger pain for the next morning.

At night, some of us would walk over to the infirmary that was staffed by political inmates who worked there as caretakers. This way we could find out how many had died on a particular day. The report said 73 dead, one of them frozen like an icicle. This day happened to be January 18, 1940. In a few days, the death toll came to 182. By the end of January, the death toll was 714 for an average population of 8300. This means that one out of 12 had died of unnatural causes, in this case, the cold wave, not to mention the mistreatment. If 714 would die within one month, that meant that the whole inmate population would have died out within one year; if it were not for the new arrivals that were daily taken into custody by the Gestapo.

On one of the next days, the *Völkischer Beobachter*—the Nazi mouthpiece—brought an article about the severe cold spell in the United States, where on January 18, more than a hundred people had died during the cold spell; this could mean one dead for about a million people. Here, it was one out of 12. What a difference. Nevertheless, at every roll call formation, day in, day out, the year long, the broadcaster on Tower A would make the same announcement, "*Nothing new to report.*"

Overtired, the inmates walked over to their sleeping quarters, trying to rest for a few hours on their straw bags. If they were lucky, they would not be scared out of their sleep and beaten up by the Gestapo. After the second bell, it was mostly quiet. Only some occasional snoring broke the silence, while the block foreman, the clerk for the registration, and the block elder had to file their report together for the next morning. Like, for instance, "*January 18, 1940—from midnight to midnight—no news to report.*"

CHAPTER 13

SACHSENHAUSEN LIVING CONDITIONS

"Concentration camps are not a disgrace; on the contrary, they are a jewel of culture. Here the misfits of society will find a friendly welcome and be educated to lead a good life, doing worthwhile work."

Fränkische Tageszeitung.

Everything was set up, like in a commune, with an officer in charge of just about everything; and, to a certain extent, one could speak of a form of self-government, under the jurisdiction of the camp's administration. Why, and for what reason, the political department got its name is hard to say because this department had to fulfill the tasks of a registration office. It was more like an administration in itself or a central office where all threads would run together. All newcomers had to appear here for their registration, and they would also get their number which they had to wear while at camp. For every new inmate, a file was made up which contained their personal papers. They had on hand, of course, the warrant of their arrest, sometimes with special instructions from the Gestapo or Kripo. As time went on, more papers with additional information were added to which, of course, were withheld from the inmates.

After that, the newcomer had to make his way to a place where all his personal belongings were surrendered. Thereafter, he had to take a bath and a shower. Next, he was handed out a zebra uniform, underwear, socks, boots, and a cap—during the winter months, he may even get one with earmuffs—mittens, and if available, a coat. His own clothes were put into a bag to be taken along for disinfection. And so, it seems as if everything went along fine, like in the army, or so. Dressed in his new outfit, he was assigned to his living quarters, a cellblock, depending on how he was classified. He could be a political prisoner, a criminal by trade, a person with antisocial behavior, a Jew, or a Jehovah's Witness. In some cases, he was transferred to the jail block, according to special orders. The jail block was called the bunker, but it also happened that a newcomer could be sent to the infirmary.

As soon as he arrived at his cellblock that was supposed to be his living quarters, an older inmate who was in charge and a custodian of the building, would give him instructions as to the rules and regulations in his new environment. At last, he would meet the steward of the mess hall, who would direct him to his place at any of the tables. The next morning, every new inmate had to appear in a hall from where they were sorted into groups and put to work in different kinds of occupations, according to their training and abilities.

The assignments to the different work commandos had been done for years by a political inmate. Only during the last couple of years, a former career criminal took over, just because the S.S. leadership always found willing helpers among these, to be used as spies; besides that, so-called professional criminals may even resort to torture upon asking. The latest clerk in charge of the working commandos happened to be a former criminal by the name of Alfred Flöbel, nicknamed "Flegel," which stands for rude person in English. He lived up to his name all right. It was he, who among others, was mostly responsible for having inmates transferred into the dreadful extermination camps.

It used to be that a political inmate was in charge of the building that housed inmates. Besides that, he was doing some clerical work, like keeping a list of names of all the men in his outfit up to date. Here, I would like to mention the names of some fine fellows. Inmates, like Harry Naujoks from Hamburg, who with the help of Rudy Gross, a clerk, and several other assistants from different offices, found ways and means to prevent quite a few of our political inmates from falling into the hands of the Gestapo killers.

By changing the names and numbers, it was possible to save not only a few of our good comrades from certain deaths, we found out. With a list of names and numbers on hand, a secret falsification system had been worked out, and not even those who were actually working at it were aware of it. With this method, one of our already deceased comrades would have to "die" again, and, if necessary, a few times more. What had to be done was taking the name of a dead person from the death file, in order to record him as "deceased" again. This was done by only one political inmate and nobody else knew about it. For several years, it happened to be my privilege to work at this kind of "secret service" job, whereby I let the dead die over again so that the living could keep on living.

One had to take the file of a deceased—preferably a foreigner with no relatives and exchange the old death certificate with a new one. Then the file was returned to the filing cabinet for the deceased. The comrade who had been "rescued" this way was dead, according to the filing system. Nobody would care about it, not even the commanding officers in charge of the inmates. The next thing to do was, of course, to let this person who had been saved so far disappear. After all, there would otherwise be one too many, and a "surplus" on the roll call list. And, the best temporary hiding place used to be the building where patients with dysentery were kept. Even the S.S. were afraid to go near this place. The next morning, when the working commandos had to line up and march to their assigned place of work, the endangered comrade would be smuggled into a larger group and taken along. Next, the head count at the gate had to be done fast enough that one more or less would not even be noticed.

At the place where the inmates worked, there were usually some civilian laborers employed, also. During the day, one of these men, a sponsor, we could call him, and who had already been notified beforehand, would see to it that the rescued fellow would get some civilian clothes besides some cash. After that, he would keep him working among the other civilian laborers until quitting time. Then this sponsor would take him along on his way home and finally let him go, to disappear into the streets. From then on, he belonged to the great masses of those unfortunate ones who may have been bombed out or who just happened to be refugees. By now, he had to have, of course, a new name. But, nobody from the concentration camp would search for him; after all, he had been reported "dead."

At this point, I would like to give some recognition to one of our very reliable political comrades who had been able to fool the S.S. commandos for years, as the actual number of inmates did never agree with the register on file. Rudi Grosse was his name. He has been an expert in using fictitious names and numbers.

However, early in October 1941, Rudi Grosse, Harry Neujoks, Werner Stake, as well as 15 other political inmates who, at that time, were also holding key positions, were transferred to the extermination camp Flossenburg. Of these comrades who were earmarked for liquidation and who evidently belonged to a leftist party, I can remember a few names like, Willi Hannemann of Flensburg, Karl Schwaiger, Albert Buchmann, Fritz Selbmann, Rudi Rotkegel, Wilhelm Görnus, Hein Meyer, Karl Schirdewahn, and Ernst Guggenhahn who, together with Rudi Grosse, were killed in a quarry at Flossenburg. The S.S. was responsible for these killings.

All of these inmates who were earmarked for liquidation were kept for eight weeks in dark cells in Sachsenhausen. The reason for this seemed to be the rather critical military situation at Stalingrad. We heard of a secret order, by which everyone who was presumably a Communist, and in an important position, had to be eliminated in all the concentration camps. This had to be done in an unsuspicious way, such as by shortening their already short food rations, and by giving them a heavier workload, like for about 16 to 20 hours a day. The pretext for being arrested, under these conditions, could be a false testimony by a double-crossing inmate. However, this time it didn't take long to identify this spy as an ordinary criminal by the name of Lammel, who came from the Sudetenland and who had already 11 arrests on his record, although he wore the red triangle on his sleeve that would mark him as a political prisoner. He had caused the arrests of the inmates mentioned before, by telling the S.S. guards that these men had formed some kind of a relief group under the name of "Red

Meal" by which they would get a better and bigger bread ration which was paid for by a wealthy inmate who used to be a consul in Uruguay.

While these eighteen unfortunate victims were still awaiting their doom and kept in a dark cell, I tried my best with the help of other inmates or comrades from the political department, to have these men set free by explaining the facts to the authorities. My assistants in this case were Emil Büge, as well as three students from Czechoslovakia, by the names of Josef Zeman, Oleg Homola, and Alex Strobach. Eventually, we caused the downfall of Lammel, the traitor. At first, he was taken to the "Klinker" and, possibly, later to a construction job where he, too, may have been liquidated, as far as we could find out. We had no mercy for inmates who would double-cross on their own comrades and, therefore, we had to find ways to get rid of these good-for-nothing ones, as well as we could. Any one of our own comrades, who were shipped to Flossenburg, was kept there for a year under strict confinement. Each one had in his cell a regular criminal as a watchdog and foreman, who had to give him extra hard labor every day; he even could put him out of misery at any given chance. There is one thing we can say about these career criminals: they had never been too enthusiastic about rubbing out any of the political inmates. They even said, "If a political inmate has to be liquidated, let the S.S. do it themselves."

Besides those victims I mentioned before, as well as Grosse and Guggenhahn, the S.S. didn't have too much success in killing more inmates through acts of terror or maltreatment. Besides that, a well-organized international resistance movement formed by political inmates at camp took care that, through collections of food, mainly the starving inmates who had to live, by now, on half a ration, or less, got more to eat so that they got into better shape again.

As has been mentioned before, the whole system was regulated within the government. There was a well-equipped infirmary in which the sick inmates could be nursed back to better health, provided the S.S. did not interfere in one way or another. A community kitchen and a special food supply department took care of the meal rations for the inmates. There was a laundry and a bathhouse, which everyone was allowed to use every other week. By the way it looked, it seemed that the inmates were being taken care of in a halfway decent way; that is, if the S.S. and other tormentors would leave them alone, instead of making it a life of hell for them.

The function of the political department consisted of receiving the newcomers and starting a file for every individual. From there, the files were forwarded to headquarters, which was in the hands of the S.S. Once the files were here, nobody could take a look at them anymore, except the S.S. They were then considered secret documents. Only after the S.S. could no longer provide enough of their own men, inmates were picked out and sworn into secrecy, never to reveal anything they may have seen or heard in this place. This was in February 1942. The threat was, of course, the death penalty for anyone who could not keep a secret. I happened to be one of those who got such an assignment. My coworkers were almost all political offenders who were working here as clerks or interpreters. I would like to mention here that a total of 36 languages were spoken and, for each one, interpreters were available. Any time a translator was needed, he was picked from among these inmates, since the S.S. didn't have that many members among them who were fluent enough in all these foreign languages. They only knew how to shout and use the sticks or anything similar to get their commands across.

Life in the reception room of the political department could be like hell for the inmates who worked here, thanks to the S.S., because they were kept under constant watch in order to find out if some kind of movement was in the making that might be dangerous to the state. All kinds of mistreatment for the inmates was the general rule, especially if the S.S. had the slightest suspicion that one of their inmates could have made a critical remark that was not to the liking of the S.S. The penalties were stiff: beatings, standing up straight for any length of time tied to a pole, transfer to a maximum security cell or the "Klinker" or a quarry.

It was prohibited to have a private conversation with a newcomer. These people, if they didn't come from a penitentiary or another camp, most often had interesting news to report, especially when they happened to be political offenders. In most cases their arrest warrant would indicate if the newcomer had something worthwhile to say, and, if so, the clerks and interpreters would mark down their names for future reference. After that, he may be questioned more, as soon as he has been assigned to his new living quarters.

One of the illegal tasks for the inmates in the political department was to establish connections between former friends and acquaintances who were already in captivity, with newcomers, who might be the right persons, but this had to be done very carefully, of course. Men who did it had to use a list of names which were kept according to cities and countries. If, for instance, a well-known political from Hamburg was brought into this concentration camp, or maybe transferred from another concentration camp, then a well-informed landsman from that town or region would be alerted to keep an eye on the new inmate, sometimes even within an hour or so and eventually approach him. It was always a nice surprise when old acquaintances would meet this way, even if these were not the best of circumstances. Better yet, if a newcomer was surprised by an old friend who brought him some of his own rations like a piece of sausage or bacon or something else to eat. This was really a welcome gift.

Unnoticeable for most inmates, and mainly for the S.S.; a fine network was formed between the politicals. And this took years. Later on, an organization of resistance came into being through all these connections. More about his will be told in another chapter.

Having a crew of clerks and interpreters put together didn't always turn out to be favorable and effective, because spies and double-crossing agents were constantly shoved from above into this group to mingle with the rest. Only a minor incident was enough to have someone who seemed to be questionable in any way, removed from his position, and maybe for good. And so it happened that the S.S. district leaders, Campe and Sorge, by name, were responsible for the deaths of five clerks and interpreters during the first days of May 1940. The first victim was a foreman, his name was Herman Kronenberg, who was put to death on the night of

May 2, 1940, in a torture cell, by the so-called cold water treatment. He was tied to a post with hardly any clothes on and then the ice-cold water from a garden hose was sprayed full force against his chest where the heart is. This was done until the body temperature dropped enough to cause death by heart failure. But, according to his death certificate, Kronenberg died of asthma and a weak heart. Actually, his murderer was Bugdalla, an S.S. blockleader and one of the most vicious ones they had at this camp.

The next victims were well-known people from Czechoslovakia, like Antonin Zapatocki and an editor for a newspaper, by the name of Paul Prokop, from Prague. Then came Ivan Sekanina, a lawyer from Prague, who was treated so terribly that he was sent to the infirmary with a broken arm. Hardly recovered from his ordeal, he was again subjected to further torture. When he had his arm bandaged again on May 1, he said to one of our comrades, "Now, I have to learn to pray." An hour later, Sekanina hanged himself, as he could no longer endure another torture that was awaiting him. Another victim, Walter Zipfel, by name, also deserves to be mentioned here in connection with the incidents just described. He had been sent to the "Klinker" where the S.S., with the help of some career criminals among the inmates, had "to take care" of him. Five times they threw him into the Hohenzollern Channel; even though he was already in a poor condition. When he returned in the evening, he was hardly able to stand on his own feet. Some comrades took the wet clothes off him and dressed him in clean ones. Here they saw how badly he had been beaten and kicked around, evidently with heavy boots, and his mouth was very swollen. As a result of his injuries, he died on April 24, 1940.

With danger always lurking around us, the nerves of the political inmates, who were working in this particular department, were under tremendous stress. If it were not for these S.S. spies, themselves, who would make life miserable enough, then we had to watch out for their hired helpers from among the criminal inmates, who tried to mingle into the political department. For instance, a certain criminal with 11 convictions to his credit, named Josef Lammel, who had been mentioned before, used to be one of this kind. With the help of several

Nazi-oriented supervisors, among them, Wiegant, Eilers, Clamsen, Schnepper, Urdmann, and several others, Lammel succeeded in getting the position of a supervisor also, and that in a rather short time. His main job was blackmailing students from Czechoslovakia. For a certain amount of money, he would promise to use his influence to have them set free in a relatively short time. But, then when he started to give untrue and discriminating reports about some inmates to the S.S. that caused their transfer to Klossenburg, the extermination camp, the rest of us comrades lost our patience. With enough proof on hand, we got in touch with one of the very few decent S.S. officers—his name was Schloef—who didn't believe in cruel treatment against inmates who did not deserve it. He was one of the very few S.S. officers who could be considered humane.

But when it came to light that Lammel used his position to torture another victim, this time a former restaurant owner at the railroad station in Rostock, by the name of Krüger, he lost his job as a supervisor, better-called slave driver, and was put to work in the infamous quarry, to which he used to ship many of his former victims. Here, he had to learn to work with his hands; hard labor he wasn't used to. According to unconfirmed reports, he possibly had been eliminated in one way or another, like by some of his own victims. In some cases, inmates took the law into their own hands and carried it out when it came to revenge, to which they, themselves, felt entitled to; everything happened under strict secrecy, of course.

But as soon as we got rid of one of these slave drivers and tormentors, it never took long before we got replacements, this time a former stormtrooper by the name of Ludwig Rabitsch, who was transferred from Flossenburg to Sachsenhausen on October 12, 1942. He had been registered under #50481 as an inmate, but it didn't take long until he, too, became the supervisor. One of his first undoings was the promotion of another stormtrooper into this office to work as a clerk. His name was Friedrich Gertz. He came from Lübeck where he used to be a gardener. Needless to say, he couldn't be used as an interpreter, as he could not even spell his own language, not to mention his messy handwriting.

During the war, this individual used to have an important position in the courthouse in Warsaw, where he served in the criminal court. While in this position he took the opportunity, like so many others of his kind, to loot and rob the apartments, thinking nothing of it. According to unconfirmed reports, he had taken along for himself about 20,000 RM (Reichsmarks) worth of household goods. Thereupon, because it was illegal, he was tried and convicted by an S.S. court, and got the red triangle on his sleeve which would identify him as a political prisoner instead of an ordinary criminal; then they sent him to this concentration camp. During the trial, it came to light that quite a few Nazis, from the higher-ranking ones down to the less important individuals, had been involved in "confiscating," looting, in other words, taking all kinds of merchandise of much greater value. One of the big shots had been transferred to Tokyo, while all the others that were involved had been considered immune to the law and, therefore, had been acquitted. Gertz, who seemed to be quite talkative, came out with these news items. But it didn't take long until the Nazis in command found out about it too.

On one of the following days, Gertz was no longer in the political department. He had been taken to the bunker, we found out. A new trial against him and his accomplice, the S.S. stormtrooper, Stullenberg, took place. After several months, they were back in the concentration camp yard again, this time tied to each other with handcuffs. That was in the fall of 1943. They even had to sleep together with the handcuffs on and, during the day, they had to run like that in the courtyard, carrying a full pack and, of course, they had to eat together in the same manner. Several weeks later, they were again taken to the bunker and were reported as "being taken off the list of inmates," according to the report. The next thing we heard was that they had been shot at the execution stand that was located right next to the crematory.

"*Taken off the list or register or removed from the roll call*" would mean either shot to death, gassed, or poisoned. The Nazi high command thought, by using the term, "*removed from the roll call,*" or whatever, they were able to fool the inmates. It never occurred to them that, among the politicals, some had found ways and means to locate the whereabouts of those exactly that "had been taken off the list." In Block #56 where the political inmates were located, right next to the building for disinfection, one could trace the names of the dead inmates through the numbers that were still on their clothes when these were returned from the crematory to the place for disinfection. Then the names were kept in a special file and, this way, it was possible to trace down everybody who had been murdered and cremated. Even the names of civilians who were taken in directly for execution and then to the crematory could be traced back by checking their clothing for any kind of identification they may still have had with them. Thanks to the "secret service" among our comrades who did the identification, not even members of the S.S. found out about it. Otherwise they, too, would have ended up at the nearest gallows or gas chamber.

Not only articles of clothing belonging to the murdered victims would pass through for identification and disinfection, but there were other items, too, that the S.S. had collected or confiscated or, rather, stolen in the countries they had occupied. Apartments and houses, as well as stores, in these countries were looted and the goods shipped by the truckload to the "Third Reich." Anything that was stolen in the eastern countries was brought at first to Sachsenhausen for disinfection, to get rid of any possible bugs and bacteria. For months at a time, the trucks arrived to unload the loot, such as clothing from men, women, and children, including underwear, bed sheets, pillowcases, quilts, blankets, tablecloths, curtains, drapes, fancy needlework, furs, rugs, carpets, in fact, anything that could be found in a good home.

Just to see with what kind of brutality the Nazis went to work became obvious when blood-covered clothes, mostly nightwear, were among the articles. Evidently, these victims had been robbed at night, taken out of their beds, beaten, and stabbed, as the bloody clothes were also torn and pierced with knives or similar tools. One could still see if the victims were stabbed in the chest or in the back before death.

There had been one incident when inmates who had to work in the building for disinfection, found among the clothes a dead baby wrapped in bloody diapers. He had been killed with a bayonet, in all likelihood, because he was pierced all the way through. And, in their hurry, the S.S. thugs had forgotten to leave the little body in his crib. But this way we got some insight as to what was going on in the outside world. We were also wondering what may have happened to the rest of his family. However, it was not advisable to report this incident to any Nazi officials. Broadcasting news like this would certainly get the eyewitnesses into a lot of trouble; it probably would mean death for anyone who knew about it. And so the baby corpse was removed by the night shift crew who shoved it into the furnace in the building for disinfection to remove all evidence.

In May of 1942, a truck loaded with empty suitcases, trunks, and handbags arrived here at the barracks for disinfection also. By looking at the few tickets that were still attached one could read that this baggage used to be the property of Austrian Jews, many of them from Vienna, who in the meantime, had been liquidated—murdered—in other words. After the evening roll call, when they had a few minutes to themselves, some of our trustworthy comrades locked themselves into a storage room next to the building for disinfection, where the luggage was kept, in order to do some unobserved checking.

In one little suitcase was a letter that the sender wanted his family to have. The contents revealed that the whole transport, himself included, was to be taken to a resort area for recuperation and that it was permitted to take along something to eat. Sure enough, there were some leftovers, bread, and some bread crumbs, as well as discarded wrapping paper in some of the bags and suitcases. However, in what gas chamber this "vacation trip" ended, could not be determined. In all probability, it could have been the Linz Crematory, as this was the one nearest to Sachsenhausen. But to conceal any evidence and to make it impossible to trace the former owners of the luggage, it was shipped to Sachsenhausen. After all, nobody around here would get the idea that these were the belongings of people who had become victims of a mass murder somewhere else.

During the evening roll call on November 17, 1941, the inmates of the building near the gate had a strange sight. An old policeman in uniform who had at least seven or eight suitcases with him, besides other items, had just been taken inside the compound. After the roll call, this newcomer was taken with all his luggage into the cellblock, and an S.S. man went to the political department to demand a number for him, without giving the name of his charge. And so he became marked as ZB #40147. It was not a rare occasion when newcomers were brought into the cellblock without identification. In most cases, these were more or less prominent people earmarked for liquidation the following day as "unknown." Their case history thus ended in the crematory and after that, they were reported as being removed from the general list of inmates.

However, in this case, the unknown person was given #40147 and then brought in for registration. He happened to be the retired police chief from Limburg-Lahn, Jacob Küchle by name who was brought here for some reason or another, evidently to render him harmless. Since the reason for him to be arrested sounded so ridiculous we tried to engage him in a friendly little conversation. But what we got out of him would have made our hair stand straight up if it hadn't been shorn off already. After his retirement he was assigned to a special job which required absolute secrecy, something he was unable to keep since he was a rather talkative fellow. And this led to his doom.

According to the tales of Küchle, we got some insight into what was going on in the outside world. Since January 1939, he told us, a systematic killing of incurable patients, insane persons, and some Jews also, took place. In this case, an injection was given which would kill these victims within minutes. One professor by the name of Heide, Heyde, or a similar name according to Küchle made some speeches, even if not openly, as not everyone was invited. He was talking about a war that was imminent and that it would become necessary to make room in hospitals and institutions for the wounded and sick members of the armed forces. Therefore, it became advisable, yes, even mandatory, to have the present ailing population "cured" in time—that is quick and easy. This can be done by a new method, an injection that proved to be 100% effective, presuming the treated patient could take it. Küchle, who would make daily observations while at his job in Hadamar, near Limburg-Lahn, admitted that the effect of these injections was indeed 100% lethal. We also found out from Küchle that from January 1939, until his arrest in the fall of 1941, alone in the cities he knew about, like Limburg-Lahn, Hadamar, Buch, Pirna, Linz-Danubve, and several more cities more than 60,000 people had been taken into custody and killed through injections. He was sure that alone in Hadamar, the monthly death total was somewhat near 25,000. As far as the Jewish people were concerned, they were also brought here and killed in large numbers. Küchle pointed out that they came mostly from Mannheim and Ludwigshafen, but they had not been killed for being invalids but on account of their wealth, which the S.S. liked to confiscate. There were millions of dollars' worth of jewelry, furniture, paintings, and clothes left behind, besides the evacuated houses and apartments.

Understandably, a man like Küchle became a nuisance for the Nazis after they heard about it. He stayed only a few days in his cell where he was waiting in vain, of course, to be set free. Then one day the S.S. took him to the prison block where he was tortured so badly, mainly by "Iron Gustav" and his helpers, that afterward he was taken to the infirmary. On December 23, 1941, he also got the injection that took him out of his misery. According to his death certificate, he died from: "Brain damage as a result of external injuries."

As soon as the office in the infirmary received notice about a death among the inmates, then this information was spread to six or even seven different places at the concentration camp, but first to the political bureau in the main office so that the relatives or friends of the deceased could be notified in a fashion that would not give the real facts, of course. Among the five to six men from among the S.S. whose job it was to send out sympathy cards or telegrams, each one tried to overdo the others by giving the bereaved a report of how well the deceased had been taken care of, and that all efforts had been made to keep him alive until the very end. We have a little example here about an inmate by the name of Nickolas Cordsen (Fig. 12).

Fig. 12. Nickolas Cordsen made the statement "Hitler is unfit to take care of the government," which was very unhealthy for him.

In April 1942, Cordsen was transferred from the jail in Neumünster-Holstein where he had spent already 18 months in custody because he had made some remarks to farmers, some of whom were Nazi-friendly, such as "Hitler is unfit to take care of the government." Cordsen became #41778. As I had known him personally for years and also that he was suffering from asthma and some malnutrition, I did my very best whenever possible to provide him with some extra food and saw to it that he wouldn't be burdened with the hardest kind of physical labor.

Then, later in August 1942, while stricken with dysentery and shingles, Cordsen was taken to the infirmary for treatment and bed rest. During this time, a Nazi overlord named Ullmann happened to inspect the barrack in which Cordsen was lying, where he gave him an injection, presumably to "cure" his ailments. That was on August 21, 1942. When I tried at noontime to visit my friend, one of our political comrades, who had taken care of Cordsen, told me he had passed away after receiving this injection and that his body had already been taken to the morgue where I could say goodbye to him before his remains were shoved into the crematory. The orderly who took care of Cordsen told me in confidence that the injection consisted of prussic acid (cyanide). Now the family of Cordsen had to be notified in a letter, which gave the following explanation:

> *The farmer Nikolaus Cordsen, born February 9, 1883, in Atsbüll, near Flensburg, with his last address in Grossenwiehe, Kr. Flensburg, died in the hospital building of Concentration Camp Sachsenhausen, on August 21, 1942, at 9:15 p.m. The causes of death are circulatory*

malfunction and heart failure, dysentery, and double pneumonia.

Signed, unreadable scribble, title.

Also included was a little sympathy letter which gave some details of how well Cordsen had been taken care of since he was admitted to the hospital.

Here is the letter:

Oranienburg,
August 22, 1942
Dear Mrs. Cordsen:
Your husband asked to be taken into the hospital on April 22, 1942 and had been admitted right away. He has been given the best possible care by the physicians as well as the caretakers. But despite our painstaking care and efforts, we did not succeed in curing his ailments. I can only offer you my deepest sympathy for the loss of your dear husband. He did not have any last wishes. I have given our department for safekeeping of personal belongings the order to have his clothes and whatever belonged to him shipped to your address.
signature of Loritz

And another letter:

Concentration Camp Sachsenhausen Commandant #11/41 778/RT.
Oranienburg,
August 28, 1942
Dear Mrs. Cordsen:
Your husband, Nik. Cordsen, born Feb. 9, 1883, died on Aug. 21, 1942, as a result of heart disease and circulatory disorders besides dysentery and double pneumonia. His body was cremated on August 26, 1942. If you can have the local cemetery send us a statement, assuring that

grave space is available, the urn can be shipped to you. Enclosed is also the death certificate.
The Camp Commander
I.A. signature.

And still another letter:

r:
Commandant K.L. Sh.
16, 9, 42 Ho Oranienburg, Sep.
the letter to Mrs. Cordsen:
    Oranienburg,
    Sept. 16, 1942
Mrs. Margarethe Cordsen:
The Commandant of K.L. Sh
    part III/16/42/Ho
    The commandant, K.L. Sh. wants to let you know as a reply to your letter, dated Sept. 12, 1942, that the urn with the ashes of the deceased Nikolaus Cordsen was sent on Sept. 7, 1942, to the administration office in Esgrus. (Another little town near his hometown.)
The officer in charge of the crematory
Signed Klein
Stormtrooper.

The urns used to be shipped home to the bereaved families upon request. During the first few years, a pre-payment of 4.75 RM (a little more than $1.00 in those years) had to be made before the urns were sent home; but later it was sent free of charge. However, then came the time of mass executions, and the number of dead inmates became too big to handle. From then on, the ashes were used mostly as fertilizer. It can also be mentioned here that upon special request the urns could be sent home to the families. In these cases, the ashes came from the big piles that were lying around. After all, who would know whose ashes were in the urns that were still being sent out? Nobody, that's for sure, the Nazis figured. In the first years of its existence, the obituary notices for Concentration Camp Sachsenhausen had been filed in Oranienburg, which used to be the seat for government and vital statistics. Here the death certificates were made out. But when the number of reported death notices grew constantly bigger due to mass executions by the S.S., the administration officers became more and more concerned because, after all, this sudden increase in death notices was something to worry about. It was obvious that news about Nazi terror acts like these would keep the civil employees in the office for vital statistics wondering. Eventually, nothing could prevent this bad news would reaching the outside world. To prevent this from happening a special bureau for vital statistics was established in the Nazi commander's office which was named: Oranienburg #II. This #II office was located in the building for inspection and was under the direction of S.S. Trooper Klein, by name. Except for a few inmates that had been married here, the bureau of Vital Statistics took only care of death notices. There has never been a birth recorded at this concentration camp.

Now comes something else again. To the big surprise of all who heard about it something new had been added to Camp Sachsenhausen: a "house of ill repute" for the inmates!! This happened in the fall of 1943. According to rumors, it was Joseph Goebbels who supposedly suggested that the inmates could be interested in some sex life. And so in the far corner of the infirmary behind the room for pathology and close to the cellar where the dead bodies were kept, ten call girls were stationed; each one living in a single cell. These girls were provided by Concentration Camp Ravensbrück, the concentration camp for women. There were six girls of Germanic type and four were Slavic in order to have the correct race on hand. The Master Race Nazis wanted to make sure that no races were being mixed in this establishment. Jews, of course, were excluded; they were already sorted out beforehand and taken to the cellblock for liquidation. Eligible to visit this bordello were only those inmates who had earned with their daily work a special premium certificate. Besides that they had to get permission from the S.S. officer in charge and that he could only get it if he didn't have some kind of a penalty on his record.

After he could fulfill these requirements, he could buy a ticket for 1.00 RM for which he could have some fun for 20 minutes in the arms of Fanny, Rosa, or whoever her name was. However, to make sure that nothing else was going on that could be labeled subversive, some S.S. men, like Kolb and Höhne, as well as several others would alternate in making observations through a peephole in the door.

It should be mentioned here that the political inmates held on to their decent and honorable reputation and therefore regarded it as below their dignity to visit this bordello; instead, they boycotted it. The same can be said about the Norwegians, Danes, Dutch, as well as some other foreign inmates, while the common criminals belonged to the regular visitors who tried to outdo each other when it came to frequency. The girls who had been placed in these single cells did not leave Concentration Camp Ravensbrück on their own free will. Instead, the camp leader, Buhren by name, picked these girls and women out himself, promising them freedom after serving here three to six months in this establishment. The girls were chosen according to shape and beauty. The most beautiful girls, if they liked it or not, were taken to numerous other concentration camp houses of ill repute where only first class, that is, only the young and beautiful merchandise was acceptable. These were for the S.S. overlords. The next best were for the concentration camp inmates. As to the girls, well I have never heard that after a stay of three to six months they were set free. Like always, promises were made but never kept (Fig. 13).

Fig. 13. Ticket for a good time. Girls were promised freedom after serving three to six months, but promises were never kept.

CHAPTER 14

POTEMKIN REVISITED

"Everyone in Germany is a National-Socialist; those few who are standing outside the party are either sick in their minds or idiots."

Hitler 1938.

Among one of the examples Hitler liked to follow was also the favorite companion and lover of Czarina Catherine II of Russia, that is Field Marshall Potemkin who became a legend on account of all the promises he made. He too knew how to deceive the empress and made her believe in things that never were or events that never happened. Hitler also did not only deceive the German people, he lied to the whole world, and even his own brown uniformed accomplices were acting more or less like dutiful pupils. And so, one can say, even in these concentration camps, Potemkin found his modern counterparts. People in the outside world were made to believe that these concentration camps were nice places to live in.

Extreme caution had to be taken at all times to make sure that nothing about acts of terror that took place inside would be heard outside these confinements. No information about the deplorable conditions, the cruelties, the mass murders behind these barbed wire fences, should leak through the walls to any outsider. Every letter, any piece of paper that passed through the gate, went through censorship. If an inmate should be lucky enough to find out that his name was on the list of those who were supposed to be released soon, then he had to go first to the political bureau where he had to sign a form letter containing the following conditions:

1. I declare that I will never, under any circumstances, be it in talking or in writing, work against the present government of the Nazi system or of its subdivisions.
2. As soon as I hear about any subversive action against the Nazi establishment, I shall inform the nearest police station at once.
3. I have never been ill or injured while in a concentration camp.
4. I know that I am not allowed to speak about any of the conditions of this concentration camp.
5. Every item of my possessions, which was held for me during my stay at this concentration camp has been returned to me. I will never ask for any compensation.
6. Forceful suggestions have never been made to me while filling out this form.
7. I have been told to report at once at the police station of my home town after my return.

Oranienburg: the date

It does not have to be pointed out that everyone who had been released signed this declaration against his will. He knew very well that if he refused to sign it he would never be set free again. He would also overlook the fact that the S.S. may have stolen anything of value to him, like maybe a watch. Instead, he would rather admit that everything had been returned to him in good condition, as good as it had been at the time of his arrest. Even though some inmates had been crippled or even turned into invalids during their stay at this concentration camp, they too would have to make a statement, saying that they never received any injuries or mistreatment.

There have been cases where an inmate had lost a hand in an accident or an eye kicked out by some of the S.S. guards. After that had happened, they had to lie to their relatives and tell them that these accidents happened long ago before they entered the concentration camp and also that they had been treated for these injuries while at the concentration camp.

Whenever a very sick person, someone who may not have long to live anymore wanted to write to his family or let someone else do it for him, in case he was no longer able to write, then he had to include in his message that he was still in reasonably good health. In quite a few cases, it happened that the death message from the S.S. guard in charge arrived before the last letter from the dying inmate.

Being situated in a central location, and also near Berlin, Sachsenhausen would receive either "high class" visitors from other fascist countries or others in military uniform. Often all kinds of Nazi outfits with colorful decorations would show up at the scene. This would remind us that it could be time for carnival, especially for Hermann Göring's uniform. Whenever an extraordinary visitor was to be expected, a special order came in to give the whole place an extra careful cleaning. Everything had to be in extra good order so that the impression of the visitors could be as favorable as possible. The sanitation department had to make sure that no piece of paper was lying around, the place for the roll call had to be raked very carefully, and everything in the adjacent cellblocks had to be in tip-top shape because it was only here where visitors would get a look inside. In other words, they were only shown the front, not what's behind it. For instance, they would only be shown the first few barracks that were for the inmates to live in, not all the others.

While passing through the gate, visitors were confronted with inscriptions on the barracks nearby in three-foot letters, saying *"There is a way to freedom. Its milestones are called: eagerness, obedience, integrity, cleanliness, justice, abstinence, honesty, willingness to sacrifice, and love for the fatherland."*

It may be mentioned here, that next to the barracks which carried the word *"Freedom"* there happened to be the walk that led to the crematory and the shed for industrial equipment.

Anyone in the belief that the Nazis in their brown uniforms would set a good example had the wrong idea. Their slogans were more like: laziness, sadism, corruption, sloppiness, dishonesty, injustice, thievery, alcoholism, indulgence, murder, and the tendency towards immorality. These features of the hoodlums in brown did not show up to any of the high-ranking visitors because, during an inspection of this concentration camp, even the S.S. had to make a favorable impression.

Under the leadership of camp commanders the "high class" visitors were shown through the gate and after that a short stop was made, a few explanations and remarks followed, especially about some unfortunate bystanders who happened to be around at this time. As these were inmates Camp Commander Loritz would say to his visitors something like this: "These inmates over there are good-for-nothing radio listeners." After that, he would shout at them: "Get going, back to your cellblock where you belong, and keep on listening over there." Then back to the visitors: "Gentlemen, you can see for yourselves, that these inmates don't even want to walk. They are also too lazy to put on their overcoats or to build a fire in their barracks." It happened to be a cold and wintry day, but nothing was mentioned that inmates were not allowed to wear overcoats or make a fire without permission. They had to stay in unheated barracks quite often.

If a visitor would take the liberty to ask one of the inmates personally, he would never get an answer; a true explanation by the inmate himself who happened to be standing at the gate would give him very unpleasant results; a thorough beating would be the least he could expect. And that no inmate, of his own free will, would stand near the gate in the bitter cold without an overcoat, just to listen to the radio from the blockleader's office or rather freeze in his living quarters instead of making a fire; well, everybody knew that, even the camp commander himself. And, everyone was aware of what kind of punishment was waiting for them, just in case they would have put on their overcoat or built a fire in their living quarters.

In case it was time for the roll call while visitors were present, then Loritz would walk with them from one cellblock to another by which he would ask the inmates in a jovial way some questions like, for instance: "How many previous penalties?" (This happened to be the cellblock for the career criminals.) Answer: "28." "For what have you been punished?" "Fourteen times for theft and receiving stolen goods, eight times for fraud, three times for forgery, two times for disturbing the peace, and once for resisting arrest." When the inmate next to him was asked about his offenses, he gave the true answer, that is, he didn't have any previous convictions before being taken here, upon the commander replied: "Then it's about time that you get some."

After asking some more criminals, by trade, why they were here, he also turned around to some antisocials and some hobos who were here on rather short terms for begging and loitering. Then Loritz would turn his head around and say with a satisfying smile to the visitors, "Here you can see for yourself, these here will be different because here they are educated to be worthwhile human beings. They used to be only thieves, bums, and good-for-nothings. But here, they are getting good training. In the first few years, they cannot come out, on account of the war, because they could be dangerous for the general public."

Eventually, Loritz, the make-believe Potemkin, would lead the visitors to the infirmary in Barrack II, in which the reception, first aid, operating room, bath and massage, X-ray department, sick rooms for those in recovery, pharmacy and dental clinic, as well as the offices and living quarters for attending physicians were located. Everything is neat and clean, no need for further questioning. The nearby room for pathology is passed by on account of the morgue being underneath, and, of course, the bordello was never shown to visitors. Instead, Loritz would lead his company directly to R II, the administration office. And that was the end of the visit to the cellblock with the infirmary.

Whatever happened behind Barrack II where people with tuberculosis and dysentery have been kept and in those barracks from where push-carts were constantly taking dead bodies to the morgue? Things like these were never shown to visitors. Instead, the inspection trip would go to the laundry where the machines were in operation, and a busy inmate crew could be seen at a glance.

Then the tour continued across the walkway to the food storage quarters and the kitchen. Here the visitors could see long rows of meat hooks loaded with pig halves which would indicate that every inmate would be able to get a daily ration of about ¼ lb. of meat for dinner, or so it seemed. And then the delicious smell of the meals that were cooking in the kitchen! Yes, indeed, it must be a pleasure to live here in this concentration camp. And, besides that, anyone who would like to take a sample was welcome to do it. Who would have the nerve to say that these inmates had to go hungry or had a hard time here in this concentration camp? Terror stories, that's what they are, which were being broadcast by some radio stations in foreign countries.

In the canteen, inmates could buy all kinds of delicacies, like salads with mayonnaise, hot dogs with sauerkraut, fried herrings, cheeses, an assortment of cold cuts, ham, boiled or smoked, candies, chocolates, cakes, pastries, cookies, in fact, anything they desired. And, for those who like to smoke, there were not only the cheapest cigarettes and tobacco but also expensive Havana cigars available; things that people on the outside world couldn't even buy anymore since a long time ago. On the way back, they would stop at some barracks where payments were being made. Talking in a friendly way to one of the inmates who just happened to be around at the cashier's window, Loritz would say: "Hi, young fellow, how much did you get paid out this time?" "Fifteen Marks, Sir Commandant," was the answer. "And, you?" "I don't have anything on my account," said this inmate. "Well, you see, gentlemen, this first fellow has been working hard last week, while the other one was just loafing around and therefore didn't get any pay." But how was it really? Those inmates who did get money by postal money order sent to them by their relatives were allowed to withdraw from their accounts up to 15 Marks a month so that they could afford to buy some extra food and delicacies. But those poor fellow's families had to go hungry themselves because their provider was imprisoned in a concentration camp and therefore, never had an account to withdraw from. And so they were described as lazy and good-for-nothing bums. Nobody would tell the visitors that the money which was paid out was the inmate's own, and that it did not represent wages for work performed.

Before leaving the concentration camp, through the gate again, there used to be another short inspection tour to some special barracks like #2, 3, 4, 5, or 6, which served as exhibition centers. Tables and benches were neatly arranged in the living quarters, and in the bedrooms, freshly made beds were inviting enough for any visitor who came here. Oh, yes, the inmates had the life of Reilly. On the drawing-room tables were some loaves of bread, which were supposed to be handed out, and besides that, some packages of the best of butter and margarine, as well as a big dish of marmalade.

Fully satisfied with everything they had seen and heard the visitors would slowly turn around and start going back to headquarters before leaving this concentration camp. Meanwhile, all the pig halves from the storeroom were put into wagons and pushed over to the canteens for the S.S. men to enjoy, because these items were not supposed to be eaten by the inmates. The meals that were cooked while visitors were around were more or less for advertising and show. After the coast was clear, the inmates in the kitchen would help themselves to these meals, because first come, first served. They knew from experience that everything had to be eaten up fast before it could be taken away. However, for the rest of the inmates, it was entirely different, like, for instance: soup made from white cabbage with some boiled potatoes that were frozen already in it. No fat could be seen swimming on the surface, and the inmates would keep on turning their tin spoons around in a vain attempt to find some traces of meat in it.

The canteen, too, had its everyday shabby appearance again. All the advertisements for the different delicacies on display were taken off and shoved into the next storeroom; the image of the proverbial meat pots of Egypt, according to an old story, was gone. Potemkin's ghost had disappeared from here but may have settled down once more over the commander's headquarters, where Loritz said goodbye to his visitors, all of whom seemed to be satisfied with what they had seen. And they were glad they had been here; the same could be said about Loritz himself.

As soon as the group of inspecting visitors had left the camp-grounds, the same routine, like harassment, maltreatment, as well as cheating on inmates, was back in force as usual. Loaves of bread that were on display for 0.45 RM were on sale now for 0.60 RM, pickles instead of 0.10 RM were up to 0.30 RM, marmalades went up from 0.40 to 0.60 RM, just to show a few examples. Sales tactics like these were prohibited by law anywhere else but were common practice here at the concentration camp. Nobody here would go by these rules and regulations; the Nazis made their own here. However, the Nazi paper *Völkischer Beobachter*, dated March 26, 1942, announced, among other rules, for instance: "The profit for the retailer may be over 6%, but for the wholesaler to the retailer it cannot be over 8.8%." Just to mention one article, like sauerkraut for instance, which was sold to the inmates at 0.45 RM per lb. in March 1942, and the vegetable salad, consisting of potatoes, turnips, cabbage leaves, and tomatoes for 0.50 RM, instead of only 0.16 RM, it was not too hard to figure out that, for instance, in February 1941, the canteen made quite some profit for the benefit of the Nazi treasury.

Now a few more sales under pressure to the inmates: In the beginning of August 1941, 20 loaves of bread were sold to each cellblock at 0.60 RM apiece, but only in case red beets could be sold too, at a high price at the same time. In the middle of October 1942, 10 kg of shellfish, together with two pails of small boiled potatoes, sold for 38.20 RM, and a pail of corn on the cobs sold for 25.00 RM. At Christmastime of 1941, every cellblock had to buy 30 mouth organs at 1.70 RM each, something nobody really wanted. Just imagine what a racket it must have been if 2000 inmates would play these instruments all at the same time. It certainly would not help calm their hungry stomachs.

"We can buy everything at camp," this sentence had to be written at the beginning of every letter that the inmate wanted to send home. It had to give the outside world the general impression that anything that could make life easier or more comfortable could be bought at camp.

Of course, the relatives would have to send the money in first by postal money order. As has been mentioned before, the goods were being sold at high prices and often together with items that were not to eat but rather something the S.S. wanted to get rid of. And, if something good to eat would arrive at the canteen for the inmates, the S.S. would probably be there ahead of them and take it, steal it, that is.

For instance, big shots among the Nazis, like Campe, the "Iron Gustav," and Novacki saw nothing wrong in it if they helped themselves for weeks, even months at the time, to items like bacon, sausages, and marmalade from the inmate's canteen. They even had the nerve to pick out articles they needed for the bakery so that some nice cakes and pastries could be baked for them. Everything was stolen that was supposed to be for the inmates!

From the meager rations that were intended for the inmates, the S.S. would steal whatever they liked, even if the inmates were entitled to it. One of the biggest thieves was the kitchen chef himself, an S.S. leader by the name of Rackers. On March 27, 1942, it came to light that the so-called kitchen chef had truckloads of food, like meat products, sugar, flour, margarine, meat, and potatoes shipped to his apartment where he would sell it on the black market. Other big shots in leading positions were also involved, as, for instance, the caretaker of the building for storage by the name of Pohlmann and S.S. leader, Birke, who was in charge of the heating system, besides another S.S. man by the name of Landgräber, who was supposed to look after the vegetable plantation and the pig pen.

Diet articles for invalids, like oatmeal, rice, and other cereals cooked in milk that were supposed to be for inmates with a weak stomach were very hard-to-get. There were never enough of these articles available just because Rackers had himself built a storeroom, as well as some cages, for about 30 rabbits, right underneath the kitchen for the inmates. No wonder there was never enough food for the invalids; the rabbits got it instead.

When on April 23, 1942, the discovery was made about what had happened, the perpetrators of this rip-off were removed from their posts; but they only got 14 days in jail, and this was only because they had kept food items in a room that was inhabited by rabbits!! Kohlmann got the same penalty because he had kept "surplus food articles" in his own apartment without reporting it.

But when it became known that Loritz, the commander himself, had his own benefits out of these illegal transactions, better-called corruption, then it all came to a "stand still" and Loritz went "on furlough." But, before that, he helped himself to items from the S.S. kitchen, as well as some storage rooms, to assorted food items like sausage, hams, bacon, butter, wine, and liquor, which according to somebody's estimate could have amounted to around 4000 RM. in those days. It can also be mentioned here that Loritz, together with his girlfriend, made a pleasure trip to Stettin-Pom. While on the way, he asked his paramour what she would like to eat. The answer was, "Roast duck." Since this delicacy was not at hand, a telegram was sent to camp Oranienburg with the request to send a roast duck with all the trimmings to Stettin. An order is an order and so, the S.S. kitchen chef, himself, prepared it and had it delivered through an S.S. man by motorbike to a given address so that these two good-for-nothings would not have to "starve" any longer.

These thefts of food from the inmates and S.S. quarters of concentration camps, had their counterparts in the defense industry, the so-called "Deutsche Ausrüstungswerke" (DAW), an enterprise set up by Himmler and under the direction of a high-ranking S.S. officer by the name of Pohl. These workshops were set up in every concentration camp and manned by cheap help, that is, inmates. Thousands of inmates were exploited here for the benefit of their Nazi oppressors. Articles that were made here like, for instance, expensive furniture, complete sets for apartments, yes, even sets for luxurious mansions were built by craftsmen from among the inmates, everything under the direction of the S.S. slave drive, the S.S. pharaoh, Pohl, a real bully according to reports.

When, on August 30, 1941, Himmler was visiting Camp Sachsenhausen again, this time in the company of quite a few Spanish officers of the Franco army, he also made a side trip to the factory where a special cabinet for liquor was being made for him, everything according to his own specifications, of course. Up to about a dozen cabinets had been manufactured at the expense of approximately 58,000 RM, according to hearsay. However, none of these cabinets that were supposed to hold and keep wine and liquors cool were good enough to meet his fancy. And, if he finally did get the desired liquor cabinet, is hard to say; no one was able to find out. But anyhow, the quantity and the value of this fine furniture, made out of expensive hardwood and, according to specifications for the S.S. gangsters and their families or girlfriends, may have gone into the millions, one could only guess.

Here are a few examples regarding orders given by S.S. members that are worth mentioning. One S.S. leader, named Hansen, in charge of the Berlin-Lichterfelde branch of the defense industry gave his request on February 17, 1942, that all work details in this industry had to be stopped immediately so that his hothouse project could be finished by March 1st. And for S.S. leader Eicke a dog bed had to be built that had to match the bedroom furniture of his daughter. The work took one week. Unfortunately for his family, Eicke, meanwhile an S.S. General, was killed near Leningrad, whereupon his wife and daughter had to be satisfied with a not-so-comfortable cot in a barracks for refugees near Flensburg.

For Commander Loritz, the Potemkin for Camp Sachsenhausen, the following little biography may shed some light into his real life, which could be made public to posterity. Loritz had absolute authority over this concentration camp from December 1939 until August 21, 1942; he could decide about life or death among the inmates. His brutality became legendary. As a swindler extortionist and by using his position for his own benefit, he, too, was on top with those who had the reins in their hands.

At Lake Wolfgang (Salzkammergut) he had one of the most luxurious mansions built for himself by a labor force consisting of up to

24 inmates, who had been handpicked and shipped on consignment to work "at the lake." The estate was located near St. Gilgen. All of the building materials, even the stones and trees, had been transported in trucks from Sachsenhausen to Lake Wolfgang and, besides that, a transportable hunting cabin, as well as material for a duck pond built out of concrete. Also, a great number of paintings had been shipped there, which had been created by some artists among the inmates. Besides that, approximately 60 rugs and carpets, also woven by the camp's inmates, had been shipped to this mansion. Lamp shades, made of fine leather, handmade laundry baskets, tables, chairs made of wicker material, letter weights, some of them with silver handles, and maybe thousands of other items, done by inmates, had been taken to his villa at Lake Wolfgang, not to mention whole sets of furniture which also came from Sachsenhausen. A place for the boat was made by dynamiting a section out of a rock, an operation which also may have cost thousands of Reichsmarks.

And who was this man Loritz? According to rumors, he started as bill collector for a gas company, besides that, he had been selling part-time newspapers, but he sure was on time when he found the opportunity to join the S.S. It didn't take him long until he could move out of his cramped quarters in a poor neighborhood to a better place by holding a rather high-ranking position within the S.S., hereby pushing any possible rivals unscrupulously aside, while making his way to a leading and powerful position. When he became commander of Sachsenhausen, he discovered among the inmates under him, his former boss, a political representative, by the name of Clemens Högg (#16003).

This man could, as Loritz knew very well, cause him some trouble. Therefore, he had to get rid of him, one way or the other. And so, he had him transferred to a cellblock where he was constantly exposed to atrocities of the S.S. An accident, by which he broke the upper part of his leg, was the reason for which Högg had to be taken to the infirmary for treatment. Here, he met his political friends who did everything for him to help him get well again. However, due to the fact that he had been kept in captivity under such miserable conditions, he had lost his will to live. Once a strong and healthy man, an ardent fighter against the Nazi regime, he had turned into a helpless cripple by now. In February, they took him to the extermination camp, Belsen, from where he never returned. Evidently, he, too, became a victim of the personal hatred of Loritz.

When the wastefulness, fraud, and larceny done by Loritz caused enough concern, a special accounting and investigating committee had to be put into action. When it became too risky to handle, even for this committee, because other high-ranking S.S. criminals were also involved in this scandal, Loritz was transferred to Oslo. After that, we heard several different reports about him and it was hard to say what to believe, until after the capitulation a news item came in, according to which he had been taken to an internment camp in Bavaria. As has been pointed out before, the high command of this concentration camp tried to avoid, by all means, to let into circulation any reports about the general conditions and the brutalities that went on. Nobody should hear the truth about the conditions inside these concentration camps. Any time a foreign newspaper or radio station would bring a report about the cruelties that were so commonplace in these concentration camps, the German press would call it lies and horror stories, and the general public was calmed down again, at least for the time being.

Meanwhile, the International Red Cross used its influence to make it possible to have food packages sent to foreign inmates, for instance, to the Norwegians, Danes, Dutchmen, Belgians, Czechs, Frenchmen, and Poles. Packages from Norway and Denmark contained mainly items like butter, cheese, bacon, sausages, some things which the S.S. liked to eat, too. Therefore, these packages were opened beforehand by the S.S., who took some of the contents, and then had them handed out to the inmates as "damaged in transit." The packages for the Frenchmen and Belgians, many of which had been sent from Switzerland, were mostly filled with coffee, tea, sugar, cocoa, and chocolates. These packages, too, were opened up and robbed by the dozens, and most of their contents were taken to the commander's offices, from where they found their way to the apartments of the S.S. bandits so that the members of their families could also enjoy these luxuries. Making out a complaint or asking for a refund was absolutely impossible; the slightest suggestion that maybe a member of the Nazi staff could have opened one of these packages, never mind taken something, could mean the death penalty in all possibility for the complainer.

During the fall of 1942, inmates were allowed to mention in their letters to their relatives that it was permissible to send them socks, stockings, or underwear. The reason was that the supply of these articles had gone down considerably. However, these packages, too, were opened by the S.S. blockleaders, in case they found something in them that they may be able to wear themselves, and then they took them. Then the same permission was given to have packages sent to the concentration camps which contained items to eat, as well as tobacco and cigarettes. That was in November 1942. Here, too, before the inmates would get their packages, they had been searched over by the S.S. who took out what they wanted, mostly cigarettes and butter. But in the letters of acknowledgement, the inmates would have to write that they had received everything in good order. After all, it had been sent to them; whether they received it or not, the relatives had to believe that their inmates got it all, otherwise, they might have stopped sending packages.

What kind of corruption was being used by the S.S. members against the inmates can be illustrated here in the clothes and wearing apparel department for all the people at the concentration camp. Among those thousands of victims who ended up at the firing squad or in the gas chambers as persons unknown, there used to be quite a few well-to-do people who had been taken to these concentration camps dressed in their best clothes. Some of these people never entered the building for registration; instead, they were taken directly to their place of execution. If the victims were to be shot, they had to take off their outer garments and the jacket, so they would not be damaged by bullet holes.

All these garments, like those from inmates who had died otherwise, were taken to the chambers for disinfection and, after that, to a room for storage. However, the chief warden in charge of the clothes department saw to it that none of the elegant and expensive garments were handed out to inmates. This selfish and ruthless caretaker, by the name of Höpken, kept on collecting thousands of expensive suits, coats, hats, and shoes which he kept in a cellblock after they came back from the disinfection chamber. From here on, he kept selling these clothes, not only in Berlin, but many other places. He also saw to it that he got hold of all the cash and jewelry that had been sewn into these expensive suits, for his own safekeeping, of course. He had collected so many suits that people could believe all these victims had been killed on account of their expensive wardrobes.

But because Höpken tried to get everything for himself only, he soon made himself an enemy of all the other S.S. gangsters who also tried to get hold of some of the loot. So, it didn't take long before he had to go to court on a special S.S. trial that took place in the commander's headquarters, where he was convicted and, subsequently, shot by a firing squad. The unsold merchandise still at hand was confiscated by the same court, but actually it only changed ownership, and other S.S. hoodlums got hold of it. In one of the next chapters, more will be said about the sale of murdered people's property.

Darkness settled over the concentration camp. Things began to move near the garbage piles and other waste materials. Must be the ones belonging to the S.S. headquarters? Hungry inmates in competition with rats, were searching through the piles, hoping to find something that could still be edible. No wonder many of these inmates died finally of typhus fever, while at the same time, the Nazi oppressors were enjoying their meals that oftentimes had been improved with the luxuries found in care packages for the inmates.

Since so much within the Nazi establishment looked appealing to the outside world but was otherwise more or less make-believe, it is no wonder that the concentration camps were sometimes described as places for recuperation. Like Potemkin years ago, who spoke to his queen, Catherine the Great, about his conquests in the wealthy villages of the Crimean peninsula, so did Hitler and his cohorts, by trying to give, not only to the German people but to the rest of the world, the general impression that the concentration camps were really places suited for well-being, education and training of its occupants. They certainly were experts in fooling the people. And, therefore, with some reservations, it has generally been accepted to believe that these concentration camps were, after all, not really the worst places to live in. But it sure was hell on earth for those inside; one could compare it with a chapter from Dante's *Inferno*.

CHAPTER 15

THE BROWN INQUISITION

"If it should be necessary, I will have a thousand Czechs shot. If that does not help, then the whole Czech nation will be liquidated."

Himmler.

We all remember the time of the persecution of the early Christians by Nero; the Medieval Inquisition, tortures, and mass killings during the Middle Ages and even before that time, which gives us the shivers whenever we come to think about it. And after all these years, we thought mankind would have changed and become more humane. It is hard to believe that, after centuries of progress in science and technology, these brutalities could happen again. Apparently, the years of wars and the following years of want, misery, despair, and disease have turned man into a beast again. We still remember from our time in school, the 100-year war which was actually longer, the 30-year war, seven-year war, among many others, and, also, Napoleon's conquests. Even Mussolini had his forerunners as dictators, but he became the most infamous. Going back to the Middle Ages many different painful methods had been used for tortures and executions. However, even among the executioners, there have been, some rather shall we say kind-hearted people, who, for instance, would rather choke their victim to death in an unobserved moment, before he would have torn him to pieces in front of an audience of eager spectators.

During conventions of executioners—they really took place—these men in their bloody trade found opportunities to exchange new ideas and methods for killing their victims. This was done in order to make improvements in their so-called "dishonest" profession. However, even they were outdone by the Nazi henchmen. Progress that had been made in the field of science and medicine could also be applied to tortures to get confessions, besides trying out different ways of killing.

As we have read in our history books, Nero, at the time of the Christian persecution, made human torches out of men to show them to an audience in the city of Rome, while other victims were thrown to the lions to be torn apart, we all were horrified to hear that things like these had really happened. We had been disgusted just to think that men must have been unusually gruesome and that it was unthinkable for murderous events like these to ever happen during our lifetime. Wrong! The sadists of the brown plague, as the S.S. was often called, could outdo their counterparts of centuries ago by far, as we shall see in a few examples.

At first, we have to take a look at that infamous thug who was very handy when it came to torturing people in all kinds of ways. His name has come up before: the Nazi chieftain, Loritz, the grand marshal of the inquisition during Hitler's reign of terror, sponsored by Himmler for his talents in finding always new ways and means of torturing their victims.

After Loritz had demonstrated how mean and inhumane he could get while he was commander in Esterwegen, Himmler, after he took notice of him, had him promoted in 1936 to the post of commander in Concentration Camp Dachau where he stayed until 1939. From 1939 until 1942 the inmates in Concentration Camp Sachsenhausen had to suffer and die under his reign of terror until, finally, even the Nazi big shots thought they better get rid of him, because Loritz had been involved in quite a few cases of fraud and larceny. Therefore he was transferred to Norway. All different kinds of cruelties had been instigated by him. Loritz was responsible for many new means of inflicting pain and misery on the inmates in the cellblocks, prison cells, and waiting rooms. Loritz was also responsible for teaching his henchmen about the shooting gallery, the gas chambers, the crematories, and other gruesome places for inflicting pain and suffering on the inmates.

In fact, it has been said that Loritz outdid them all, so that even Hitler had to admit, Loritz was one of a kind in the concentration camps.

In a prison cellblock that was somewhat isolated from the other buildings, the S.S. thugs tortured their victims to death in many different ways. An inmate of a Slavic background who was first disrobed and chained to a post had a cage with two hungry rats attached to his body with a rope. At once, these hungry rats started eating the flesh of the abdomen of the helpless victim. Despite his cries for help to get out of his misery, the two S.S. henchmen kept sitting at a nearby table rather unconcerned, smoking their cigarettes, while watching this horrible spectacle with great satisfaction and enjoyment. The unfortunate man finally died, after collapsing within an hour.

In another case, the S.S. murderers thought they had found an even better way by tearing their victims into pieces, similar to the methods of the Middle Ages. Here the S.S. henchmen would fasten their victim in a frame with a loop for the head, two for the arms, and two for the feet. By pulling on all loops, the victim's skin would become very tight, whereupon the henchman took some razor blades to cut the arteries and, afterward, watched the blood spurting out high. Luckily for the victims, death came from loss of blood before he was torn to pieces. Eyewitnesses from among the inmates who had to watch these gruesome murder ordeals were taken to the quarry the same day in order to be liquidated. However, one inmate who became an eyewitness to these horrible spectacles escaped detection and told the writer of this book. The inmate's name was Erwin Rathmann.

Other ways and means used by the S.S. consisted of putting a water hose into the victim's mouth or rectum and letting the water run in at full force until the inner organs would burst, causing a very painful death. More often, the victim had the water hose directly hitting the region of the heart which would cause death by heart attack a short time later. During the winter months, S.S. thugs found out that by making the victim stand against the wall and soaking their clothes full of water; they would turn into human icicles after an hour or so. Afterward, the victims would be carted off directly to the morgue.

It also was not unusual for the Nazis to hold their victim's head in a barrel of water until he drowned. The cause of death according to the death certificate would read: "Accidental death by drowning." S.S. leader Saathoff, whose name had been mentioned before already a few times, had pushed a political inmate, an invalid, into a snow pile. That happened in January 1940, in front of Barrack #44. After that, he stepped on his victim's head and kicked him until he died from suffocation.

Several inmates just happened to witness this gruesome spectacle from the window of Barrack #45, while Saathoff was not quite sure if someone saw it. Therefore, he stepped into the day room of this barracks, demanding to know who had been looking out of the window. When the barrack steward, Jakob Adorf, from Cologne, assured him that nobody would have been able to see through the window panes because they were coated with a thick layer of ice from top to bottom, Saathoff got rid of his rage by hitting an inmate, who just happened to stand next to him, with a heavy stick. A Polish inmate, who couldn't understand a question, got kicked in the face and lost one of his eyes. Only after Saathoff had left the barrack could the injured man be taken to the infirmary.

At the beginning of 1940, the S.S. invented another painful method to kill. Next to the crematory used to be the infamous slaughtering place with the shooting stand. About a yard in front of the wall for catching the bullets was a cemented ditch, about a foot wide. Attached to it was a lid with hinges that would fit around the feet and hold them down, like in a trap. A movable gallows was rolled into place above the victim's head, the sling fastened around his neck, after which the henchman would set the winch in operation, hereby slowly but surely suffocating the victim, but also tearing his spine into pieces, causing an unusually painful death. As far as it is known, this happened to a minister from Brieg in Silesia who had been executed in this murderous manner, after being accused of treason. The author of this book had the opportunity to witness this execution through a hole in a wooden plank of a shed. If the victim happened to be a prominent person, or even a member of the S.S. who had fallen into disgrace, in that case, the firing squad was the usual method of execution. While the victim went down to the shooting stand that was located in an excavation, two S.S. men who had been ordered with the execution, would take a position in the background and in front of a shed holding some coffins. As soon as the unfortunate person reached the ditch with the trap, several shots would hit him in the back and put him out of misery.

After that, the corpse was thrown into a coffin by the same S.S. men and taken to the crematory by inmates who worked there (always inmates with a criminal record). One of these was the infamous Hans Gärtner, who was well-known for his cruel behavior. After being undressed, the corpse was thrown into the oven. Sometimes, members of the S.S. would undress their own victims, especially if they happened to be persons who might be identified by the crematory crew. Corpses of the S.S. men were always undressed by the S.S. gang themselves.

Bodies that were taken to the crematory were not only concentration camp inmates; they were also delivered by the truckloads from the inmate prison of the government security building at Prinz Albrecht Strasse 8 in Berlin, after they had been painfully tortured to death in the cellar underneath. Among these dead people were many prominent citizens, as could be seen from the way they were dressed.

In some cases, an order was attached to the boxes with the request to shove them unopened into the oven. When, however, these boxes were too big for the doors of the furnaces, then they had to be opened first with the consent of the foreman in charge of the crematory. In one instance in February 1941, a large box had to be opened. The corpse inside was wrapped in barbed wire and a black pitch-like substance had been poured over the face to conceal any kind of identification. According to the clothes he wore, it looked as if the dead person had belonged to the upper class. By the way, the crematory that was used at first had only two furnaces, which obviously was not nearly enough to take care of the workload of bodies that were being delivered for cremation every day.

When, after the massacre in Poland in September 1939, the portable furnaces were not used as often anymore, four of these transportable crematories were shipped to Sachsenhausen and put next to a lot of buildings used for industry. One look into the furnaces left no doubt about the fact that people had been cremated in them. Remnants of partly burned bones, even bits of clothing that once belonged to Polish women and children became a gruesome testimony of what had taken place here after the mass murders among the civilians.

A special way of choking, similar to one formerly used in Spain, had also been tried by the S.S. sadists like, Saathoff, Fickert, Schubert, Knittler, and some others, while they were walking through the rows of inmates who had to stand at attention. If a piece of a handkerchief or a shawl would stick out too much, according to Saathoff and the other henchmen, they would pull it tight, turn it, twist it until the unfortunate victim would choke to death, and drop to the ground. Rolling through the snow after being kicked down could also bring doom to the inmates as they were forced to keep rolling through the wet snow until fully exhausted. Nobody was allowed to pick them up or assist them in any way. In most cases, pneumonia would set in, followed by death, often the same day or the next.

Death at the gallows was the method used more often than any other in order to get inmates out of this world. A portable gallows was set up on the exercise plaza because this kind of execution took place in public. In fact, all inmates were forced to witness these spectacles and, in quite a few instances, these onlookers became unconscious and fell to the ground. Quite often, men who were scheduled for execution didn't even know it before that they were doomed. In most cases, the victims were kept interned in the penal section for some days before, but there have been exceptions where, for instance, the doomed prisoner had been working all day long, and at his return and entrance through the gate, his name was called, followed by the order to march directly to the gallows. This way, the condemned man wouldn't even know why he was to be hanged. However, the death sentence was read to him, often giving only a flimsy excuse. Interpreters had to translate these so-called death documents into several languages so that every inmate who had to attend the hanging would understand that "justice" had been done.

At an execution that took place on August 13, 1943, the rope tore in half and the unconscious victim dropped to the ground. The henchman, Höhn by name, asked the unfortunate victim if he would like to hang for a second time, or if he would prefer to be shot. Apparently, unable to give a quick answer, Höhn killed him with a shot in the head.

In July 1944, a slightly built young fellow from the Ukraine was taken from the penal section and brought to the gallows. He had been accused of sabotage, that is to say, he was under suspicion of having cut a pair of shoe soles out of a knapsack. Anyway, the boy couldn't understand what kind of crime he had been accused of. Now the medieval method of torture was put into action. He was tied to a block and a leather-covered steel whip came down on his back for about 50 times, until he became unconscious. After that, he had to be carried to the gallows. Hans Gärtner, a criminal by trade and also a beast in human form, was on duty this time so he put a loop around the victim's neck, then pulled him up on the gallows, which already exhibited the remnants of the knapsack and the pair of shoe soles.

When on the evening of December 24, 1940, the decorated and lighted Christmas tree stood in full glory on the exercise plaza; one could see the gallows in front of it. After the roll call, a prisoner of Polish extraction was hanged, and while his body was still swinging in the strong wind, Christmas songs blared over the loudspeaker, like "Silent Night, Holy Night" and others. Not much has changed since the days of the Inquisition when, for instance, in Spain and Portugal, and especially on religious holidays, scores of heretics were burnt at the stake after being forced to light the candles at the altar before stepping on the piles of wood and rubble to be burnt at the stake or choked to death from the smoke. So why should Hitler stay behind when we think of the Inquisition of the Middle Ages? These spectacles which served, not only as a warning but also as an act of entertainment for the general public, took place for many years. Until the beginning of the last century, hangings in public were not unusual in quite a few countries, so why shouldn't Hitler at least revive some forms of execution?

There is nothing that can hurt human dignity and emotion as much as being forced to witness the execution of a fellow man. Some were forced to watch close by until their former roommate would expire at the gallows. The atrocities of the S.S. went so far that even some dance music was transmitted over the loudspeakers during an execution.

Now let's take a look at some unfortunate people who had been hanged. What were the crimes they had been accused of? They were not criminals; all they wanted was freedom which the Nazis took away from them. In other words, they were more or less fugitives from Nazi law enforcement. The human bloodhounds among the S.S. caught up with them and had them hanged when they were innocent people who only didn't agree with the Nazi doctrines. Among them was Willy Novak, a political inmate, who originally came from a village in Mecklenburg. Well, he and a comrade were escaping while being assigned to a job at a plant in Lichterfelde. They were caught and returned to this concentration camp. Handcuffed together they were forced to walk side by side. While being searched, a bread knife was found in one of Novak's pockets. This became his doom. Possession of a deadly weapon meant the death penalty. For weeks, he was kept guessing as to what kind of a fate could possibly await him until on one August afternoon in 1944, Novak was taken from his cell by a blockleader and put on a wagon for his last ride to Lichterfelde. Here his execution took place. On his way, he had to sit on his coffin. A transportable gallows was also lying on the floor of the wagon. This reminds us of Jesus Christ, who had to walk while carrying his cross to the crucifixion, although Novak didn't have to carry the gallows—one improvement.

In order to enforce an admission of guilt, the S.S. and the Gestapo used several ways and means of torturing their victims, similar to those of the cruel Middle Ages. One of the worst was hanging from a pole which, until 1943, was being used in all concentration camps, partly as a punishment, but mainly to enforce admission. Here the inmate had to step on a stool that was standing in front of a nine-foot high pole, from which a strong chain was hanging down. With his arms in the back, the inmate was handcuffed to the chain. This, alone, could be uncomfortable enough, but to increase his suffering one of the henchmen would kick the stool away from underneath him so that the unfortunate victim was kept suspended in midair, unable to touch the ground with his feet. And so he had to hang, oftentimes with dislocated joints, for hours in this horrible condition. After finally being taken down, the tortured victims were, in most cases, no longer able to move their arms.

In quite a few cases, the victim's comrades had to feed their crippled friends as they could not reach their mouths with their hands anymore. Sometimes these pole-hanging victims stayed paralyzed for the rest of their lives. If a victim was still able to use his feet, he might limp from the pole driven from behind with a stick held by a henchman who also used his boots to drive him forward, towards the roll call plaza.

However, this didn't mean that the ordeal was over. No, because now these unfortunate victims were strapped upon a table, face down, and then the tormentors kept hitting them on their backs with a leather-covered steel whip, up to 50 times. By then, blood could be seen dripping through their clothes. Finally, they were taken down and brought by a blockleader to their own quarters, where they ripped off the bloody clothes and poured salt and pepper into their wounds. After that, these unfortunate human beings were thrown outside on the exercise plaza. Only then, could the comrades from the infirmary pick them up and take care of them. However, in many cases, it was too late, and so they had to be brought to the morgue.

At random, the S.S. thugs would pick out their victims from among the rows of inmates who were standing at attention on the exercise plaza. Apparently, whenever they didn't like the looks of an inmate, they could be picked out for a treatment of torture. One could even overhear remarks made by blockleaders like, for instance, Schubert, when he talked to a subordinate who just happened to be in charge of a cellblock, such as: "The face in the last row, the fifth one from the left, I don't want to see that one anymore by tomorrow." Now, in case the block elder couldn't find a way in time to transfer a doomed inmate to another location or into a commando for work outside the concentration camp, then it was pretty certain the inmate with a face not to Schubert's liking was picked out and taken to the penal section from where he was "eliminated" in one way or another.

Newcomers, especially, were victimized by sadists among the S.S., who evidently enjoyed experimentation in tortures. On March 2, 1940, a transport of newcomers was brought into this concentration camp. However, this time the people had to wait outside the reception barrack for a long time until they were taken inside. And during this time about half a dozen S.S. men, under the leadership of a sergeant from the political department, by the name of Clausen, kept on hitting the new arrivals, who were trembling in the cold with their fists and boots. One man among them who had been spared so far, his name was Josef Gaschler, from Munich, later to be known as #20614, became enraged and shouted, "What's going on here? Are we among the robbers or do these hoodlums still consider themselves members of the so-called human race?" A moment later, a shot was fired which, however, didn't hit Gaschler but instead three pairs of S.S. hands grabbed him and pushed him to the ground. Then he was kicked in his face and his mouth ripped wide open with the blood running out. After that, he was hardly able to speak when he finally arrived inside the building at the reception table. And, if this kind of ordeal was not enough, more S.S. men kicked him in his stomach and against the bones of his legs. The next treatment took place in the penal section with the result that he was reported dead in less than 24 hours.

It seemed as if the S.S. guards were trying to surpass each other while trying out various methods of torture on their victims. One beast in human form by the name of Suhren, who came from Bremen, was a former commander of the concentration camp for women in

Ravensbrück. He never missed an opportunity to assist whenever tortures were taking place. For instance, another inmate had been caught while trying to escape. His name was Zimmermann. Suhren gave the order to have him dressed like a circus clown and stationed at the gate, where he had to greet the homecoming troops of workers with words like, "Hi, fellows. I am Zimmermann. I am back here again." After the last man had passed through the gate, he was tied down to the platform where he had been standing on and got at least 50 lashes with a leather-covered steel whip, administered alternately by several S.S. blockleaders. And, because he cried out loud in pain, Suhren kept on kicking his face much harder and pressed it down on the platform, while ordering his assistants to use more force.

Apparently not satisfied, Suhren, himself, hit upon him with all his might. By now, his blood was running from his back and legs. The victim kept on screaming until he finally became unconscious. He was hit more than 50 times. He could not get up from the block any more so, finally, the inmates from the infirmary were allowed to carry him into the hospital barrack. Strange as it seems, Zimmermann eventually recovered, after a long time. However, not every victim came back to life again. Many were suffering from their injuries for the rest of their lives and quite a few died a short time after their ordeal.

"What, only nine dead today? That will be something if hardly anyone is going to 'kick the bucket' anymore." With these words, Sergeant Knittler, from the Russian prison camp, shouted at the interpreter, Wilhelm Beuche, after being informed by him that only nine Russian war prisoners had died during the last night. This was on November 28, 1941. The following evening Knittler ordered all Russians to stand outside the barracks, dressed in only a very few clothes in the bitter cold, after having taken a hot bath. The next morning Beuche could report to sadist Knittler that 37 Russians had died due to exposure.

It also happened that former criminals among the inmates were eager to assist their S.S. supervisors in their evil tasks. Outstanding in this category was a prison guard named Richard Mandel, a dreadful individual, nicknamed "Perronje." He took orders from the blockleaders to handle the inmates in the prison cellblock that were earmarked for special punishment. He tortured them so severely that they only needed a so-called "final treatment" to get them out of their misery. One of his victims was the inmate Otto-Karl Hill #52027, whom he had beaten so severely that his kidneys were torn so that he had to stay in bed. Now Perronje was afraid that in case this inmate should be taken into the infirmary he, himself, could get into trouble. And for this reason, Hill was not taken in for medical treatment but to a prison cell instead, where he died a few days later on November 18, 1941. The following case brought Perronje his doom: On a Sunday morning in July 1943, Perronje ordered a prisoner by the name of Fiedler, who had been accused of stealing bread from his comrades, to go to the gate of the soccer field and hang himself within half an hour, hereby handing him a strong piece of rope. He really did hang himself, which was witnessed by other prisoners who had to stand at attention in front of the prison barrack. This was even too much for the concentration camps commander. Perronje was dismissed immediately. After all, only the S.S. has the authority to order inmates to commit suicide, and not a person only in charge of the prison colony.

The tortures received in prison cells were not enough. They were followed up by transfers to the brick factory, called the "Klinker." Already on the march over which took about half an hour from this concentration camp, the tormentors were upon their charges again. Anyone who stumbled or walked out of line could be shot, especially if this individual was already earmarked for liquidation. Since this method "shot while trying to escape" was well-known among the inmates, they did their best to walk in perfect order. If the S.S. hoodlums didn't get a chance to shoot an inmate they wanted to get rid of, they would take off his cap and throw it into a nearby ditch. Hereafter the S.S. guard would order the inmate to pick the cap up again. If he didn't obey immediately a deadly bullet would hit him or several bloodhounds chased after him to rip him to pieces. There have been cases where inmates were killed by these ferocious dogs.

This reminds us again of the time when the early Christians under the reign of Nero were killed by the lions.

The chief tormentor in the "Klinker" or brick factory was a Nazi by the name of Van Deezen, a willing instrument of Loritz, capable of committing any kind of painful atrocities. As his assistant, he had not only some S.S. henchmen, but also foremen taken from among the list of dangerous criminals. But one should also admit that some good human beings have been found among the foremen, men who were fine comrades like, for instance, a man from Czechoslovakia by the name of Kranepuhl. These men sometimes treated their charges better than some of the political inmates or those who wore the red triangle on their sleeves. The most notorious command post was Post #16, under the temporary leadership of criminals like Staniczek, a foreman, Heinrich Eichler, an antisocial, and the two criminals by trade, by the names of Berthold Missuhn and August Möller. These savages were able to murder about 50 inmates each during a few months. They were just eliminated one way or another. While it was finally possible to get Eichler on his way out so that he passed away on November 10, 1942, the other two were transferred to Auschwitz and were never heard from again.

The most notorious place to get murdered was the "Klinker," especially a ditch from where only very few men returned alive or even unhurt. Here, like in penal colony #16, men had to work like slaves, pushing heavily loaded cars or carrying heavy loads of stones and unloading these stones into the boats that were waiting in the channel, whereby everything had to be performed at a very fast rate. Anyone from among the worn-out, exhausted, and underfed prisoners who could no longer keep up would feel the whip of the foreman or sometimes blocks of wood would be thrown at them to keep them moving until they finally collapsed. A few hard hits with an iron pole as well as some kicks from a heavy boot did the rest so that, by nightfall, more inmates could be reported as having passed away.

Most of these very unfortunate victims used to be homosexuals who seemed to be the target of these painful and inhuman treatments done by the S.S. and their criminal helpers who were employed as foremen. Only very few of these victims were still alive when this concentration camp was finally closed. A great many of them went their way through the chimneys of the crematories. In July 1942, a special group of victims that were earmarked for liquidation, arrived at the "Klinker" where they were handled like has been mentioned before; the reason for their punishment was "assumption of power."

Just a few cases may illustrate how many murders had been committed on these people in a comparably short time. According to statistics, from July 1 to 18, in 1943, 55 people were reported dead, and for the remainder of the month, another 23. Then, until August 18, there were eleven more which shows that it didn't take long to get rid of these victims. Some of these were suicides, which were often easier to endure than being beaten or kicked to death. One of these was George Fennekohl, a block steward. He had lived together with us inmates for over three years and had always been a helping hand to people around him. But when he was taken to the "Klinker" where he was subjected to some very painful tortures, he became desperate and ran into a high-tension wire, where he got a deadly bullet from the watch tower.

When the daily number of victims that were killed at the "Klinker" continued to increase, so that on January 13, 1943, 23 victims were counted as being dead, an investigation took place, and the block steward, a political prisoner by the name of Oskar Eckhoff, was summoned to the commander's office for an investigation. During this trial, he could only acknowledge that everyone at camp knew about these cruelties committed by the S.S., who also had no mercy for the sick and exhausted members in the labor force, and also that the prisoners had to work until they collapsed, with no chance of being taken to the infirmary from this horrible "Klinker." And sure enough, after this day, an improvement must have taken place, since not nearly as many prisoners died. There is a possibility that somehow foreign broadcasting stations found out about these conditions and spread the news around. And even though the Nazis denied everything they were accused of and called it horror tales, quite a few people became concerned. It can be said here that when the news about these atrocities committed by the Nazis became more widespread, the whole establishment came into a bad light. This included even Goebbels and his broadcasting speaker, Hans Fritsche. Also, the Nazi papers were bringing stories about the gruesome conditions in enemy territories. Like, for instance, an article in the *Völkischer Beobachter* dating back to January 1, 1941, where it said that in England the cows are better off than the laborers. On June 1, 1942, it said "Punishment with the whip is a sign of English culture." On May 18, 1942: "Hateful treatments were applied to German people in United States who were imprisoned together with negroes and guarded by Jews." "For the first time, Roosevelt interned women." During the middle of May 1942: "The hell in Khabarovsk" by S.S. war reporter, Erich Kernmayer, and some other stories. Quite a few of these horror storytellers have been taken to these concentration camps, where many of them died or were later quickly put to death. Since even minor offenses against the concentration camps organizations would call for punishment, these mistreatments often were without reason. However, not in every case have the inmates been subjected to severe maltreatment. It could happen that someone could get away easily like, for instance, being kept in a dark chamber for three days with a hard board to sleep on or standing at the gate. This could be for a short period or from early in the morning to late at night, it could be in the hot sun or in the freezing cold, in rain, storm, or snow, without getting something to eat or being allowed to go to the bathroom.

As a collective punishment, it could happen that the whole camp's force would have to stand on the plaza for hours or even through the whole night, sometimes with knees bent or hands stretched out high or behind the neck. Another penalty consisted of taking part in "sport," but not the kind that would mean enjoyment to anyone involved. What happened was making the inmates run back and forth, rolling in dirt until exhausted, after which they would get a kick with a heavy boot in the ribs. This is what the Nazis, the so-called Master

Race, would call the right way to treat human beings while, on the other hand, there was a law protecting animals against mistreatment. In a concentration camp, man was of a lower order than the animals. For pulling heavy wagons loaded to capacity, 14–22 inmates were put into harnesses. On the large estate, "Stollhof," near Oranienburg, that belonged to Heydrich, the horses were too valuable for hard work like plowing and pulling heavy wagons, therefore, human labor was put into action. The lady of the estate, Frau Heydrich, who was also the daughter of a former school teacher from Burg-Fehmarn, ordered inmates to be put to work instead of the horses. After all, what are the inmates for? Once she lived on a government estate near Prague where she had 15 inmates and Czechs at her disposal who had to work for RM .60 (about 15 cents) a day. Late in June 1949, Frau Heydrich was standing trial at the De-Nazification court in Burg-Fehmarn. She was put into group #1V with the order that she had to give up everything and return what she had gained through the use of Nazi government property. During this trial, Frau Heydrich at least acknowledged the destruction of Lidice as a crime against humanity.

It may sound like a hoax when Loritz had an artificial tree erected with a nest for storks on top of it. And, finally, a pair of these beautiful birds moved in. Since storks like to eat frogs in their daily diet, they had to fly to a nearby pond to look for them. Evidently, there were not enough. What happened was that a special commando, the so-called stork commando was formed. Members of this group, inmates of course, were sent out to look for frogs in every possible little brook or water hole. Loritz gave the order to handle these frogs very gently until they were put into the pond. Strangely enough, a man who can be a brute in dealing with humans has some kindness left for little creatures like these.

CHAPTER 16

THE ANGEL OF DEATH WALKS THROUGH SACHSENHAUSEN

"On every telephone pole from Munich to Berlin, the head of a prominent Jew should be stuck up."

Rosenberg.

"This Christmas season we are going to celebrate in the empty houses of the Jews. Heil Hitler! May the Jews perish."

It has never been a secret that people around Hitler and Himmler would not miss an opportunity to commit a bloody crime against concentration camp inmates. During the winter season, cold and hunger did their part to get the worn-out inmates out of the way. More and more seemed to die so that the unwritten law of the Nazis to eliminate as many of the human beings unworthy of staying alive, became a reality even without their actual help. Always welcome were the unauthorized attacks upon the innocent by the masses of the Nazi establishment. This way they had the best opportunity to commit atrocities without being penalized, as there was always a chance to blame the victims, themselves, or those people they wanted to get rid of anyhow. For the November 9, 1939, assault on Hitler that took place at the "Hofbräuhaus" in Munich, the Polish people were blamed. What happened was that several dozen of the Polish inmates were picked out, making them believe that their release may be possible. Hereupon, the S.S. selected 33 inmates, and had them take off their coats and wet their foreheads, to have their names and numbers written on it with a special kind of pencil before they were shot to death. Here is the list of names and numbers of these victims: Bleszynski, Stanislaw (23996); Bielski, Anton (24284); Choczewski, Marian (52896); Chrabalowski, Czeslaw (24103); Figat, Henryk (24524); Golabek, Szalislaw (23871); Grabowski, Edmund (23757); Kalinowski, Wieslaw (24481); Kopek, Richard (24496); Kroczynski, Peter (24251); Latko, Tadeus (24186); Lepianka, Johann (23723); Lewszynski, Lewczuk, Alexander (23807); Marczynski, Josef (23811); Michalczak, Josef (24105); Mosiewicz, Bleslaw (24621); Müller, Artur (24404); Mosecki, Eugen (24044); Polkowski, Czeslaw (23921); Przadacznik, Ryczard (24615); Ryll, Thomas (23..7); Sopinski, Mieczyslaw (24329); Swiniarski, Zanusz (24202); Stasinowski, Henryk (24529); Stojczyk, Maximilian (23777); Strozok, Wladislaw (23802); Trojanowski, Tadeus (24420); Tyszewski, Wladislaw (24053); Wanicki, Johann (23914); Wieprzkowski, Bronislaw (24490); Witkowski, Czeslaw (24534); Wolmann, Heinrich (23739); Wybranowski, Jerzy (24616).

Only later, it became evident that the assault against Hitler was prearranged. The culprit was a certain Georg Elser who was arrested and removed from the scene. Everyone was waiting for the trial, but nothing happened. Finally, Elser was taken to concentration camp Sachsenhausen, where he got two cells which he was not allowed to leave. He received his meals from the S.S. kitchen (better meals) and did some carpenter work as a hobby. Whenever he was taken outside, he wore a black cloth over his face which gave him the title "man with the iron mask." None of the inmates found out about his name until this concentration camp was dissolved, and an S.S. watchman discovered who he was. Whatever happened to Elser afterward, I have never been able to find out, but it is more likely than not that he, too, was eliminated in one way or another. When the bloodhound Heydrich, himself, was assassinated, the Czechs had to take the blame in some way and for that reason, some orders were given. One was to wear a black ribbon around their sleeves. Since none seemed to be available, they took a piece of black thread to express their "sorrow."

On almost every occasion, the Jews were the first to be blamed for any misfortune, followed by foreigners, mostly Polish and later, Russian inmates. In the early summer of 1941, the loudspeaker on the plaza announced that the long-expected war with Soviet Russia was now a reality. Of course, the Soviets had started it and invaded Germany and, therefore, Hitler had to defend his country. Hitler was only involved in defensive wars, nothing else, as he tried to explain to the German people, what most of them most likely believed, especially those who did no longer think for themselves. According to the broadcasts, the action taken against Soviet Russia went at a fast speed—Blitzkrieg—and in case someone liked to believe the news, the fall of Leningrad was only a couple of hours away.

"The enemy seems to feel that destruction is near," and similar slogans originated by Goebbels were transmitted over the radio; however, there was never an acknowledgement of the expected victory. All of the incoming news reports seemed to move around the same platform like, for instance, "The Soviets were completely removed from the surface; Communism is finished; thousands of war prisoners taken into custody; the Red Army was completely wiped out." These were the reports made by Goebbels, which were further broadcasted by his chief in the radio industry, Hans Fritsche. As had been said before, there was never an announcement that the expected victory had really taken place. That is, of course, according to Goebbels war propaganda after the war with Russia was about 14 days old. There was nothing else to do for Hitler's Army, except maybe some kind of police action. The best description was made by the political inmates who said in effect, "All that is now necessary is an army of street sweepers to sweep the battlefields clean of any possible debris."

All of these news broadcasts that were merely premature failed to sound authentic. They also failed to make an impression on the inmates; only the S.S. gang enjoyed them. The inmates were convinced that after entering the war with Russia, Hitler's fate would be doomed and maybe one could count on the war being over in a few months, followed by the destruction of the Nazi establishment. However, it turned out to be a long time of waiting. For the political inmates who never gave up hope, the war kept on and the German army moved further and further into Soviet Russia.

During the first days of August 1941, Concentration Camp Sachsenhausen received the first Russian war prisoners; around 2,000 men, who were being housed in isolated cellblocks. One kept wondering why prisoners of war who were under the protection of the Geneva Treaty were bought into this concentration camp. It was also a surprise that so many young soldiers who were still of high school age were among them. Yes, it was really astounding that the Russian newcomers consisted of so many young kids. This gave the S.S. reason enough to make the statement the Soviets were using school children for their army as they may not have enough soldiers of normal age. Only much later did we hear the truth behind it: The German Army took hold of schools in session and after that, these boys were taken into custody. This way they proclaimed they had taken so many prisoners.

The first transport consisted of 448 POWs: 426 were Jewish civilians and 22 soldiers. Besides that, three corpses had been taken along. In this transport were also a 14-year-old boy and four, 16-year-old boys. At this time identification cards were still made out and it was possible to trace these newcomers back to Minsk and places like Lebedewo, Gredno, Roszany, Oszniany, Dubrow, and others. At the reception, these Nazi chieftains would show up: leader of the group Suhren, Campe, another big shot, Nowacki, as well as Blockleaders, Häring, Kessler, Knittler, Zwejn, and Fickert.

Since the Russians did not understand enough of the German language and were, therefore, unable to give quick answers they were kicked and beaten by the Nazi hoodlums. Suhren ordered to withhold any food from the hungry Russian POWs. They were herded into a cellblock where they had to lay on the floor without any mattresses or blankets, only dressed in the clothes they wore. The next morning seven of them were dead already.

It may also be added here that during the last days and even before the first Russians arrived, a building within the industrial section was remodeled, also somewhat in a hurry. One room was done over to serve as a waiting room where people had to disrobe, and next to it were several smaller rooms, all partitioned with plywood between them. They were supposed to be the offices for the doctors. The first of these rooms was furnished, with a desk and a chair for the doctor and an extra table with a vase of flowers on it. Everything was painted white; even a white tablecloth was there. Sprayed with enough disinfectant, this room gave the atmosphere of an efficient doctor's office. In the adjoining room, the patient was measured and put on the scale. Nothing would indicate that anything could go wrong here or that this establishment happened to be a slaughterhouse. The so-called doctor was an S.S. man in a white uniform who only pretended making an examination. The inmate who was supposed to be the patient was ordered into the room to be measured and weighed. Here another attendant took over. Everything took place under soundproof conditions.

Behind the scale with the measuring block, an S.S. sharpshooter was hiding. Just as soon as the wooden block went down on the victim's head, a shot was fired through his neck, killing him instantly. The place on the wall where the bullets would penetrate was well covered with draperies so that the victim had no idea of what would happen to him. The dead person would then drop down and slide along a ramp into the next room where the bodies were collected. Then some inmates from among the criminals would lift the dead on a conveyor belt which brought them into the newly installed and transportable furnace.

To make absolutely sure the shots and possible outcries could not be heard, the radios were playing full blast. The killer hand was always well supplied with cigarettes and liquor as a reward by Commander Loritz who, himself, brought in a record player with extra loud music to make sure any outcries of those who were not killed immediately could not be heard elsewhere.

The first massacre of the Russian POWs started on September 2, 1941, and went through the night until the next morning. And, as the ovens could not consume all of the bodies fast enough during this short time, several hundred corpses were left in the storage room of the morgue. While working outside this slaughterhouse, some inmates discovered a large pool of blood coming from the back wall of the "examination building." One of the political inmates, Hermann Dettmer from Lübeck, got the job of digging a trench to let the blood flow away and maybe sink into the ground. A wooden board from the building also came loose and made it possible for some of my comrades and me to take a look inside the morgue. It was a gruesome sight. Bodies piled upon bodies only partly rinsed off with a water hose. Among them, the crew from the crematories were busy picking the bodies up to get them into the ovens.

These bloodthirsty helpers for the S.S. could even look forward to a reward given out by Loritz. But only after having committed one hundred murders would they receive a ribbon as a decoration. For another hundred committed murders, they would get another band as a special reward. And whoever could prove that he had killed 300 Russians or more would get a paid vacation in Italy. This would take two weeks. Years later, while working in the administration office, I found letters of complaint from Italian resort hotel owners, which gave an insight into what kind of items had been stolen in these hotels, besides the vandalism that took place while these S.S. murderers were on vacation. These letters also asked for payment for all the damage done to their hotels and for all the items that had been stolen.

It must also be mentioned that the S.S. mass murderers were looking carefully over the clothes of their Russian victims and if they found anything of value they certainly would keep it for themselves. Furthermore, it can also be said that some of the political inmates who were well acquainted with what was going on here had noticed that victims who were not killed with the first shot received a second one after they dropped down to a kneeling position. Plenty of ammunition had also been used because the wounds were badly torn.

With all the ovens in operation to their full capacity, it still was not possible to get rid of all the bodies as fast as the victims had been killed. Therefore, death took a holiday. What happened was that one had to wait a day. This time was put to use by showing some Russians the industrial section of this concentration camp where they were told that they could be put to work as a carpenter, cabinetmaker, mechanic, or in similar jobs. However, they first needed an examination by a physician, stating that they were able to work and could get their working papers.

Also encouraging, was the news that they were offered a so-called workman's portion of 200 g bread, 50 g cold cuts, and 10 g margarine. This they had to tell their comrades upon their return into the cellblock. That this information made a big impression upon the starving Russian POWs, who had not been given any food since their arrival, is easy to understand. No wonder they could not get out of their cellblocks fast enough and into the transport vans which took them in intervals of about 10–20 minutes to the so-called medical building. Like lemmings, they rushed forward, trying to get into the little vans that would take them to their "medical examination," not knowing that this would be their last ride. Some 50 to 60 POWs at a time would squeeze into the little vans that brought them to their place of death.

From now on, more and more POW transports were taken to this concentration camp so that the interpreters of the political department had to work day and night. It was no longer possible to make out cards for every newcomer who was transferred from the Stalags. They were only given some tokens of identification to wear. This kind of work was done in some isolated cellblocks where the Russians were located, between Blocks 11 and 12, as well as 34 and 35. As a rule, between 1000 and 1500 POWs arrived at the same time.

On September 2, 1941, a small transport with only 254 Soviet soldiers arrived, transfers from Stalag X, all good-looking and healthy, in comparatively good uniforms. 203 of these were listed separately; the remaining 51 were on a special list marked #3, with the remark Stalag X in Wietzendorf Kreis Soltau, Bez. Lüneburg, and, according to an order from Stapo Hamburg as of September 9, 1941: these POWs were to be taken to Concentration Camp Sachsenhausen for "special treatment" which, of course, meant liquidation and was signed by an official by the name of W. Meyer.

The next day, these POWs got a quart of watery soup with some turnips and carrot pieces in it. Through interpretation, they were also informed that they would get some bread for their supper. S.S. man Fickert even made that promise. However, on the same evening, 50 of these men were taken by cars to the slaughterhouse. Some of these POWs became very suspicious and refused to leave the cars that took them and stopped not-too-far away from the crematory. The stench from the burning flesh and the black smoke drifting over from the ovens made them nauseated and scared. Hereupon the S.S. men entered the car and shot every one of them, killing them instantly. But, on account of some enemy war planes flying overhead and over this concentration camp around the time of this massacre, the slaughter came to an end, at least for this day, but of course, it was resumed the next morning to execute the remaining 50 victims.

On October 10, 1941, something new was being added. Here, a transport of 174 POWs was forced to sing their own funeral hymns before their execution; it happened to be a Russian melody (Fig. 14).

Fig. 14. Notes of a Russian melody.

I am only bringing this unbelievable expectation to paper as it makes my own blood curdle, just thinking of such an outraged atrocity. It is not even possible to describe all of these horrible crimes committed against humanity; there were so many ways and means when it came to liquidating people. One of the most gruesome experiences was the transport of October 11, 1941, which brought 600 men from Stalag #323. On arrival at this concentration camp, the big trucks had already 63 dead and nine dying POWs in them, who were dumped like dead animals in front of the insulation cellblock for the Russians by the chief henchman, nicknamed Crematory-Böhm. Among the dead were some who had their eyes stabbed out with knives or kicked in with the heels of heavy footwear. All bodies were covered with blood. The next morning, I found in a cellblock two fatally injured men. They had been shot from the watch tower while standing during the night at their window. All I could do while being unable to help was to spend the final hours with them, comforting them as much as I could, under these circumstances. The name of one of these men was Alex Gawrilenko, born September 1, 1921, in Grefenowka. After they died, some comrades carried them to a wagon that brought them to the morgue. And what happened to these helping hands? They were kicked mercilessly and thrown with the other bodies right upon a big pile of corpses, waiting for the crematories.

While entering the Russian cellblock on October 13, 1941, in order to see how many of these men had died during the night, I was confronted with a horrible sight when I opened the door to the lavatory. All of the dead had been piled up there. Upon further investigation, I noticed that from one body the ears had been cut off, from another the nose, and for one body, a piece of flesh was cut off the right arm. Next to it, a POW was sitting on the floor, his face the expression of a madman while he was eating from the flesh.

The following morning I saw a repeat performance of cannibalism in another Russian cellblock. Here, two prisoners, insane from hunger pain, were fighting for the lungs and liver which they had just cut out of a body. These cases had been reported immediately to the camp's high command and the inmates from the political department pleaded with the commander in charge to let the Russians have some bread to eat. But instead of an answer, camp leader Suhren gave the order to take the temporary cannibals outside and have them shot immediately. The political inmates made another unusual observation that some other starving POWs were pulling grass from the lawn and eating it, and so the only thing we could do to help these hungry people was that some of our comrades went to the inmate's soup kitchen and asked the cook in charge to bring a few pails of soup and some other food over to the starving Russians. Outside of that, the comrades, themselves, took some of their own meager rations and some extra bread and brought them over to the starving POWs.

But it didn't help much, cannibalism still prevailed. On the morning of October 23, 1941, one could notice again that from 15 dead bodies among the Russians, parts of their arms, legs, and inner organs were missing. When one day a soup kettle spilled accidentally over the floor, while the man who was carrying it stumbled over something in his way, the hungry Russians rushed forward and licked the whole floor clean with all the dirt on it. In just a few minutes the whole floor was clean, perhaps cleaner than ever before.

Then there was still another Russian transport which arrived on October 18, 1941, with 1800 POWs. It was during the early morning hours. Besides 18 dead in the van, there were also about a dozen dying men who expired within the next few hours. While checking all these prisoners, it came to light that there were two men too many, who had no identification cards. Both of them had escaped from a previous transport but were caught again when this one came along.

The next morning—it happened to be Sunday—both of them had to pass between the gate and the window of the blockleader's office. When after the noontime meal the inmates marched outside and toward the exercise plaza, they could hear two shots. They had been for the Russians who dropped dead to the ground. Attendants from the morgue picked them up and placed them into coffins and afterward into the storeroom, next to the crematory. The next morning, the inmates who had to work in the crematory opened the door and saw that one of these men was only seriously injured and had dragged himself out of the coffin. When he asked the inmate to please spare his life, a bullet from S.S. leader Klein, who happened to be in charge, killed him instantly.

The number of murdered people became immense; entirely too high for the two furnaces of the crematory to consume. The piles of murdered victims became higher and higher; a day of rest had to be put in, that is to say, a day on which no Russians were shot to death.

In anticipation of the ever-increasing demand for furnaces to get rid of all the dead—not everyone was a murder victim, many had died a natural death—the high command ordered the construction of a new and larger crematory. This building got the nickname "Wärmehalle," which means something like a heated waiting room. Besides that, another slaughterhouse with gas chambers also went into construction. Two of my comrades, Walter Frank and Karl Sieck, who were working in the political department that took care of identification, told me in confidence that a large amount of Agfa-Photo material had been set aside for the filming of all the piles of corpses that were lying in front of the crematory and elsewhere. These men had to develop these kinds of pictures and, of course, they kept some of the copies for themselves, which they showed later to me and my comrade, Büge. Unfortunately, both Franz and Sieck later lost their lives during a bombing attack.

When soon after this, Joseph Goebbels, in his Berlin broadcast, spread the news about the "Bolshevik terror in the Soviet paradise" and had pictures displayed in newspapers and magazines, we had the opportunity to notice that these were exactly the same pictures that were previously made here. These were the pictures the S.S. had made here, showing the piles of corpses lying in front of the crematory.

The murderous activities continued, nevertheless, until the dead Russians took their own revenge. While still alive, they had brought with them dysentery and body lice that carried the organism of the dreadful disease known as spotted fever. It didn't take long until a number of inmates became infected. However, not only inmates were endangered and died of this plague, but it also spread to the S.S. quarters. One of the first victims happened to be group leader Homann, one of the very few Nazis who never laid a hand on anybody. After verifying his death, due to spotted fever, a quarantine was put into effect, as already several inmates had died from this disease, too. This took place on November 16, 1941. From that time on, no more Russians were brought into this concentration camp. After all, the crematories had been working at full capacity just to get rid of the "regular dead."

In the meantime, news about these horrible murders of their countrymen had reached Moscow. No prison wall or barbed wire fence seemed to be impenetrable whenever urgent news had to be transmitted. No strict censorship of letters or the watchful eyes of the outside commandos, who had contact with civilians, could prevent the dreadful news from being spread beyond this concentration camp. But, somehow and somewhere, tales of these horrible murders reached the outside world.

The camp's high command had no idea that for quite some time a close-knit group of political inmates from various backgrounds had been formed; men who did their very best to compete with Goebbels by making use of short-wave radio broadcasts. More will be said about it in a later chapter that deals with the underground movement.

By now, the Soviet press must have given Goebbels and his propaganda machine a hard time because the Nazi mouthpiece, *Völkischer Beobachter*, dated November 26, 1941, had this to say in the headline news: "From the battlefields around Moscow, reports are coming in according to which Soviet soldiers are running over to the German lines. To counteract such a crisis, Stalin's government felt obligated to report the atrocities by German soldiers against Soviet prisoners of war. The German Army and its allies are reading these false reports which are supposed to cover up the gruesome methods of the Soviets and to boost the morale of their own soldiers." And, toward the end of this bulletin, one could read: "Hypocritical note of the Moscow war criminals: According to reports of the army's high command, special victories at the Eastern front have been accomplished and, again, the Russian soldiers were joining the German forces. This unfortunate situation for Stalin prompted the Kremlin leader to publish rumors according to which German soldiers committed atrocities against Soviet POWs. Lies like these could only be the brainstorm of a madman, who after living in bloody tyranny for over 20 years, would like to prove that the life of a man is less important than that of a grain of dust."

Several days before, another Nazi paper *Das Reich* had this to say on November 23, 1941: "The distribution of rumors that Soviet soldiers have been killed in German war prisons are only propaganda stories of the commissars and intended to make the Soviet soldiers more eager and willing to fight." With this publication and others like it, Goebbels had made it clear again to the German people that "no child, no angel" is as clean as the S.S. He concealed from the world at large the fact that in concentration camps, prisoners of war have been forced to fight in special formations among the S.S. and, therefore, against their own countrymen.

They were given a special name, "Landeseigenen Verbände," something like unions of their own country, of which the name "Wlassow" soon became prominent. First of all, it became necessary to halt the spread of the dreaded spotted fever and dysentery because the S.S. were worried about their own health and lives. Nothing was heard about these terrible diseases outside the concentration camp. Goebbels kept this news concealed from the German people; however, he had the Nazi press announce that in other countries these diseases were rampant, in order to divert the attention away from here and toward other places as it was usually done by the Nazi press and broadcasts.

In order to combat spotted fever, the Nazis used cyanide gas, manufactured by the firm Tesch and Stabenow in Hamburg, which also delivered the gas for executions of inmates in gas chambers. But here, in this case, the inmates were transferred to other quarters for some days while their cellblocks were fumigated. Windows and doors were shut tight and sealed with strips of adhesive material. Even the inmates themselves became disinfected and, if possible, handed out some sterile clothing. After being fumigated, these cellblocks were aired out to make sure every trace of this poison gas had escaped before they could be used again. In one of the Russian blocks, this precaution had not been taken. After being aired out, only superficially, the Russians had to sleep in it the following night already, while the other cellblocks were aired out at least two days after they had been fumigated. Since this poison gas was odorless, the Russians didn't even notice it. However, on the next morning which happened to be the 24th of December, 1941, 42 Russians had died during their sleep.

It should be pointed out that the Russian POWs had been divided, from the beginning, into two groups. One was earmarked for extermination and the other one, a smaller group, was picked out mainly for hard labor. This group consisted mainly of big and strong individuals who had been trained and were skilled in some trades. Whenever people in the political department who were working at the reception of newcomers, were notified that a particular Russian individual was not supposed to be kept alive, he would put on his usual identification paper an extra form saying, "in case of death," so that his relatives who were left behind could be notified. After all, the death rate was pretty high anyway. Then it happened one day the officer in charge of registration, S.S. leader Friedrich by name, looked through all these papers and cards and saw the advance prepared death notices. He never saw something like that before and asked, "Are these people to die here or to work?" After that, there were no more pre-death notices filled out.

On October 16, 1941, a day when some high-ranking visitors were making a tour through the concentration camp, a big sign was erected on top of the Russian block, which said, "Working force of war prisoners." Of these so-called "working Russians" on this specific day, the working force was listed as approximately 2500 men of whom, until the end of the month, 209 were marked as "officially" deceased. Although the number of POWs increased to 4355 men, as of January 16, 1943, there were only 965 alive by that date. Through poisoned injections alone, 674 were wiped out, 247 were transferred to the extermination camp Auschwitz, 340 had been taken to the "Klinker," the quarry from where there was hardly a return, seven had been hanged at the exercise plaza, 35 were taken to the murder institute known as Mauthausen, and the remaining few expired one way or the other at this concentration camp. All in all, 3390 men had been liquidated.

For every Russian transport into this concentration camp, a list of POWs had to be made fivefold, which was checked very carefully by an S.S. man in charge who had to make sure that no extra copies were made by those who made these lists. It was only possible to make another list on the reverse side of an old wall calendar. This list showed the names of over 1400 men by the middle of January 1942. Altogether, more than 13,000 Russians died here, most of them by a shot in the neck or in the gas chamber. Since all the remaining clothes, uniforms, underwear, or whatever belonged to these victims were returned from the crematory to the chambers for disinfection, it became evident that around 10,000 more Russians had died here in the gas chamber without first being taken through regular registration in the political department. As a conservative estimate, it can be said that in Concentration Camp Sachsenhausen, under the direction of its infamous super henchman Loritz, around 24,000 Russian POWs may have been put to death.

After the construction of a new and permanent building for the slaughtering of people was finished, the mass murders through gas and poison could be continued in larger numbers. Until this concentration camp became evacuated in April 1945, the number of men killed that were listed, came to way over 137 thousand and the names of many others had never been on file. In waves, these transports came in, as soon as some kind of punitive action had taken place in a newly by Hitler-occupied territory. Sometime after the Mussolini affair at the end of July 1943, which was published in the German press and over the radio about two months later, something they did very reluctantly, of course.

There always seemed to be a certain kind of action taking place in the offices of the high command; special meetings were going on involving many Nazi spies floating around this concentration camp. Soon after these meetings, well-known and also prominent inmates from among our good and reliable comrades would disappear in smaller or larger groups. Either they were put to death secretly in gas chambers or they were taken to another camp for liquidation. The usual explanation would read, "Removed from the camp's registration files."

There were always groups of victims earmarked for liquidation, oftentimes political offenders who had to disappear in a hurry. Not to mention all those who were thought to be involved in the assassination attempt against Hitler, which took place on July 20, 1944. Quite a few of these people used to be members of the Communist and Socialist parties and in prominent positions. At this time, the transports came in large numbers with arrested people who had nothing to do with this plot against Hitler but who had made the bad mistake of saying something like, "Too bad," after they had heard Hitler had survived, with not even a scratch. A remark like that was, quite often, enough to get the offender into the gas chamber. Those who openly doubted that the final victory for the Nazis would not be certain could also meet the same fate. And so it happened that they, too, came to Sachsenhausen where they were removed from "the registration files," in other words: liquidated.

The increased worsening of the daily meals and the lack of food helped to increase the breakdown of the inmates' health, especially the older ones, the sickly, and the invalid. Getting them out of this world was the solution, according to the opinion of the Hitler government and its henchmen. The farther the Allied armies pushed into the heart of the "Third Reich" the more critical became the situation for the Nazis themselves. They wanted to live and not deprive themselves of anything. The dwindling food supply looked catastrophic, considering all the people who had to be fed. Therefore, the useless eaters, the worthless elements among the inmates had to disappear faster. A solution came to the mind of the Nazis. They called it "selection." This means anyone who was considered "ripe" for the gas chamber had to be picked out. It took almost a year while a constant and thorough check-up took place among the inmates, not by any doctors or nurses, but by S.S. leader Böhm and his side-kick Horst Hempel, also nicknamed at camp "the parachuter with the hump on his back." They went through the blocks, the workshops, repair shops, among those who had to mend the clothes, in fact, everywhere, and if they thought they had found someone they considered not fully capable of doing his job, then his name was marked in a red folder.

The angel of death went through the camp. Woe and behold to any older person, any crippled one or one who did not look too healthy among the inmates, anyone who did have a cough or did not make the impression of a healthy individual, well then, the catcher of invalids would mark his number down, which could be seen on his jacket, on a leg of his pair of pants or elsewhere, and his fate was doomed. Next, they would get the order to come to the registration office and go for a checkup, where they would get an "injection" to make them feel better, whereupon they were promised a cure in a nice sanitarium for some time.

For quite a while, two prominent people were held in the infirmary as patients. One was a well-known Berlin nursery owner by the name of Späth and the other was an official, also in a high-ranking position, and his name was Lorenz Breunig. These people were told, like some other patients, that they should get ready for a transfer into a sanitorium. Those selected were furnished with some sandwiches and woolen blankets for the trip to make sure nothing would happen to them on the way. It was in February 1945, a very cold day and, of course, these patients had to be protected against the cold. This was pointed out to them to give them more confidence.

Before he said goodbye to his political friends, Lorenz Breunig had already a good idea of what this "sanitorium" was going to be. However, he couldn't think of any way to escape when the ambulance arrived to pick him and the other "selected" patients up. The trip went through the main gate and out on the road, while the direct way to the crematories went towards the right side, just behind the first gate. Once on the road, the ambulance went crisscross through the streets of Oranienburg, in order to confuse the patients inside as to where they would be taken. After a 20-minute ride, they were at their destination: the gas chamber, which would "take care" of all the patients. It may not be necessary to describe the inside of the gas chamber, but just to get a rough idea, this is what it looked like. It looked more like bathroom stalls with fake shower heads. All the windows were made of dark blue glass. After the victims were inside this structure, the door was closed airtight. Then, either the gas was led inside directly or a can of cyanide would drop into a basin and turn to poison gas. This was done with a lever from the outside of the chamber. After several minutes, the vents under the roof could be opened again because by that time the victims had died already. After a lengthy and thorough ventilation, all doors were opened, so that later the workers from the crematory could take out all the bodies.

After engaging some scientists with a criminal record and knowledge about methods of mass murder and the disposal of dead bodies, some experiments took place. One wanted to find out about a method by which the soft parts of the bodies could be separated from the bones. Here they came upon a strong acid that would dissolve the flesh. Water was added to it and then a slimy-looking mess was allowed to run its way. The skeletons were broken into pieces and shipped by the truckloads to factories for the manufacture of fertilizers. It can be pointed out here that purposely Jewish inmates were picked out to break up the bones. Possibly, this was done to remind them that this would be the way they would have to go one of these days after they had been liquidated in the gas chamber. However, this kind of experiment didn't seem to work too well because soon after that, the dead bodies were taken to the crematories again.

When after January 12, 1945, the general outlook for Hitler and his armies became more desperate than ever before, and while, at the same time, the Russian Army was marching closer and closer toward the middle of the Third Reich, the concentration camp gave out a secret order. This time it meant to get rid of every prominent political German, as well as foreign inmates. This action took place during the night of February 1st and 2nd, 1945. One hundred seventy-eight victims were taken from their cots and escorted by a large number of S.S. men. Destination: execution at the shooting gallery in the industrial section. On the way, resistance took place which was natural as everyone knew what was in store for him. Among these condemned people were also some men of military rank from Luxembourg, who didn't want to be slaughtered without a fight, seven British war prisoners under General Goodwin, a navy officer, and some French and Russian people of military rank.

After all these men had been shot to death during that fateful night of the murder, a new action with more arrests took place against some other political inmates. Block 58 had been kept aside already, since the summer of 1944, to house mostly prominent political inmates. The man in charge of this special committee was a Nazi stormtrooper by the name of Ballhause. This is what happened: On October 11, 1944, in the early morning hours, 27 of these political inmates were taken outside and led to the gate. Later, after being transported, we found out in confidence, of course, that they had been shot at the quarry. Here are the names of our good, we may also say excellent, comrades: Erich Booze, (from the office), Josef Tschub, Alfred Ahrens, Andreas Bergron, Fritz Bücker (a radio expert), Emil Dersch, Willy Grübsch (from the infirmary), Arthur Henning, Otto Kröbel (a nurse), Rudolf Henning (a chemist), Erich Mohr, Roger Robine, Dietrich Hornig, Josef Rutz, Gustav Spiegel, Kurt Spolek, Heinz Bartsch (office worker), Ernst Schneller (member of the Parliament), Hans Rothbart, August Sander (from the infirmary), Ludgart Söllighofer, Siegmund Szedski, Wilhelm Sandhofer, Ernst Fürstberg, Mathias Tesen, Rudolf Mokry; the name of the last victim was Benoit, a young Frenchman only 16 years old who used to work for Heinkel. Unfortunately, these were not all. The angel of death went through the concentration camp continuously, picking out more victims for the gas chambers, the shooting gallery, or the gallows.

Meanwhile, a new decree came into effect which didn't look too favorable. Considering the possibility that this concentration camp may have to be evacuated, all inmates who didn't seem fit enough, all the old ones, the sick and ailing, and those unable to take a long march on the road, all these had to be transported by railroad to the western part of the country. At first, volunteers were asked to come forward and make use of this opportunity. But there were not too many who were interested in such a free ride. Therefore, a new screening took place, by which the workshops for clothes repair and other easy manual labor shops were combed through again. Everyone was promised two woolen blankets, besides plenty of food such as sandwiches for this trip. Around 10,000 inmates who didn't seem to be strong enough for a long march were brought together. Clothing, originally belonging to them, was taken from the storage rooms and loaded into freight cars. Some inmates who were in charge of the wardrobe department took a ride in this car too. The destination was given as Bergen-Belsen, near Celle, Hanover.

All reports from Bergen-Belsen that were received in Sachsenhausen sounded somewhat controversial. But, then again, the camp's headquarters used their own instigators who had to picture how wonderful a life was provided for the inmates in Bergen-Belsen. Very good quarters seemed to be over there, as well as plenty to eat. Besides that, excellent care was being taken of their sick and invalid inmates. Only someone who had never been in a concentration camp before may have believed fairy tales like that. What was described as heaven on earth was merely hell on earth in concentration camps. Through the grapevine, the political inmates found out very soon that the general conditions at Bergen-Belsen were as bad as in Sachsenhausen but, most likely, worse.

Meanwhile, the camp's commander gave the order to several of his helpers, all men with a criminal record, to use their judgement when picking out inmates for these questionable transports. The names of these hoodlums were: Beier, and the other Alfred Flegel. Needless to say, they picked first from among the political inmates to be shipped to Bergen-Belsen on a one-way trip with a pitiful end. Among these victims was a Professor, John Verweyen, and also a member of the Parliament by the name of Klemens Högg. By the middle of February 1945, almost all transports for Bergen-Belsen had left. From then on, several others went to Mauthausen and some smaller camps lying in the western part of the country.

The total camp's force did not decrease as newcomers were shipped in daily, mostly from concentration camps in the east that were lying within the territory of the advancing Soviet Army. One of these transports that had left Hungary, with about 800 men aboard, arrived here with less than 100 men, who were hardly alive. All others had perished on the march on foot which was about several hundred km or had died from hunger, cold, and exposure. Of those that did arrive, many more died of frostbite, followed by gangrene, and even amputations. Autopsies on some of the dead showed that the intestines had rotted away due to disease.

After bombing squadrons had destroyed the smaller working camp, Auer, and some others near Sachsenhausen, their inmates, women in this case, were also taken to Sachsenhausen, where they were put into the insulation block including some children they had with them. Without an end, the angel of death went through this concentration camp constantly, picking out victims here and there in increasing quantity. The gas chambers, too, were working at full capacity, thanks to the method of "selection" used by thugs Böhm, and his helper, Horst Hempel. When these two murderers were very busy, everyone in this concentration camp knew only too well that another sadist, Moll by name, as well as his assistants, had their hands full too, working in the crematories. Moll had made his way through every large concentration camp and finally became a leader in the process of mass poisoning of people by gas on a grand scale.

CHAPTER 17

SWASTIKA PHARAOHS

> *"When Lord Halifax made the statement he was representing culture, I had to reply: Sir, we do have a culture of which you do not know anything yet. This new Germany has no intention to lead or even start a war."*
>
> — Hitler

The concentration camps were serving three purposes: first of all, the Nazis wanted to get rid of all the undesirables from the general public, mainly to protect themselves. Secondly, the concentration camps were supposed to eliminate as many of the sick, the infirm, and those who could no longer work, besides the enemies of the Nazi system, like the Jewish people, foreigners, and Germans who were not pro-Nazi. All these had to be disposed of; after all, they happen to be "unnecessary eaters" to say the least. The third category consisted mostly of strong and hardworking individuals and skilled laborers. If there were not enough of these among the inmates, a special search took place among tradesmen like electricians, plumbers, roofers, tailors, carpenters, cabinetmakers, painters, and so on. In this case, the Gestapo arrested them for the same usual reason, such as "endangering the safety of the country." Next thing: they ended up in one of the concentration camps.

With the ever-increasing demand for labor, it became obvious that the Third Reich could not supply all the skilled laborers that were needed. Therefore, tradespeople had to be taken from the occupied countries as well. These people were promised they had a very good opportunity to work and earn good wages. If these people could not be taken voluntarily, then they were obtained by force, "shanghaied," as the sailors would call it. After the occupation of Denmark in April 1940, the Nazi man catchers were looking first for skilled workers of all kinds. The hourly rate at that time was between 80 pfennigs to one Reichsmark. Obviously, the Nazis didn't keep up with their promise in the German labor camps. In fact, they didn't even intend to but had in mind from the beginning to exploit the hired help without any pay. It didn't take long until the Danes found out their countrymen had been taken for a ride. Nobody was interested any more to be hired without any pay. It didn't make any sense; why should they work for nothing? And, so, the Nazis looked for help in other countries, like France, Belgium, and the Netherlands, and even in the eastern European countries. For a while, they seemed to be successful, because what they were hiring were young people for work on a farm. But, it turned out to be the same: these young workers, also, didn't get any wages. Next, the Nazis were looking for former German people, who were now living in Russian territory like, for instance, Galizien, Banat, and others. But, after they had found out they had to work without wages, they were no longer interested. Now, the Nazis had to use another trick: catching people in movie theaters. The method was like this. In German-occupied countries, the people were invited to see free movies. These movies were selected according to age groups; if mostly young people were needed, they would show what they would like to see. And, as soon as the theater was filled, the doors were closed for good. After that, the whole audience was marched out of the building and off to trains which took them into German territory. While on the way, a sorting out took place by which strong-looking young men and women were escorted from the trains and handed over to agricultural establishments who were looking for help. The remaining people were shipped to labor camps or concentration camps. It didn't take long for the people to find out about these free movies. After the Nazis couldn't get anyone anymore to see free movies, the next move was to catch them right from the streets. And, so, street by street, whole villages were combed through to pick up people for slave labor camps. And, of course, the first ones to be picked out were the Jewish people. They were taken from the occupied countries like Norway, Denmark, Netherlands, Luxembourg, Belgium, and France, and mainly from the eastern European countries, the Balkans and Hungary. Most of these people had been earmarked for elimination already, since according to the Nazi program these people as well as the Jewish ones, had to be "rubbed out."

Exceptions were made with highly skilled craftsmen like watchmakers, opticians, and members of the printing trade, as well as for drawing and engraving skills. Orders were given already to the reception office since 1941, to mark down on the registration cards of incoming Jews, if any of them belonged to one of these trades. Watchmakers, jewelers, and opticians, totaling around 100 men were transferred to a special barracks. Here, they had to repair all those watches, jewelry, and optical instruments that the Nazis had robbed from the occupied countries, so they could be used by the management of the S.S. under the leadership of S.S. Obergruppenführer Pohl. With these repaired watches, jewelry and so on the Nazis did a great business.

The Jewish engravers were kept isolated in small places; at first in Block 18 and later Block 19. Both of these blocks were enclosed with a high barbed wire fence, which made any contact with the other blocks virtually impossible. After the last bell in the evening and during the night, machinery and instruments were frequently taken to these blocks, so that anyone who heard about it had to become suspicious about those things that were going on inside, which could really not be called kosher. Well, no one outside was supposed to find out what was going on. Even meal rations were taken by carts to the gate of these barracks where an S.S. man stood guard and took the food inside. While being taken to the shower, the Jewish people were under heavy guard so that nobody could talk or have any contact with them. The same precaution took place whenever one of these Jewish craftsmen needed medical attention and had to be taken to a doctor or a dentist. Whenever these patients were alone, after the guards had brought them into the waiting room, there have been instances when a few words could be exchanged with these craftsmen while one of the S.S. guards was busy bringing in another patient to another doctor or dentist. On these occasions, the Jewish patients sometimes had a chance to talk with the caretakers or someone of the political department. By giving them either some cigarettes or maybe some much-wanted food, some of the secrets in Barracks #18 and #19 came into the open.

And what happened in these two barracks? It was the illegal mint of the Third Reich, which the S.S. had fabricated a very extensive operation for printing counterfeit bills. Not only German notes were manufactured here, but also American Dollars, British Pounds, Dutch Guilders, Swiss Francs, Norwegian and Danish Krones, in fact, any currency of countries that were favorable at the exchange. Not only paper money was manufactured in these barracks, but all kinds of documents could be falsified to suit the higher echelon of the Hitler government and the Nazi party, one of them in particular: Josef Goebbels.

When after the occupation of a country or the fall of its capital, the Nazi press, especially the *Völkischer Beobachter*, gave an account of what terrible crimes the enemy had committed. They would insert facsimiles, which had been printed in this counterfeit workshop, right here in Sachsenhausen. This way, they would also blame the "foreign diplomats." Through skillful processing of photos, it was possible to reconstruct pictures which gave the general public an entirely different idea of how it was in reality. Like, for instance, showing several political figures together in a picture who had never been at the same place or the same time together.

Hitler had been shown in "photos" in places he had never been, but this way it was another method to represent him to the people like, for instance, at a battle zone or other dangerous places. He was well-known as a coward who used the airplanes that flew under the protection of the International Red Cross, across the dangerous battlefields. He considered himself a "valuable person." This, however, did not deter him from disregarding the Geneva Convention and so he would give orders to slaughter defenseless POWs and wounded soldiers.

Maintenance workers for this concentration camp, such as repairmen, tailors, shoemakers, carpenters, and others, were only in the minority as compared to the workforce in the war industry like, for example, the Heinkel airplane factory, as well as Speer's defense industry.

Due to a lack of manpower in these war industries, inmates were rented out to these industries whenever they were needed most. In case there was a demand for certain craftsmen, and not enough were available, retraining took place under the promise of larger food rations. An order was given on May 23, 1942, to take advantage of these retraining courses with the promise of better living conditions. But, when not enough volunteers came forward, almost every tailor was trained to become a mason.

Every concentration camp was somehow connected with a branch of the German defense industry. It could happen, at times, that more than 100,000 men were employed In these workshops of the DAW (Deutsche Ausrüstungswerke). Anything could be made or repaired in special shops like furniture, electrical appliances, upholstery, carpentry, cabinetmaking and picture framing, plumbing, bookbinding, and cars could also be repaired. In fact, anything necessary to keep the houses and apartments for the Nazi leadership in good shape and working condition could be provided. No special care had to be taken when it came to the waste of material. Not at all; sometimes expensive pieces of plywood were cut up just to be used in a certain spot where it had to match the grain.

That these DAW workshops didn't make any profit is not hard to understand, even though most of the materials on hand had been stolen in one of the occupied countries. Order forms about material used and labor needed were filled out with the number on it, everything was done in quick order. If the number on these forms looked too large then another form was filled out with the next number, indicating a different order. Besides Loritz, Himmler, and several other Nazi bigwigs, there was also S.S. chief Pohl, who was constantly keeping these workshops busy for his benefit. He had quite a few orders going of which form #901 became well-known. On it, one could notice that large numbers of furniture had been specially constructed, not only for him but also for quite a few other Nazi big shots as well.

The Speer Industry employed mostly inmates who had to dismantle broken down cables, motors from ships, airplanes, and automobiles, wires from destroyed telephone establishments, also search lights, radios, and other items, everything that had been taken from occupied countries. Around 3,000 inmates alone were kept busy taking broken telephone cables apart. Total salvaged material for September and October 1942 came to approximately 112,230 kg copper, and 321,320 kg lead, all other metals were not as plentiful or valuable; but it amounted to something. Although the Speer Industry didn't pay any wages to inmates, the Nazis still had a deficit of approximately 1 million dollars or 900,000 RM.

Numerous private industries rented laborers from the concentration camps for which they had to pay the Nazis between 3 and 8 RM a day for one man, all depending upon qualifications, starting from unskilled to highly skilled labor. Not before 1942, did some of the inmates get some premium tickets, starting at 50 pfennig a week, up to one Mark a day. In some special cases even more had been paid. For these premium tickets, inmates could buy some extra food in case there was something available in the canteens. And, yes, these premium tickets were also honored for a visit to the camp's bordello. Here, it can be said that former criminals among the inmates made a lot of use of these tickets.

Also in the film industry did inmates find employment. That is to say, when many of them were needed like, for instance, in the film, *Kolbarg*, one of Goebbel's and Hitler's propaganda films. For weeks, hundreds of inmates were shipped to Bernau, where they had to play combat scenes, defending Kolbarg by inundation and things like that. This, the inmates didn't mind at all because, for acting, they even got some good food and treatment and were never harassed by the S.S. gangs. No wonder these pictures were taken to be shown on the screen—none of the well-known Nazi big shots and sadists should be seen by the public.

However, it was amazing that for the film, *Jud Süd*, no Jewish inmates were picked out from the concentration camp; but, it is possible that some were selected from another source. Salaries for playing in these films were never paid to the inmates who were the actors but, instead to the concentration camp leaders who very probably used this extra income to have a good time for themselves during the days and probably during the nights as well, who knows? Even if one figures the money spent for one man per day—and this includes food, shelter, and clothing—at maybe 1.20 Mark, it is not hard to understand that the concentration camps earned large amounts of money through slave labor.

Over 5,000 inmates from Sachsenhausen were employed at the Heinkel airplane plant, housed in a special working place. And since a large percentage of these men were first-class specialists in their field, it is easy to understand that large sums of money went into the S.S. cash registers. Besides that, many private industries made a profit by being supplied with cheap inmate labor; maybe thousands of workers had been used this way.

How much the S.S. and the cooperating industries were working together for profit can be seen in a letter from the S.S. in Berlin to the Speer war industry, in which about 30 names of business enterprises in Germany were listed. It was prohibited to buy or to deal with these firms mentioned or to supply them with inmate labor. The reason was obvious: the S.S. could not get their products cheap enough or they did not meet the demand for high enough wages the S.S. wanted to collect for their rented inmates.

Regarding the Speer Industry, it can be said that they paid an average of only 4 pfennig (0.04 RMark) an hour for an inmate, while other so-called private industries whose bosses often belonged to the Nazi party, had to pay up to 30 pfennig an hour for an inmate. However, none of these inmate employees would get between 1.10 and 1.60 Mark per hour, besides other benefits that the civilian employees would earn. It can also be pointed out here that some of the private firms belonging to the Nazis and their S.S. officers often didn't have any assets of their own or any kind of machinery, but instead would borrow these from other industries whose owners were described as "enemies of the state" and who subsequently were interned. In other words: the former owners were taken into protective custody—a concentration camp—and their belongings were confiscated by the S.S.

Understandably, the inmates who had to slave for these low wages were not too enthusiastic about their work. Whenever possible, they would sneak away from the job. It would have been crazy to work at full capacity and kill themselves. Suffering from malnutrition for quite a long time, they were no longer able to do heavy work.

Of course, from time to time, some of the S.S. overseers or foremen would push them to get more work done, using a bat, if necessary. But, there were always moments when nobody was around so that they could take it easy for a while. There were penalties for laziness, and one of these regulations has been found among the Speer Industry documents in which orders were given about what to do with these loafers. Here is one example:

"Inmates trying to avoid working have to be punished: Form #…, to be whipped…times, inmate #…fasting and strict security…Not to be released. For inmates willing and able to work, cash and food premium." In one of these papers dating back to the years 1940–41, also from Speer, stated: "The inmate's ability to work has to be utilized to the utmost. Those in charge as foremen (most likely former criminals) have to be trained according to specifications by which their body structure has to be taken into consideration." It is, therefore, easy to understand that criminals with powerful bodies were picked out as foremen, preferably so that they could easily brutalize their charges.

However, it must also be emphasized that some humane foremen were among us to protect their inmate laborers. No, not everybody would get violent. But, in some cases, the tables had been turned around, so to speak. It could happen that during the dark hours, at an isolated spot on the camp's grounds, some of these brutes got their rightful punishment, too, by being beaten up by a gang of maltreated inmates. Cases like these are some satisfaction to the oppressed and, at the same time, serve as a warning to bad foremen, even though they may be running around in inmate's clothes instead of their own S.S. uniforms. If one of these henchmen happened to be caught off-hand, it could be possible under favorable circumstances for him to be eliminated also, just like it happened so often to his innocent victims.

Here is the case of a foreman who was earmarked with the red triangle of a political inmate, but who caused the death of several inmate laborers while working in the quarry. Finally, he was demoted and shipped back to Block 47. None of the other inmates looked at him or said "hello;" everyone avoided him. When he got his lunch tray served, he found on it a strong piece of rope with a note attached to it, ordering him to make use of it by noontime. This happened on a Sunday morning. Unable to get out of the dormitory and just before lunch was being served; he finally hung himself from this rope on his bedpost.

His accomplice who used to work together with him at the quarry knew also that he was in trouble. And so he played sick and was taken to the infirmary, but it didn't take long to have him sized up. And, therefore, he was shipped with the next transport to Flossenbürg, but not without special orders for his guards on the way. It took hardly eight days until the news came in that he had "accidentally" been killed while breaking stones, a fate that he had figured out for others more than a dozen times. And so he found the same kind of death as did his comrades before him. The same explanation: perished while working in the quarry.

Sometimes one could almost get the impression that even the S.S. acted somewhat humane towards the inmates of whom they were in charge of. This could happen to someone with specialized skills who was then released from this concentration camp to work for a private concern. In this case, he was on an assignment for full-time work for this particular firm. He had an easier life this way but didn't have the freedom of a civilian worker who could come and go on his own free will during his free time. Compared to a civilian worker he was more or less like a dog on the leash, and there were still several stages or steps he had to go through before he got his assignment to work outside the camp.

It was also necessary to have a form filled by an S.S. chief in Berlin, W 50, Geisbergstrasse 21. Here is an example, dating January 1942:

> "The person mentioned above—name, date of birth, occupation—will be trained in an S.S. Workshop and employed. I also request to have him released at a convenient time."
> Signature of the S.S. in charge.

Here is one example: An inmate who did get an assignment for outside work had to have been at this concentration camp already for many years. Besides that, his papers could not show any penalties while being held captive. In most cases, foremen didn't like to lose some of their inmate workers for the benefit of outside employers and, therefore, tried to give a not-too-good impression of the inmate in question. A stereotype sentence could be found in all these forms which would say the inmate didn't show any improvement in his political orientation. Besides that, he was accused of being lazy. Even if the inmate was a good worker and did everything to the satisfaction of his supervisors, his foreman would never admit that he deserved to be released to work outside of the concentration camp; for instance, in the case of an inmate by the name of Hans Chech who, incidentally, carried the inmate number 1.

Chech, who had been at this camp for about nine years already and who had even worked at its construction, as well as several years at Speer's, was supposed to be transferred to Speer for full assignment. The chief of operation requested this transfer but the personal officer refused to let Chech go by saying he was one of the laziest inmates at camp. When the Nazi chief of operation requested an explanation about this case and how it could be possible that a presumably lazy and unreliable worker like Chech could have been in a leading position at Speer's, the camp's commanding officer intervened and wrote a letter explaining that the camp's supervising foreman had, by mistake, given an unfavorable report on Chech. But, thereupon, he was transferred. However, this was a rare example where an S.S. commander had been helpful towards an inmate. In this particular case, one can see that inmates were always pawns in the hands of their Nazi oppressors, and it was the same when family members made a petition to have one of theirs released.

Just like it used to be under Egypt's pharaohs of long ago who let the Jewish people slave for them and worked them to death at the hardest jobs, so it was with the Nazis of modern times. The life of a Jew was considered worthless. He was not even allowed to report sick with the exception that he may be dead within the next few hours. When, during the winter months the snow was lying high on the exercise plaza, the Jews had to get out in the morning before roll call to remove it. They were only dressed in raggedy, skimpy clothing, regardless of their condition or state of health, and it didn't matter if they were sick or crippled. Always one could hear the same call: "Jews, get out!" No day went by in which the death list would not indicate at least one Jew dead; mostly there were several. When, during April and November strong winds blew clouds of sand from the surrounding country upon the place used for roll calls, the Jewish inmates had to get out with water hoses. But, in order not to damage these water hoses on the ground, they had to carry them on their shoulders. Sometimes, up to 20 Jewish inmates had to drag these water snakes around and beware if one of them should collapse under the load due to fatigue or weakened condition or on account of a cold or such. At once, the S.S. torturers were on hand, hitting them with a club until some of these unfortunate men succumbed and were put out of their misery.

The Nazis didn't only profit by the work of the Jews; they also robbed them of all their valuables. In some cases, well-to-do Jewish people made large donations, and thousands of Marks were given away for medical instruments, the infirmary, and even for the establishment of a library for the inmates. They did everything, hoping that this way they might be treated halfway like a human being, which had even been promised to them. But nothing like that did happen. The S.S. and the Nazis in general never kept their promises, especially not for Jews, who according to history, had already been persecuted repeatedly since time immemorial. Now, under Hitler's leadership, the Nazis tried their very best to exterminate them entirely. During the years of 1940–1941, when normally 150 men were kept in one block, the Jewish blocks were crowded with about 375 inmates. Later during the year, the number of Jewish inmates held in one block by November 1941, rose to almost 500 men.

For any kind of offense, even if Jewish people had not been guilty, the punishment was dealt out collectively. In fact, they had to suffer more. A special punishment consisted of withdrawal of some meals, either no lunch or no supper or no bread and what goes with it, and this could happen for several days. No wonder so many of the Jewish inmates looked like skeletons slowly moving over to the place for the roll call where many of them collapsed and died.

The assassination of the mass murderer Heydrich in Prague in May 1942, created another wave of terror, with mostly Jewish inmates as targets. Simultaneously with the liquidation of the Czech village of Lidice, a mass killing of Jewish people in concentration camps took place. On May 28, 1942, the S.S. picked 96 Jews from the infirmary and the Jewish blocks. They were taken by car to the place of execution, a yard within the industrial section where they were shot.

Upon returning from work one evening, a gruesome spectacle took place when the S.S. took victims from among the labor colony several more Jewish inmates at random and pushed them into a waiting car that would take them to their execution. Among these men were Leopold Ingwer (a man without a country) with the number 18975, b. July24, 1920, and Solomon Neumann (#12850) b. June 24, 1922. Hearing their outcries for help, anyone around knew right away what was going to happen to them. They tried to free themselves, but the S.S. henchmen caught them again. While they threw themselves on the ground, holding onto the legs of their captors, Camp Leader Suhren shot them with a pistol. Meanwhile other Jewish inmates tried to escape from the death car, but Suhren kept on shooting them and even joined the S.S. killers by kicking and stepping upon these unfortunate victims. Afterward, they were thrown into the transport car, many of them more dead than alive. One could hear their outcries in the far distance, but nobody was able to intervene as the rest of the inmates were locked in their cellblocks.

According to the list of names that had to be kept on file in the registration office, there were 13 Jewish inmates between the ages of 20 and 30, 18 between 30 and 40, 28 between 40 and 50, 26 between 50 and 60, and 9 between 60 and 70, while two invalids who had been transferred from Ravensbrück were 72 at the time they were killed. Among the murdered victims was the Dutch Jew Ephraim Potsdamer, #38856. As the camp's commander was afraid of a reprisal, his name was removed from the list and replaced by the name of one Jewish inmate who just happened to die a natural death on the same day. His name was Erich Boronow #34329, born August 25, 1906. And since the murdered Dutchman could not be brought back to life again, his relatives had to be notified about his death just the same. They were told that he died as the result of an illness.

The S.S. leadership was not entirely satisfied with the number of murders that had just been mentioned; they were looking for more killings. And so from the incoming transports of May 28 and 29, 1942, another 154 Jewish prisoners were picked out for the next slaughter so that Sachsenhausen could make the statement that 500 Jewish people altogether had been killed as an act of reprisal for the Heydrich assassination. It may be said here that following an order from above, these last murdered 154 Jewish inmates had not been listed among the dead. Someone in command must have been concerned about the large number of victims killed. Among the 96 Jewish people reported killed earlier, happened to be among others a businessman by the name of Selmann Löwenstein, b. February 3, 1868; a tailor Josef Flink, b. December 16, 1868; businessman Adolf Brand, b. February 25, 1869; florist Heinz Stargard, b. January 20, 1921; salesman Heinz Lewitzki, b. August 8, 1912; and harness maker Heinz Rosen, b. November 1, 1911.

The majority of the Jewish prisoners came from the eastern countries and the Balkan states. Many of these people could be classified as penniless; however, quite a few were apparently well-to-do who came into this concentration camp, in not so small numbers. Evidently, they were afraid of returning to their own country and still hoping to start a new life someplace else. For this reason, they had taken their valuables along with them, besides some large amounts of cash which they had sewn into their clothing, hoping to save it from being confiscated.

They were wrong. The S.S. robbed them of everything. One of the greediest among them was S. S. leader Brandt, who was in charge of the department for safekeeping the prisoner's belongings. He tried to steal all he could lay his hands on until he was finally relieved of his post and transferred to a cellblock. Nothing more happened to him afterward; too many other big shots had been involved too, whose names should not be made public. It was remarkable that somehow so many Jewish newcomers from the eastern part of Europe had quite an assortment of footwear with them, even some new shoes. Since these were made of fine leather, these boots and shoes were sent to the concentration camp's shoe repair shop—for inspection. It didn't take long until the news spread that when this footwear was taken apart, new treasures had been discovered. Carefully hidden in the heels, between the soles and underneath the linings, a sizable amount of bills (dollars), jewels, and even gold, had been found inside the footwear that used to belong to some Jewish people. A real treasure for the workers who worked in this repair shop! Now they had something in hand to trade with. This meant they could buy cigarettes, food, and even so-called luxuries. For a $10.00 bill, a laborer from one of the eastern countries with not much knowledge of the value of currencies could buy 10 expensive cigarettes, which he thought was very reasonable.

But, it didn't take long for the ordinary criminal to find out about this gold mine in the shoe factory. The next thing was they formed their own "business organization," and by dealing in gold, jewels, and foreign currency they were in no way discriminating. They sold wherever they could make the biggest profit. No wonder that, in turn, the camp's supervisors got wise, too. The S.S. gang, for instance, became very interested in dealing with the criminals and, therefore, gave them the finest cigarettes in trade, all kinds of liquors and delicacies, all without the knowledge of their commanding officers, of course. It didn't take long and one would hear the question: "Who is mining the gold?" "The men in the shoe factory," was the answer.

However, it didn't take long until the commanding officers, too, heard the news. But they not only wanted to do some business, no, they wanted the whole operation, with all the profits from the shoe factory, all for themselves. There was nobody more interested than Blockleader Grünwald, who couldn't get his mind off the new source of income. Now something like a search party was introduced. Everyone around was ordered to surrender anything he had in jewelry and foreign currency and bring it to the blockleader. And now, the blockleaders who collected all this valuable stuff had no intention to hand it over to the commanding officer. But now the super racketeer, Grünwald, took over with some scare tactics, threatening any inmate who may still have something valuable on his person, even some foreign currency, with a least 25 hits with a stick or club. But punishment didn't help. Anyone who got hold of some precious items, tried to hide them somewhere, hoping to find an opportunity to get them out of the concentration camp. And so, the search continued. While searching under the mattresses and in the lockers, under the floor boards, and other places, these valuable articles were found. Upon discovery they were confiscated by Grünwald as merchandise without ownership but for the benefit of the S.S. However, the S.S. were left outside, because Grünwald tried to hold onto everything, and his holdings increased quickly.

One of the most valuable items was a very expensive platinum chain which Grünwald finally brought into his possession after a long struggle. However, eventually, all these racketeers ended up in the penal station where they had to march 40 km daily trying out newly constructed shoes for the military. This was done around and around the exercise plaza. To make sure that everyone else knew why they had to march, a big sign was attached to the back of their jacket saying "Swindler."

In order to discourage any more dealings in valuables in competition with master gangster Grünwald, the inmates would get 25 hits with a bat after the first offense; so-called hard-core racketeers among them were tied to a block and got an extra beating. However, it is hard to believe that Grünwald, in the end, was able to hold on to everything. He lost his position suddenly after he shot an inmate down from a tree as if it were some kind of game. Most likely, the real criminals among the inmates took hold of all the valuables as they knew their way around and also how to get them out of the concentration camp's territory. This was mostly done with the help of the outside commandoes. Even after Grünwald was gone, there were still valuables that belonged to the murdered Jews hidden away at the concentration camp. After the evacuation on April 21, 1945, this came to light again, this time to be used for all kinds of trading. So a golden watch could be used to buy a loaf of black bread or something else to eat or whatever. Evidently, in those days food was more important than precious metals.

The Bible didn't tell us how many Jews had been enslaved by the pharaohs but we can read that a great many of them, after marching through the Red Sea and walking through the Sinai Desert, finally returned to Canaan, their beloved homeland. Of those Jews who survived the Hitler tyranny, only a fraction were saved because millions of them perished together with untold other victims in gas chambers, besides from hunger, cold, and exposure, as well as the results of different kinds of murder methods.

In Concentration Camp Sachsenhausen the former inhabitants of 42 nations who used to communicate in 36 languages had been enslaved. It was a different kind of Babylon from the one of Biblical times, where the workforce did not seem to get along too well for lack of understanding each other. It could also be that the working conditions or the pay was not satisfying enough either and that the working crew left the Tower of Babel somewhat unfinished while looking for better jobs and higher pay elsewhere.

The crew of slaves that were assembled in Hitler's concentration camps couldn't quit working in order to move to another place.

While working under inhumane conditions with very little food to keep them alive, poorly dressed, and housed in tight quarters, they were under pressure to work for their Nazi masters and their helper's helper. Woe and behold the poor fellow who would try to take a moment for himself or look for a possible escape route. Chances were that a bullet shot by the nearest watchman would hit him, or perhaps he could be torn to pieces by a hungry bloodhound.

Even though the Hitler dynasty had been precalculated to last for a thousand years, this reign of terror actually came to an end after 12 years without leaving enough time to erect a pyramid for Adolf. However, Hitler himself had in mind to have a victory pyramid built, hoping that the so-called "end victory" as prophesied by Goebbels would materialize. The victory memorial was supposed to be higher than the Cheops Pyramid, which is the highest of its kind in Egypt.

Actually, this victory pyramid should have been built of marbled black granite, which was to be quarried near the Swedish township of Örkened. A great many of these granite blocks had been delivered to Germany already and presumably paid for too. However, most of this stone material was still left in the quarry. This means Hitler did not succeed in having a pyramid built in his honor after the example of the Egyptians of long ago who also enslaved the Jews for their labor.

Possibly, Hitler had in his mind already to have a chamber for himself built inside the pyramid which would most likely scare the visiting public for hundreds, maybe thousands, of years to come, hereby reminding them that this had been the place where one of the most notorious murderers of all times had been laid to rest.

Was it fate or prophecy that, in the end, changed the destiny of Adolf, who finally committed suicide in the bunker of the Reich's Chancellery? Instead of being preserved as a mummy, he went up in smoke and ashes so that only the memory of the swastika dynasty still lingered on.

CHAPTER 18

RESISTANCE AND SABOTAGE AT CAMP

> *"An intellectual occupation is a risk for the building of characters. Lies can neither confuse the emotions of the German people nor bother them."*
>
> Goebbels

Man is supposed to be free even though he may have been born in bondage. In every living creature, especially in man, there is a wish for freedom whenever he has been kept in chains. Man, who loves freedom and who also has enough brains, will not tolerate tyranny. The more force he is subjected to, the stronger his will is to struggle free. History has taught us, that in the end, every tyrant has found his master to keep him in line and that reigns of terror have never lasted for very long. The more brutal the oppressor, the stronger the will of the victim to get free. In not too many cases were the oppressed stronger physically than, for instance, in the case of David and Goliath. Here we have seen that in the end, it was intelligence that led the way to victory.

Hitler's National Socialism had its opponents already, in the very beginning, among the members of the left-wing parties and the clergy which he also tried to subdue. In his blind rage against people who didn't cooperate with his doctrines, he also antagonized those who were still passive and waiting to see what the future would bring. "And if you don't want to be like my brother, I'll crack your skull," was another slogan the "Führer" liked to go by. To defend himself against the ever-increasing number of unseen and unknown enemies in his own country, Hitler had concentration camps set up where he wanted to keep everyone who, according to his opinion, belonged to the so-called "unsafe elements" which included primarily the intellectuals. How wrong Hitler was in his calculations, came to light sooner than he had expected. Any of the intellectuals and their friends as well as relatives in Germany and other countries, too, who had not yet been arrested or imprisoned, could become carriers of the resistance movement.

For those who were interned in concentration camps under so-called "protective custody"—a term that sounds rather harmless—the orientation was by no means easy. First of all, they had to be screened in order to find out what kind of people they really were. It never took too long, however, to spot pro-Nazi spies infiltrated among a group of newcomers. They had been taken into a concentration camp for different reasons, oftentimes the result of a criminal conviction. Instead of being put into jail, they were sent to a concentration camp where they had to wear the red triangle just like any political prisoner. Camouflaged this way, they could serve as spies for the Nazis. This has been mentioned in one of the former chapters.

We have been dealing here with former S.S. and S.A. members who had been found guilty of some kind of criminal offense. However, they were not marked with a green triangle as the regular criminals were. In addition to political offenders, who were kept in "protective custody," there were also members of religious groups, like Jehovah's Witnesses, who had to wear a purple triangle, while all others were grouped together and referred to as being in custody as a preventative measure. The placement of all the inmates was taken care of by the camp's leading officers, more or less at random.

As happened occasionally, some offenders with several convictions and also hardened criminals, while under the influence of alcohol, had been cursing Hitler and his regime. They, too, were registered as "political" and marked with a red triangle. At the same time, political opponents who had been found guilty for being involved in a job action or some minor offense had been grouped together with undesirables or antisocials, instead of giving them a small penalty as given out by the police.

Newcomers had to be kept at a safe distance until they could be identified by some of their comrades who had been at this concentration camp for some time. As a rule, it didn't take too long for an acquaintance of one of the political offenders to come forward and give assurance that a certain newcomer was trustworthy and here, for political reasons only, or one who could be considered not dependable or friendly to the Nazi cause. As had been mentioned before, it was up to the political department to get in touch with newcomers to get all the information they could from them about themselves and their relatives or friends who had been here before them. However, it has happened that despite a most careful screening, criminal elements and spies had been successful in masquerading among the others as political offenders. As time went on, they would denounce anyone who was against the Nazi regime. The result was that the accused had to endure severe penalties dealt out by the camp's commander and his helpers.

Through the political newcomers, it was occasionally possible to get more information as well as opinions and voices of critics from all over Germany. The same was true in cases of transfers from other concentration camps, jails, and prisons. Transferred people from among the politicals would also bring in some news about what has been happening in other countries. In this way, it was possible to get an overall picture of the general situation all around us. However, it was more difficult to get in touch via letters with family members.

Every letter went through censorship and in case it had some message that could sound suspicious or had been interpreted in a way the concentration camp's censorship didn't like, then this letter would be returned to the sender with a warning and a penalty which meant no more letters could be written and sent for a certain length of time. Outgoing mail also went through very strict censorship. And, of the incoming letters, a great many of them had been cut into tiny pieces so that the receivers could not make heads or tails out of them. In some cases, only the empty envelopes had been forwarded.

Smuggling letters out of camp also had its difficulties; it has never been easy to find a reliable messenger to take them along. Furthermore, there was always a good chance that the home post office inspector might open these letters before they were delivered. The letter writer who made some unfavorable remarks could face a penalty of being hit with a bat at least 25 times for the first offense.

Communication from and to a concentration camp didn't present too many difficulties as crew members who worked outside of a concentration camp came in steady contact with civilian laborers, and these often had sympathy and understanding for inmates who were in contact with them. It didn't take too long until they became buddies and getting together with them became a real help. The outsiders, too, would get a more realistic description of how things were at camp. However, any contact of crew members with civilians and the resulting consequences, like discussing viewpoints and exchanging information, could not always remain undetected by the camp's leadership. It didn't take long until the inmates from the outside commandos were exchanged rather frequently, especially the politicals. But even these methods were not too effective because it still could be made possible to find some kind of contact with someone working on the outside. Not only that, but the number of buddies between inmates and the people on the outside increased as time went on. Friendships even developed because of the sympathy the outsiders felt for the inmates. Besides that, dislike for the Nazis grew more and more intense.

With the establishment of more and better workshops inside the concentration camps, the number of specialized workers increased too, for instance, in the line of electronics and radio communication. S.S. vehicles equipped with transmitters came in for repairs, which were done by the inmates who specialized in this field. These men certainly knew their jobs. While doing the repairs, the crew could listen to the foreign stations, mark down the messages, and forward them to key members among the inmates, who in turn would spread the news to their political allies. And so it can be said that, as time marched on, we, the inmates, became more and more independent of the Nazi broadcasts and Goebbel's propaganda speeches, and their regular news broadcasts sounded more or less like fairy tales.

There was only one easy step from the receiver to the sender and, during the summer of 1941, the construction of secret transmitters took place in Sachsenhausen, but only under very careful circumstances. The necessary material came from the salvage piles of the rather extensive radio workshops. The very best specialists, like engineers and technicians, were among our political friends. Yes, we even had the chief engineer in our group. He was the expert who also constructed the transmitter for the Turkish radio broadcast.

With the help of a confidant in the outside commando, the first transportable secret transmitter was constructed in a workshop several kilometers outside the wall. This was done with spare parts originally found in the S.S. repair shops. All this material had been smuggled out of this concentration camp on a Sunday morning by some crew members under the pretense that they had some urgent repair work to do somewhere around the camp. The items for the construction were hidden in a truck under some building material. Since only one harmless S.S. guard came along on this mission, it was also possible for the radio engineer to hide undetected among all the stuff.

Inside the camp, another radio station was put into operation. After mutual agreement, it was hidden inside the infirmary. To be exact, it was located in the barracks where patients with dysentery were kept in isolation, because admittance was prohibited, on account of the danger of contamination. Not even members of the S.S. guard dared to come near this section. Of course, the "dysentery transmitter" had only a limited power but he could make contact with the secret radio station outside the camp's wall. Furthermore, this transmitter could even reach London and some other foreign stations through connection with another in-between transmitter. This way it had been made possible to broadcast some information on how things were inside this concentration camp to the outside world. Hours for operating were generally around noon and after the evening roll call.

There were only three people who knew about this arrangement and thanks to this disguise; it has been made possible to keep everything secret until the time of the capitulation. Of course, each one of these three men was also in contact with a few reliable buddies of his own, who would either get some messages for distribution or they could come with some news items of their own. And, nobody would ask where the news came from, just get the news across. The go-between, that is, the man who operated both secret transmitters and receivers, and who also had been under oath to keep silent, is believed to have been a former Trappist monk; he has been referred to as "Moltke."

Only a few people knew this name and nobody had any idea who he was. Unfortunately, he didn't live long enough to see the end of the Nazi terror because shortly before the capitulation, he was killed in his place outside the concentration camp during a bombing attack. He used to be the foreman of the so-called forest commando; Josef Adorf was his real name. He came from Cologne and had been one of the best and most reliable comrades we ever had at this concentration camp. He was always willing to help even if it could endanger his own life. Since 1939, he had been among the political inmates, and he did accomplish what other inmates would regard as downright impossible.

Obviously, the news from the secret transmitter could not be introduced to the camp's inmates as it was, instead, it had to be somewhat tarnished. It used to be the job of a certain group of inmates, referred to as "latrine patrol," meaning that this was the place where an inmate could get the extra news, which didn't come from the camp commander's loudspeaker. Even the camp's leadership used similar tactics by sending so-called very important news down the line through the ranks of their commander, supervisor, blockleader, and, finally, foreman for the different quarters. Most of this happened to be propaganda. Special news of alleged victories with the so-called new weapons and then, of course, as always, Goebbel's speeches with promises of the latest weapons, which practically guaranteed the end of the war and victory for the Nazi empire. At times, these different messages mingled and one had to figure out what to believe. However, this could only happen to the uninformed inmates who had not much contact with others and who were unaware of the secret sender and receiver establishment.

Although the S.S. was constantly on the lookout trying to catch inmates listening to foreign radio stations, they did only occasionally surprise one. So it happened that the electrician, Fritz Bükard, had been caught in the summer of 1944 by a blockleader, while using a receiver in a toolshed, next to workshop #28 that was used for drying material. He had installed the receiver himself. Besides that, a typewriter holding a message with some news on it had been found. The camp commandant traced two more political associates, Dietrich Horning and Willy Griebsch, who were also arrested. These two were taken to the penal station where they had to wait until their trial.

Several weeks later, when everybody thought that things had long been forgotten, all three were taken to the infamous Block #59, from where they were supposed to be "transferred." Only later it was announced that all three had been shot by the S.S. The special commission with S.S. group leader, Ballhause as prosecutor, was supposed to be the people's court, where almost every witness happened to be a hired inmate, willing to denounce any of his comrades, on the promise of being released from this concentration camp very soon. Here, it became obvious how many regular criminals were masquerading as political prisoners by wearing the red triangle on their jackets.

The camp's Gestapo was located in receiving Block #14, within an isolated territory and opposite the prison block. The director was Rudolf Haas who also wore the red triangle. There were rumors that his stepbrother was his assistant. Being fluent in quite a few languages, it had been easy for him to get acquainted with the new arrivals. He came originally from a borderline country between Austria and Yugoslavia. He was able to hide his real identity and had a great talent for getting along with people. But then Haas was transferred to the prison block for several weeks without any warrant to indicate why he had to be placed there or for what kind of offense.

Then, from the prison block, Haas was promoted to block elder for the receiving office, which the inmates took for rather a suspicious kind of a move. It didn't take him long to send out damaging reports about political inmates to the commission for special trials. Soon after that, the accused inmates were taken in large groups to an inspection station outside the camp from where quite a few were taken to cellblock #59. Next, they seemed to disappear. That is, their names were being taken off the roll call list, which means that they had been eliminated in one way or another. Then one day in the fall of 1944, Haas "had it made." He was released; nobody knew to where. Only after the capitulation did he appear again, this time as an interpreter, in May 1945, for the British military government in Flensburg, where I recognized him. Seeing me again, together with two more former political inmates from Flensburg, was not exactly a pleasant surprise for him. We were even more surprised when Haas introduced himself as Rudolf Kuchan, a representative of the Yugoslavia Red Cross. Dressed in a fancy uniform and riding in an expensive car, driven by his chauffeur, a Serbian, he would enjoy sightseeing trips. However, it didn't take long until he was arrested in Lübeck, not only for racketeering, embezzlement, and stealing Red Cross packages, but also for his spy activities during his term at Sachsenhausen.

More people were acting as agents for the dreadful so-called special commission, like, for instance, two carriers of the red triangle on their sleeves. Their names were Herbert Volek and Ernst Siegel, both adventurers from the Baltic countries. As these two were also fluent in several languages, they, too, spread horrors among their political inmates through espionage. This way they got their promotion. Volek became supervisor and Siegel got a position as interpreter. Incidentally, Siegel, an internationally known racketeer, was arrested in Paris together with about 1000 Frenchmen, with whom he was taken into this concentration camp.

Volek, a writer, was a man who didn't have a clean record in his past. In fact, I recognized him when he was first brought here as the man behind a revolutionary organization among farmers—the so-called black flag with the white plough as its symbol—which around 1930 planted bombs in buildings like courthouses, finance buildings, and similar administration buildings in Schleswig-Holstein. Afterward, the Communists got the blame for these acts of terror.

Volek, too, hoped to buy his freedom by making damaging reports about the political inmates; however, he was not aware of the strength of the secret resistance movement with which the political inmates confronted him. When it became known that he was one of the guilty ones in connection with the death of 27 older politicals, many of whom had been held in the concentration camp already since 1933, he was ambushed on a dark night and beaten up so thoroughly that, afterward, he could not be recognized anymore as the man he used to be. His position as the supervisor was gone and some politicals who, at that time, had some control and power over others, took advantage of this situation by having him shipped to an extermination camp from where the news soon afterward arrived that he had been fatally injured while working in a quarry.

There was still another spy doing his evil work, an unsociable person by the name of Kuhnke, who also held a job as supervisor and who had great hopes of improving his position and general standing by making devastating reports about his charges. It didn't take long to get hold of this vicious individual. On a transport into another camp, he found out for himself that being beaten up with fists and kicked around with boots on one of these transports was quite another thing than dealing it out to others. Also worth mentioning is the former criminal, Erwin Rathmann, who became very efficient in his role as an informer and spy for an S.S. commission. He was a good actor and tried to give the general impression that he was trying to find out which of the S.S. men were guilty of cheating and mistreating the inmates so that this could be reported to this special commission for severe punishment. What happened was that he, himself, landed in this concentration camp after being found guilty of grand larceny back in 1943. It didn't take him long to make his way up the ladder because, after only a few months, he had advanced to the position of a blockleader for the camp's prison, a move that could be interpreted by the political inmates that he, Rathmann, may not have been too innocent in the murder of 27 political comrades.

Already while working as a go-between in the Russian isolation block, it became evident that he worked hand in hand with the criminally inclined blockleaders like Knittler, Fickert, and Kaiser. Together, they did a fine job exploiting the Russian work commandoes. It all started by making out false order forms for the daily rations of food like bread, margarine, cold cuts, cheese, and so on, by not only ordering the daily supply for the Russian workers, but also for those who had died already a few days ago. This way they had a surplus for themselves. However, on May 1, 1942, Rathmann was caught while handing out a full carton of margarine to the S.S. Blockleader Fiekert, to take home to his apartment. It didn't take long for the political inmates to find this out also.

Then, one winter evening around 1943, while paying a visit to the Russian block, he got a really good beating and was put into a prison cell. Although he needed medical treatment, he refused to be taken to the infirmary, fearful he might get more of this kind of treatment over there, too. After he felt somewhat recovered, he got up and took revenge on those who gave him well-earned beating. What happened then was that several politicals, among them comrade Söllighöfer, disappeared in the infamous Block #59. Later, his body, too, was found among the 27 murdered political comrades.

Outstanding among other Nazi watchdogs was a convicted criminal and S.S. man from Chemnitz, Arthur Wirth. He, too, carried the red triangle to make-believe he was a political inmate. He finally became foreman and also in charge of some cash but he, too, wanted to get out of this concentration camp. Nazi leader, Rossner, assured him his freedom if he could pick out someone from among the politicals who was involved in spreading anti-Nazi propaganda, one who was picking up those horror stories from foreign broadcasts. This was around the time of Rommel's retreat, and when the German Armies couldn't keep a foothold in Sicily anymore. Also in the news were reports of the King of Bulgaria being shot along with some members of the Gestapo. It also happened that Mussolini was under arrest.

On July 26, 1943, I was talking in the infirmary about the news with Dr. Rudolf Pechel, the editor of *Die Neutsche Rundschau*. At this moment we must have been overheard while unaware of it by some watchdog, this time the Nazi spy, Wirth, who, in turn, informed his supervisor, Rossner, about this incident. Of course, Rossner lost no time reporting to concentration camp leader Rolb. Soon after that, we had to appear before him individually for questioning. Naturally, we denied everything.

When soon afterward the informer, Wirth, entered the scene, there was no escape left for us. The result was that both of us landed in a solitary dark cell. The next day I had to appear before the chief of the political department, Erdmann, and sign a statement composed of accusations made by Wirth which were absolutely untrue. On July 28, 1943, in the evening, Kolb visited me in my cell to inform me that Dr. Pechel and I were going to be hanged following the last roll call for the day. It really looked bad. We might as well say farewell to the world.

On the next day, around noon, camp commander Kaindl came to tell me that instead of being hanged, I would be kept in isolation. How could that be, I wondered. According to Nazi justice, any person marked as a delinquent had to go to the gallows. Something must have changed their minds. And, sure enough, this time our political comrades had used their influence by pleading with the camp's commander, arguing that all these questionable reports had been received through regular channels and then they were spread among the inmates, maybe something had been added and some of the so-called news items were downright jokes. And Dr. Pechel, the editor, revealed in his statement that any remarks from me could only be taken more or less for satire. This time we had been lucky to get away with it.

However, this was not always the case because spreading critical and downright unfavorable reports—so-called horror stories—could have serious consequences. But it gave us a warning. One had to be much more careful and make absolutely sure nobody was around, especially no one who could be Nazi-minded and close enough to listen into a conversation. Regardless of this incident, foreign news bulletins kept on coming in until the day of the capitulation, without the camp's high command being aware of it. Even my internment did not keep me from getting hold of the foreign news. One had to have connections.

When on October 22, 1942, all the inmates were standing at attention for the evening roll call, one could hear shots and cries for help besides the cursing of the blockleaders coming from Barrack #56 (disinfection). Then, suddenly, we could see between the blocks a group of Jewish inmates being chased towards the road by the blockleaders.

"Why don't you go ahead and shoot us?" we could hear them calling with fearful voices. Some of the fugitives threw themselves down on the road, waiting for the shots to kill them. Hereupon, camp leader Sauer entered the scene to find out what was going on. Well, the Jews were supposed to be shipped to Auschwitz to the gas chambers. They found out about it when the blockleaders stole their last belongings from them with the remark, "You don't need these things anymore in the gas chamber, that's why we are taking them, you lousy Jews."

For the first time the Jewish inmates tried to revolt against the S.S. who started to shoot. Meanwhile, some Jews started breaking doors and windows to get outside. After that, they ran to a place where the camp's commander had a chance to calm the excited-looking and frightened men down with the promise that they were not going to be transferred to Auschwitz but would be taken to some workshops instead. After that they were marched through the gate to the outside, and it seemed that the first Jewish revolt came to a quick end. However, later we found out from the political department that all Jewish inmates who were taking part in the revolt had ended in the gas chamber. That was the end of the first Jewish revolt at Sachsenhausen.

Among the inmates who were working on defense and war material, the will to resist the establishment became more and more pronounced. Whenever possible, acts of sabotage took place. This could be in the automobile assembly plant or while working on airplanes. After all, over 5000 inmates were employed and in the fields, too, where the heavy war machinery, like tanks, were tried out. Members of all nations were working together side by side, always doing their very best to damage the war material and make it as useless as possible. However, it was done very carefully so it could not be determined if the finished product had been damaged deliberately or if the parts used in the assembly could have been of inferior quality. After, all, there was always an excuse like war merchandise using substandard material. The young Russians who were working in the Heinkel Airplane Plant used to remove little valves from parts of the planes from which they could later make some cigarette lighters for themselves. Replacement of these valves used to take a long time as the suppliers were located in different parts of the country.

Another hard-to-get item used to be plexiglass for the pilot's cabin and for "one-man torpedoes" as they were called. And when finally another shipment of this badly needed item arrived, then it never took very long until most of it got lost again or maybe stolen. Plexiglass could very well be used to make cigarette holders, and the demand for these was very big because the outside work brigades wanted them, too, for trading with civilian workers. These are just a few examples to show what went on and how the much-needed material for the war industry would end up and disappear.

For quite a few months the Heinkel technicians had been working on a special type of airplane, the so-called "Fledermaus" which was to be towed along as a glider, loaded with high explosives and piloted by one man only, who, naturally, would become a death candidate once he made a hit into enemy territory. Almost daily, this type of airplane had been worked on and tried out in flights, but there is no report of it ever having been used in combat.

For almost a year, from mid-summer 1943 until early 1944, we saw these planes cruising over Sachsenhausen. Why was there no progress? On experimental flights, an inmate had to sit in these gliders since he was considered a (more or less) worthless human being anyhow. Everything worked out beautifully, so why not try them out with a valuable S.S. man in the same seat? However, in this case, everything never went right. There always seemed to be malfunctions of one thing or another, even accidents when some of these S.S. men were injured or lost their valuable lives. Until the time of the capitulation, these experimental flights continued, but that was all. They never made it to the battlefields, thanks to the acts of sabotage that constantly took place.

The article "Panzerfaust," a hand grenade, could be used by school children, according to the press and radio. It was more or less a toy, but just the same, it was supposed to be very effective as it could smash enemy tanks like a bomb, but it was still safe enough to be thrown from behind a nearby tree or wall. That's what the people were told. The stories one could hear about these grenades were downright outrageous.

After the throw, there should be four explosions. That is to say, four times in a row, the tank was subjected to explosions before it would disintegrate. One could hear the loud noises in the nearby woodland from early in the morning until late at night when finally a total of six detonations could be heard.

Obtaining these explosives, as well as other ingredients, to make these hand grenades, seemed to become more and more difficult. First of all, the needed material arrived only in insufficient quantities, and the little that did get into the workshops was hardly enough for experiments. For the real purpose, that of using these exploding grenades in the real war, there was never enough material left. The inmates did their best to have these items get lost or disappear.

Being involved in any kind of sabotage was, for the inmates of all nations, more or less common sense as everyone was against the Nazi terrorist regimes and, therefore, they tried to shorten the war by making the required war material as useless as possible. Everything had to be done to defeat the Nazis. Inmates were certainly more enthusiastic as saboteurs than in the regular workforce of the private war industry where people were somewhat afraid of being caught. But the inmates stuck together because by being treated like slaves they felt they had nothing to lose.

While sabotage and a general passive resistance took place in every corner of the concentration camp, as well as elsewhere, my friend, Emil Büge, and I were working overtime in the political department. If the hours in the evening after the roll call were not long enough, we worked on Sunday. This work had to be done. And what was it? Making notes of everything that went on here. Yes, everything that I heard or observed while walking from barrack to barrack and through the buildings, had to be recorded. For this purpose, a large envelope was used, disguised with a red cover—the kind that was being used by the "express service" of the political department. Not even the S.S. blockleaders showed any interest in it. They may have taken it as a regular index file of a commanding officer. Besides some form papers to be filled out, there was not much of any value in this "express folder," except the tiny little remarks written around the margin where one could hardly see them. These were my own shorthand notes I had learned many years ago, but as this system was no longer being used, I may have been the only one still able to use it.

As soon as I got ahold of my friend, Emil Büge, I would give him all the information I had picked up and recorded and he would add his own reports, made in a similar fashion. (Fig. 15)

After that, he wrote his reports in very small letters with a colorfast ink on tiny bits of paper. Meanwhile, he had made himself some eyeglass holders into which he would glue these tiny papers until these folders were so filled with papers that there was hardly any room left for his glasses to fit in. During the year Büge had made about ten of these cases for his writings and filled them

Fig. 15. My friend Emil Büge, the Spanish interpreter.

with any glasses that were no longer useful; some of them may not even have been his own. Now he had to keep these eyeglass cases with their special contents in a safe place until it became known that one or the other of the trustful political friends was supposed to be released. If so, these people would take the eyeglass holders, with contents, along and forward them to family members or friends for safekeeping. It also happened that sometimes a friendly S.S. man could be trusted with delivering these cases, for a little cash, of course, because these eyeglass cases looked just like any other cases that could no longer be used. They were just mementos; nobody knew what was inside.

When it became known around the middle of April 1943, that my friend Büge was scheduled for dismissal on Hitler's birthday, we were confronted with the problem of having to smuggle at least four of these cases besides a bundle of unprepared notes through the camp's control center. It was considered normal to carry two pairs of eyeglasses per man, at the time of his release from camp, and so Emil put two inside his pockets. All the rest I shoved into my red-covered "express folder" with some registration forms and walked off with it rather unconcerned, right through headquarters, where Hitler's birthday celebration was already taking place. Then I arrived just in time for the departure of the former inmates who were lucky enough to be sent home. These men, about a dozen of them who had already passed all the control spots, were waiting for their own papers of identification to be handed out, as well as the tickets for transportation. And while these homebound comrades were still signing some of the required forms inside the office, I walked outside to check the luggage that was in the hallway. I found Emil Büge's suitcase, with the one empty pocket on one side, and used it to hide the last written mementos that had to be smuggled out of this place. A final handshake with all our comrades—maybe a dozen—who were leaving us now and then the S.S. guards came and took them along to Oranienburg. Now they were free again, that is, under some conditions.

I still had two more years to go until the capitulation but I kept on making notes of whatever happened in my daily notebook like before. Fortunately, I was able to keep all of my records, which I took home with me on the day the Allies took over and made free men of us.

It took more than a year until Büge and I came together again. Meanwhile, he had dissolved all of his eyeglass cases in warm water, and all of the little pieces of paper were swimming in the bowl. After they were sorted and dried out, they were smoothly put together and were very helpful in getting this book together. If in the current trials, or those of the future, the atrocities committed by the S.S. leaders should come to light, they can find out for themselves who was responsible for these crimes against humanity. And they will also notice that when it comes to intelligence, the inmates were well ahead of them in some instances. Neither sabotage nor resistance, passive or active, communications by radio or through memos, has been prevented by the Nazis—they don't know how—the political inmates always made sure to be a step ahead of them.

CHAPTER 19

THE MASTER RACE WITHOUT ITS MASK

"Be aware of it that you are standing in front of the greatest German history that has ever known."

Hitler.

It could have happened only during the Nazi regime that another race was invented and included among those already known by anthropologists. They "created" the so-called "Master Race," which they liked to identify with the northern Europeans and regarded as a superior race. However, one could really not be quite sure if the northern Europeans Hitler had picked out as superior were identical to the Master Race, which during the time of the Nazi terror, became known to the world around them as a race with a rather low culture and morale standard.

The truth is that Hitler's preference for the Nordic type and his effort to include his followers among them was more or less a come-on, a sort of advertisement and a desire to form a society with which he hoped to subdue all other races and make them his servants. At first, he had only two main races in mind for his political arena: the Aryans and the Jews.

It is not the purpose of this book to go into details concerning the different human races as even well-known scientists refused to regard the Aryans and the Jews as special races. Not even the Nazis, themselves, were too sure about which race they would have to place individuals like Hitler, Rosenberg, Streicher, Goebbels, and thousands of others who they thought were members of the "Master Race." In fact, it was really funny to see that those who thought they belonged to the Master Race liked to make fun of their own people, if one or the other didn't resemble the Nordic race too well as in the case of Goebbels, himself, who had been labeled "Rand Deutsch"—a borderline case—and even "Schrumpf Germane"—a German dwarf—while others, Göring among others, were bold enough to point at Goebbel's nose, hereby hinting that his mother apparently had an affair with a Jewish fellow which could be the reason Goebbel's nose did not have that Aryan look.

When it came to Hitler himself—alias Schicklgruber and Schicklhuber—we can refer to an article in a Copenhagen newspaper, *Politiken*, which appeared soon after his rise to power, showing two pictures with the explanation that Hitler's grandmother was Jewish and that, therefore, he ought to be tolerant and benevolent toward the Jewish people.

The persecution of the Jews under the Nazis followed the examples of recorded historical comments according to which they had been victimized for centuries in many countries. There was a group of so-called antisemites that wanted to blame all the economic ills, since Germany was defeated in World War I, on the Jewish people. Hitler, too, blamed them for everything that went wrong in Germany. Using mass hypnosis, Hitler started the war against the Jews with one thought in mind: getting hold of all the capital and property owned by them, preferably as cheaply and as easily as possible.

As has been pointed out before, it happened already before the onset of the war in 1939, when Hitler had the sick and incurable Jews transported into extermination camps. The reason: they were not worth the effort to be kept alive. He did the same with the wealthy ones to rob them of their belongings.

With the occupation of the surrounding countries, confiscation of Jewish property took place, in addition to their extermination. The self-proclaimed Master Race was nothing more than a band of criminals that would overshadow even the worst criminals known so far. No wonder, they didn't hesitate to take some of the most hardened criminals out of jail in order to put them into their service.

During the spring of 1941, the names of certain convicts were called out repeatedly at the evening roll call, asking for those among them who had previous experience in cracking safes. After the last request, about ten of this trade responded and were subsequently shipped to Dublin where they had to use their talents by opening the safes in banks and industrial enterprises while being careful not to damage any of its contents. They got strict orders from their Master Race contractors not to use dynamite for any of these safes. For their efforts, they were assured a really good profit.

It has never been made public if these safe cracking experts did get their promised benefits after finishing their jobs which consisted of emptying all of the safes in the eastern territories. However, it finally leaked through that after they did their part, one by one, they were eliminated or they just disappeared after handing over all of their collected treasures from the safes to their Master Race employers. This was later discovered from the death notices that reached Sachsenhausen. We also found out that the next group of safe crackers that was employed at a later date met with the same fate as their predecessors.

The Master Race was also aware of the Latin proverb, *non olet*, meaning money does not smell and, therefore, they stuck to it. They didn't only steal money or money's worth from the Jews, no, they also took it from other people who had either been banished from their homeland or murdered. Some examples of what happened has already been mentioned in one of the previous chapters. It can be said that Hitler's Master Race did not consist of only the German people, preferably, the northern German types, as well as northern Europeans, no; it was a combination of all kinds of criminal elements with some international character. They were gangsters who, for the sake of money, did their best to get rid of the wealthy people just to get ahold of their possessions. The new inmates—arrivals—had to hand over all of their belongings. Some S.S. blockleaders were bold enough to take gold watches, jewelry, etc., away from their charges without making any record of them, as was supposed to be done.

Through a little hole in the wall of a wooden shed in the yard of the industrial section, it was possible to make observations, like for instance, when the S.S. blockleaders were on their way to an execution. Before taking their victims to the galleys, they robbed them of their valuables, because these items had not been registered in the registration office of Sachsenhausen. In most cases, these used to be prominent and even wealthy people who carried everything they had left with them, all of their money, jewelry, securities, and other valuables. Not before they were inside the dressing room of the barracks next to the crematory, were they informed that this had been their last and final ride.

In case these victims put up a resistance and refused to take off their coats or jackets, they were undressed by force, whereupon they were dragged out to the shooting stand. In every case, they had to face the wall of the shooting gallery that caught the bullets. If any of these victims wore some expensive clothes, the S.S. men took them from them; after all, they were only "unknown" persons who were to be shot and, of course, no one could ever find out that members of the Master Race had committed some extra murders; at least that's what the Nazis thought.

It was on May 1, 1942, when a group of well-to-do people from Holland arrived, 96 persons all told, were housed in the prison block. All of them had been sentenced to death by a court-martial in Maastricht; however, they didn't know it. While in their cells, they were told to put their coats neatly folded on the seats where they would find them again after their hearing. But instead, they were herded right away into trucks that took them to their execution. Here they had to strip down to their underwear. S.S. leader, Suhren read their names and then the verdict. After that, the S.S. murderers, six of them, killed every one of the victims with shots in the back.

Later during the day, while staying in the barracks for disinfection, I had a chance to take a look at the clothes that were left behind and noticed that all shots had been fired into the backs of the people. Shirts and vests were soiled with blood. All had been wearing expensive clothes and shoes which were picked up by another S.S. gangster named Höpken. He has been mentioned before, he did this in order to sell these items for his own profit. All I could discover were two names among the piles of clothing: Fauchey and Postema. Any other possible identification had already been removed by the S.S.

Himmler's orders to the commanders of the concentration camps, not to let any reports of the existing conditions in these places reach the outside world, tried to be strictly enforced. The general public was not to be informed about any of these robberies and killings that went on in the concentration camps. The so-called status symbol of the Master Race was not to be tarnished in any way. Whenever an order from the high command came in with the request to "take care of" any invalids, the very sick, and those who were no longer able to work, well that meant elimination, then the final transaction took place in a manner that looked almost harmless.

Out of a hundred invalids who had been transferred from Concentration Camp Ravensbrück to Sachsenhausen on May 21, 1942, five Jews were picked out for a special treatment to restore their health quickly. Here are the names: Jakob Ajchenbaum (42375), Fritz Mizes (42388), Pinkus Mlynek (42424), Markun Münz (42384), and Chaim Willig (42377). This special treatment consisted of an injection that caused death instantly. These victims were between 50 and 60 years of age.

Whenever the elimination of a larger number of qualified victims was at stake the commanding officer could arrange for some trips to a "health resort" which under the name of S-commandos soon got a bad reputation among the initiated, since one could rightfully suppose that behind this kind-hearted gesture, more atrocities and meanness were concealed. At the beginning of June 1941, a transport of invalids, amputees, lame, and sightless persons took off with the destination Pirna-Sa, but another name for this place was Sonnenstein near Erfurt. Altogether 303 people were supposed to recuperate in a resort town.

However, only after a few days, this vacation trip came to an end; all the participants got rid of all their problems and ailments once and for all. Personal items which had been shipped back from these so-called health resorts had been returned to the storage rooms for safe keeping of the inmate's belongings. Among these shipments were crutches, artificial limbs even glass eyes, besides purses with money and other valuables. Therefore, it became quite clear that the previous owners did not need their possessions anymore: they had passed away, all victims of either poisonous injections or the notorious gas chambers. Whenever these transports took place some individual inmates the concentration camp commander wanted to get rid of in a way that did not look too suspicious for people who had to take care of the records, had to come along. Maybe one could read a notice saying that so and so was to be included in one of these trips for the purpose of experimentation. For some time a village near Bernau got a real bad reputation: instead of being a village for vacationers, it happened to be a place for gas chambers. Again people, mainly those with TB, invalids, humpbacks, and also those who were hard of hearing had been taken there. As an "extra" this time the brother of a famous actor, Fritz Junkermann (38490), had also been included in the list of those to be eliminated. Evidently, he was not to the liking of members of the Master Race.

This commando (group) had the rather harmless sounding name "herb garden;" it left with 118 "vacationers" on October 5, 1942. After everything seemed to be ready for departure, another victim was taken from Block #23, this time the owner of a large estate in Mecklenburg, Wilhelm Japp (32876), b. September 2, 1878. What happened was that among his belongings was a letter from his lawyer's firm, Kassow and Kayser in Schwerin Meckle that had been found according to which he had three sons in the army, and working on his estate were Russian prisoners of war who received special kind treatment while working for him. For this noble act, this good-hearted employer had to be put to death.

Hardly had the remaining belongings been returned to the concentration camp—that is, whatever was left of the victims from the first "herb garden" transport, another transport by the same name was put together only two days later. There were 146 men sorted out as vacationers, consisting of 38 Jews, 6 Gypsies, 63 Poles, 11 marked as "gay," 2 from Belgium, 8 from France, 3 people without a country, 5 from Russia,

5 from Czechoslovakia, and 5 from Holland. Still, further transports had been planned but had to be postponed as quite a few inmates grew very restless and uneasy at camp. Therefore, another name had to be found for the next transport.

Then, on November 13, 1942, the members of the Master Race that were in charge were ready to transport 203 inmates to Dachau. Yes, Dachau was the place to go; here they had nice and comfortable nursing homes with excellent services for room and board, as well as pleasant surroundings, and even plenty of entertainment.

With envy, some of the sick who had been left behind saw these "fortunate" ones, consisting of ailing, blind, amputees and very old ones depart. Along with them, several Russian prisoners who had beforehand been kept in the infirmary were included in this transport as well as nine Norwegians from Tellevaag, near Bergen, Norway. However, this time, no crutches or similar items were returned to Sachsenhausen, a precaution to prevent further rumors from spreading among the camp's inmates. Then finally through return transports from Dachau, news leaked in according to which the whole transport had been taken to a gas chamber right away after arrival. One of the reporters had been an eyewitness when this mass murder took place. He also told us that the cause of death had been described as either bleeding from the lungs or an "18-minute twitching of the heart."

In case the gas chambers didn't seem to work efficiently enough for the Nazi bureaucracy, then other methods could be used for mass killings as can be seen from the following report from Dublin, given to me from a former prisoner. The Jews had to dig a ditch approximately 220 yards long and 30 feet wide near a fork at some roadway, as protection from enemy bombers or so they were told. Later in the evening, some 5000 Jews—men, women and children—were herded into this ditch by the S.S. The reason: enemy aircraft was on its way. Scared and confused, these people jumped into the ditch. A moment later, several big explosions took place, one right after the other, so that the thrown-out chunks of dirt could bury everyone alive in one mass grave.

Even though the subhuman Nazi villains tried their best to present themselves to the world and to the public in general as the Master Race, it was not surprising when they tried to conceal their murderous activities. In case some rumors had leaked out, then they did everything in their power to minimize any reported cruelties and labeled them "False" or "Prefabricated." The newly constructed human slaughterhouse which had already been described before, together with its gas chambers that resembled showers from the outside and the ovens of the crematories right next to it, this whole complex had been called by a harmless name: "Warmehalle" which could mean something like "heated waiting room." Strict orders were given not to call this place of hell by any other name.

However, as time went on and more and more murders took place, it was no longer possible to keep its existence secret any longer. This "heated waiting room" created such a terrible smoke and stench in the air that not only the inmates at camp but also people living in nearby villages and even Oranienburg could smell it day and night. It became obvious that this kind of air pollution came from the burning of corpses.

Whenever the outside commandos marched through the streets of Oranienburg, the school children would shout at them, hereby making remarks like: "We can't stand the stench from your smoking furnaces anymore; how many people did the S.S. fry yesterday?" or similar questions like this. In the eyes of the adults, one could see fright, anger, and concern, too, which was meant for the inmates who had to pass through the streets. One could hear them whisper something like: "Oh you poor people, what terrible times you have to go through…"

The higher the number of deaths caused by the Master Race rose, the more concerned they became about having the news leak through to the outside world. Following these mass killings, the inmate's relatives had to be notified, meaning that death certificates had to be made out and sent away in large numbers. At first, the family members of inmates from the eastern countries had been notified.

Here is a letter issued by S.S. brigade leader Glücks, who later committed suicide in Flensburg after the capitulation. This form letter had been sent to the commander of every concentration camp.

"I am referring to the method by which the relatives of deceased inmates are notified in case of death in a concentration camp has occurred. It has happened lately, repeatedly, that death notices had been addressed directly from the camp's administration office to members of the family of the deceased inmates from the eastern countries and occupied Ukraine. Therefore, I want to make it clear once and for all that any death notices are going to be sent only to the police department of the respected home town which in turn will give these messages to the employment offices of the district so that these bureaus can forward the information to the relatives of the deceased. The employment bureaus are not going to fill in where death has occurred. By sending death messages directly to the relatives the general public has already been alarmed too much about the fact that inmates died at camp and this kind of publication is, therefore, very unfavorable for our future propaganda campaigns, especially if the administration is unable to give the relatives a satisfactory explanation as to why the deceased had to stay at the concentration camp anyway."

The reputation of the Master Race had suffered already; it really couldn't get any worse. The above-mentioned form letter had already been sent to every police station of every nation, including Germany. And, therefore, the relatives of the dead of all the countries would never get any more death notices directly. Nobody could find out where, when, and why one of their family members lost his or her life because the police bureaus gave out no further explanation.

Return shipment of any mementos, belongings, and valuables that used to be the property of the deceased came to a halt if they happened to be foreigners; however, soon it didn't make any difference if these arrivals came from dead Germans either. The Master Race collected these belongings, too, which made them ordinary plunderers of corpses—a real low scum. Yes, one could say their reputations could hardly get any lower, because they even sold these items, such as gold watches, rings, and whatever they could get ahold of in the line of jewelry. Besides that, what they could not sell, they would give to their wives or girlfriends, or whatever the case might be.

In their own opinion members of the Master Race considered themselves superior human beings in every respect; they were therefore much too valuable to be sent to the fighting front where they could possibly be injured or even killed. The ordinary population had been sifted through, time and again to get the much-needed soldiers together to serve as cannon fodder. Boys of high school age, as well as old men, were also picked out to be sent to the front. Meanwhile, the Master Race took over positions as so-called members of the S.S., where they could sit in comfortable offices, well-fed and far away from any war zone. They also bribed any health officer or physician with food from warehouses intended for the general public or whatever they could steal from the concentration camp's storerooms, even by the carload. And, they would also buy their own freedom from military service with items like jewelry that they had taken off the dead victims.

After they could no longer get enough soldiers together from among the German people, the Master Race would press men into service from the occupied countries. First, they did it by promises and, later, by force, after including them in the rank of the so-called "Volksdeutsche" party. However, not even with these men in the army did the Germans have enough soldiers. The next step was to get hold of all the Russian prisoners of war. They had to fight against their own people; even Russian Army officers were forced into service.

During the spring of 1942, Camp Sachsenhausen's Barracks #10, 11, 34, and 35 had to be vacated by transferring the former inmates to different buildings so these barracks could be converted for other purposes. The work had to be done by craftsmen from among the inmates. Especially Barrack #10, which looked after reconstruction more like a motel with single rooms, as well as rooms with two beds. It also had a dining room complete with chairs and tables, covered with tablecloths and napkins, as well as fine silverware and dishes. To make it look even better, beautiful flowers in handsome vases were placed on the tables. After everything was ready, high-ranking Russian military personnel who had been captured at the front were taken into these fancy quarters. The reason was to make tools out of them for the Nazis by programming them in such a way that they would fight against their own people.

Barrack #34 was not quite as elegant after its conversion because here no higher-ranking men than lieutenants were stationed while military personnel below that rank had to be satisfied with Barracks #11 and 35 which were rather plain looking and without comfort. The meals came from the camp commander's kitchen. The curriculum, or rather, re-programming, happened to be theoretical as well as practical. To make it more pleasant, some entertainment was provided like for instance for the officer's regular visits to the theaters and movies on a daily basis. However, this reprogramming was not 100% effective because some of the higher-ranking Russian officers didn't want to do what the Master Race had ordered them to do. So-called cases of conspiracy were uncovered and, consequently, some of the higher-ranking officers were taken during the dark hours "for a time." Several days later, their uniforms had been recognized by some inmates in the barracks for disinfection. This way it became clear that these officers, among them one general, two lieutenants, two majors, and three sergeants had been shot. Evidently, using foreign military personnel was not too reliable after all.

After the news spread among the inmates of what had happened to the Russian officers, it didn't take long until the remaining ones had been removed from the motel or hotel barracks and relocated. The converted barracks were no longer used as before but were turned over again to their former tenants as living quarters or for isolation purposes. The Russians had to live from now on in some barracks outside the concentration camp. Later on these Russians were sent to the front lines and had to fight against the Poles. Ukrainians and White Russians had already differences among themselves, so it could be possible to let them fight against each other, or so the Nazis thought.

Policemen, officers, and soldiers from Luxembourg who had been brought to this concentration camp were forced into service for the S.S. police system to be used in Yugoslavia. But when they refused to be "re-educated" at the police school in Dresden, in order to serve the Master Race, they were returned to Sachsenhausen penal barracks.

The treatment was severe. They were forced to run long distances and the foreman in charge, Wilhelm Jakob, a former S.A. man who had deserted, had strict orders from his supervisor, the infamous camp leader Kolb, to have no mercy with the men from Luxembourg, but to neglect any kind of ailments and not to bother to have the sore feet bandaged.

Atrocities against mankind, and mistreatment of the defenseless, were always the order of these Nazi sadists. They didn't stop when they got hold of children or the very old; anyone who came in contact with members of the Master Race was likely to become a victim of their acts of violence and cruelty.

It was compulsory to greet the meeting of a Nazi official by taking off the hat. Every inmate had to go bareheaded as a sign of courtesy. One could always hear "Hats off." To make things worse, Suhren, one of the camp's commanders, ordered the barbers to cut an alley about one inch wide from front to back across the inmates' heads. For about a year this so-called "Suhren Alley" persisted. But after his transfer to Ravensbrück, inmates were allowed to let their hair grow in again. But otherwise, the cut-off hair had to be saved and collected; another sacrifice by the inmates.

Any consideration as to the age or social standing was completely disregarded by the Nazis whenever victims were taken into custody. Everywhere, the Nazis tried to make it understood that they were the Master Race. Here is one more example: a clergyman, by the name of Orier, from Esch in Luxembourg, who came alone to this concentration camp in 1942, happened to be old and physically in poor shape. The inmates from the political department did their very best to have him transferred to the infirmary where other inmates would take care of him as best as they could. Somewhat later, being included in another transport to a different concentration camp with other clergymen he, too, became a victim of the Master Race.

In the Duchy of Luxembourg where the people were fighting against the Nazi terror and showing resistance in every way possible, nine people were tried in a special court and shot on September 3, 1942, as we found out through our own secret radio communication. Here are the names of the victims: Betz, Bruck, Kons, Lommel, Meieps, Schneiger, Toussaini, and Weels. From the little country of Bupen-Malmedy, some inhabitants, including the mayor, were taken to this concentration camp on October 2, 1940. The mayor died on November 11. The reason for all these people being taken into custody was according to the opinion of the Master Race: they could endanger the safety of the Third Reich! Oh yes, the people of the Master Race had their worries.

The race a person belonged to was of the utmost importance to the Master Race. It didn't take long until the whole world found out that the Nuremberg Laws had only been written to make it legal for the Jews to become penniless and without rights so that the Nazis could take over their possessions without much trouble. Therefore, from the wealthy Jewish people who were already held captive at concentration camps, large amounts of money and bank account deposits were taken, with some persuasion, hereby promising them to use this money for the improvement of the facilities used by the camp's inmates. All they had to do was to sign their funds over to the Nazis and things would look much better—at least that was what they had been told. The unsuspecting Jews paid for new facilities for the hospital, the infirmary, new equipment, instruments, and medical supplies. In return, they were promised an early release from the concentration camp and also a trip to foreign countries. Of course, these promises were never kept. Here is only one example. There were many others.

Bank president Adolf Rothschild, age 67 (34530), reminded the Master Race about its promise. As a result, he was beaten and kicked through the door with heavy boots. To avoid more punishment, he tried to take his own life by running into a barbed wire fence carrying a wire with high voltage on top. This was behind Block #56. Caught in a very painful situation, one could hear his cries until he finally died. Before that, a guard from his post shot at him without too much success. It took about another 15 minutes until he was relieved from all his pains and suffering. Then the electrical current was turned off so that the inmates from the morgue could free the body from the barbed wire. And so this camp had one less Jewish inmate to feed while getting hold of his wealth. One has to realize that all these confiscations taken under duress became the property of the Master Race, instead of being used for the improvement of the conditions under which the inmates had to live.

For the Scandinavians and the northern German people, the Nazis had the highest regard because they were, in their opinion, the "Nordic race." They even invented words that appeared more often over the radio and in the newspapers, such as "aufnorden" meaning people resembling this type could be regarded and treated as a better race. Nevertheless, even though these people were considered as being superior, both Denmark and Norway were invaded by the Nazis in April of 1940. Of course, the excuse was that they were bringing these countries under the "protection" of the Third Reich. After, at first, the Jewish people had been picked out of these countries and taken to the concentration camps where many of them died or had been killed, the so-called "Aryan race" was next to be put into custody and thousands of them ended up in concentration camps also.

However, it cannot be said that the preferred Aryan race did get better treatment than the rest. Oh no, they, too, had to feel the fists and boots of their Nazi captors and members of the Hitler gang who found in Norway just the right helper they wanted, the well-known traitor, Quisling, who was very willing to give the Nazis a helping hand. Years ago, Quisling went with a well-known philanthropist and North Pole explorer, Fridtjof Nansen; he also went under his leadership through the Caucasus. Quisling didn't see anything wrong with betraying his own people. He didn't even stop to protect Nansen's son, the architect Odd Nansen, but helped the Nazis to get him, along with many others of his own country, shipped to Camp Sachsenhausen.

Among other Norwegians who had been taken to this concentration camp by the Nazis was the poet Arnulf Överland, a philanthropist, who may still be remembered by his fellow inmates sharing with him this concentration camp. Norwegian Prime Minister Gerhardsen, and physician Svend Oftedal of Oslo, did their very best to make life easier for their fellow men whenever possible. The same was true of Bjorn Deichmann-Sörensen and Carsten Ösebö who was murdered later in Beksen. Anything that is said here about the Norwegian comrades is also true for the Dutch and Danish inmates. We will never forget men like Johs Fosmark and H. C. Steen-Hansen, both from Copenhagen, who were always ready to help their fellow comrades when were caught in a dangerous situation. It didn't matter what and how many they happened to be. And, I may add, I am still in correspondence with them. (This was circa 1948.)

In the beginning, one could get the impression that inmates from Norway and Denmark did get better treatment than the others. For instance, they could wear their hair long, the regular way, like the Germans, Austrians, and those from Holland and Luxembourg, while inmates from the eastern countries, like the slaves and also Romanians, had to have their heads shaved or their hair cut short. However, a great many of the Danish and Norwegian inmates had the letters "NN" imprinted on their files. It didn't take long until the secret of these letters came out. NN stood for "Nacht and Nebel," meaning night and fog. Inmates whose files were marked NN had to be handled with care outwardly, but in the event an order came to get rid of them, then they, too, had to be eliminated, like the rest, during the dark hours.

One of the Norwegian transports, the one dated May 27, 1942, is more or less outstanding. Among these 114 newcomers were 66 inhabitants from the island of Tellevaag, near Bergen, a place where, according to rumors, two S.S. men had been killed. Without any further investigation as to how these S.S. men died, the whole island village of fishermen was burned down after a great many of the houses had been destroyed by explosives. Women and children were taken into custody in case they had been unable to escape beforehand into the mountainous regions of the island. The whole male population, old and young, including some cripples and two insane ones, were transported to Sachsenhausen. Unfortunately, these Norwegians, being used to a diet of fish and other wholesome ingredients, did not do too well on menus consisting mainly of cabbage and turnip soups, and a great many of them got sick and eventually died.

The very fact that the "superior race" did not always succeed when it came to confiscating other people's property happened in the case of a ship owner by the name of Georg von Especom from Bergen, Norway. He made sure his whole fleet had left the harbor just in time. Not a single little boat was left behind for the Germans to confiscate. Very angry about such a disappointment, Especom was taken to Sachsenhausen on November 26, 1942.

The question of the Japanese being included in the Master Race, because they happened to be the eastern allies of the Nazis, came up at camp also, but could not be answered directly. After all, there were no Japanese at camp, so maybe they could be taken for the Master Race of the Orient. Inmates from the south, such as Italy, were not treated like members of the Master Race after "Il Duce" had been set aside and done away with in such a shameful way. Even his soldiers refused to fight for him anymore. The same happened to the Spaniards. In fact, it didn't make any difference if they had fought for Franco or against him, as both categories had been taken to Sachsenhausen. Neither of them were treated with any kind of consideration.

After the occupation of Holland, where the Master Race acted with brutal force, Dutchmen were taken to this concentration camp. Among them were many people who were members of Jehovah's Witnesses. They seemed a threat to the Nazis, just like those from Germany who almost always ended up in a concentration camp.

After the occupation of France, the first Frenchmen arrived at Sachsenhausen on July 7, 1941—a total of 244 men. They happened to be miners from the department Pas de Calais whose wrongdoing had nothing to do with politics but they had demonstrated against insufficient wages. The Master Race had set up the daily wage schedule at 3.00 RM, up to 3.80 RM per hour, and that was at a time when 1 RM was worth 20 Francs, which was, by far, not enough to live on. For instance, a pound of butter would cost about 60 Francs, and other food items went up in price, too. Of course, besides that, whatever the Master Race could get hold of in the line of food was confiscated for their own use. Further action against the miners took place as well. According to some reports, approximately 1500 miners had been taken into custody.

The Frenchmen were under suspicion by the Master Race of being infiltrated with Communistic ideas. That's why it was of the utmost importance to have them rounded up in large numbers and shipped to concentration camps. Continuously, these transports were on their way to Dachau, Sachsenhausen, and others that, in the meantime, had been turned into extermination camps. France as a "Grand Nation" was unthinkable for the Nazis since that title belonged to the Master Race or so they thought. It was not surprising when on January 23, 1943, a remarkable transport from Paris arrived at Sachsenhausen.

It happened to be mostly the intellectuals who had been rounded up with the Socialists, Communists, and also some policemen. In this transport, which was named "Luna action," were some Gypsies and quite a few hardened criminals with red triangles on their sleeves. With brutal force, all these prisoners were forced into transport wagons, and it even happened that innocent bystanders who were at the railroad station or those who wanted to say "good bye" to their departing friends or family members, ended up in the same transport.

When these uninvolved people tried to resist and get out of the transport, the S.S. started shooting into the crowd, which resulted in injuries and even death. As a result, some dying people arrived at Sachsenhausen among the others. Help or medical assistance was not available during the train ride on the transport. Two young Frenchmen had been shot in the head and were blind afterward. They died soon after their arrival, despite the greatest effort of the physicians among the inmates to save their lives.

How unorganized this transport had been put together can best be seen when we take a look at the names and places from where these people came. There was Fernand Maurice from Lore/Orrne, Van Hijams Anroy from Den Haag, Adrien Hebard from Paris, Josef Staus from Utrecht (Holland), Jean Demarsy from Amiens, Ernest Tregaut from Arpajon, Herrman Damfeld from Bergenop Zoom (Holland), Maurice Royer from St. Germain, Charles Beaudou from Tholen, Willem van Wyk from Den Haag (Holland) and some others. The policemen from Paris were Francois Cachot, Maurice Pierre, and Albert Briolot, and also the brother of the former prime minister, Pierre Chautemps (58030), who were all on the same transport. All told there were 1603 people.

Hermann Göring always tried his very best to give the impression of being a jovial fellow, but he was anything but that. He certainly portrayed the Master Race as he was one of the most cruel members of the gang. After the occupation of Austria in March 1938, falsely called "going home into the Reich" action, it was Göring who used all his power to subdue any members of the so-called left-wing parties, as well as those of the Starhemberg party, all of whom he had arrested without reason. This also happened to both of the princes of Hohenberg, the brothers Max and Ernst Hohenberg, sons of the late Austrian heir to the throne, Franz Ferdinand of Austria-Este, the same one who, with his wife, the princess of Hohenberg, Countess Sophie Chotek, was assassinated in June 1914, in Sarajevo.

Both of the princes had been arrested in a hotel in Vienna, following a rumor that a Nazi flag had been torn down from the building. Afterward, Max and Ernst von Hohenberg were taken to the concentration camp Dachau on Göring's orders. The arrests were not enough for Göring because he wanted to demonstrate that he held absolute power over the princes. Therefore, he sent a telegram to the commander of the Dachau concentration camp which read:

> *Dr. Stl. Wien, #1229 March 30, 1938, at 6:55 p.m.*
> *To the Concentration Camp Dachau:*
> *"The General-Field Marshall, Göring, is giving the order that both of the princes of Hohenberg will be given the dirtiest and most unpleasant jobs."*
> *Signed by the inspector of the Sipo. Full service in Vienna.*
> *signed: Sinzger.*

According to this command by Göring, the princes were to clean the latrines, as well as the stables, a labor assignment that did not make them lose any respect in front of their fellow workers. In fact, they did this kind of a job well, as if they had never done anything else before.

The intended degradation of the Hohenbergs by Göring did not affect the other inmates. The political inmates, especially those formerly connected with the left parties, recognized the game. It was nothing but government hatred for members of the aristocratic family. Because of it the inmates were always helping them with their dirty work; they were just like comrades to them. Göring and the officers of the camp's administration made a wrong speculation by instigating hatred among the classes. Unity prevailed instead and the great masses of degraded and oppressed political against the savages for whom human rights for the imprisoned people did not exist.

In February 1939, Ernst von Hohenberg was transferred to Camp Sachsenhausen after his brother Max had been dismissed from Dachau. However, here the commanding officer got the order to put Ernst von Hohenberg to work with a clean job and, therefore, he was assigned to an office position in the infirmary, where he stayed until his release in April 1943. During his stay, he sat with us at the same table in the mess hall and he surely proved to be a real comrade. He went through the same misery as we all did. We all had gone hungry and we also were left freezing together whatever the case may be. Whenever it was possible to buy a few items in the canteens, then everything, including his portion, had to be divided up equally upon the prince's request so that the less fortunate inmates, who never got any extra money from friends or relatives on the outside, would also get their share.

Together with Prince E. von Hohenberg, came also his personal file to Sachsenhausen. Being one of a couple of inmates who sometimes had to work in the political department, I also had a chance to take a look at these papers which otherwise were only intended for the use of the S.S. I had to take every precaution whenever I wanted to see any of these special files. As a rule, I would choose a Sunday morning for this kind of mission, because during these few hours, the political department was only guarded by one watchman from the S.S. Since there were two guards, they changed position with one another from time to time. Neither of them interfered with my presence. They even admitted that they didn't care to keep an eye on me and as it turned out, I was never disappointed by either of them.

Included in the above-mentioned file on Hohenberg was also the original telegram from Göring which I, of course, didn't dare to remove, since I couldn't think of any possibility to hide it. Therefore, I asked my friend Emil Büge, the Spanish interpreter, to read it and make a copy of it. This he did and, afterward, the original telegram was returned to its old place. During the Nuremberg trial, this telegram was used as evidence against Göring, who tried his very best to explain that he never heard of any inhumane treatment and hard labor for the concentration camp's inmates. After the capitulation, I had a copy of the same telegram made for the Allied commissioner for war crimes who interrogated me. I had to make a statement under oath that the evidence I was handing over to them was absolutely true.

The elite of the Master Race became well-known to the world through the Nuremberg trial. Its purpose was to eliminate mainly all of the intellectuals of all countries and races. Destroying culture, art, and science became a legacy to them. Anything that was not of value to their political concept had to be destroyed according to Goebbel's orders.

Even foreign scientists and professors of universities got no pardon when it came to brutal beatings with boots and fists. It didn't make any difference if the victims were members of the so-called preferred race from the northern nations or if they were scientists from France, Poland, Russia, Hungary, Holland, Belgium, America, Asia, or anywhere else because in the opinion of the Master Race, they were only "low-class," far below their own order of human beings. They didn't even respect German and Austrian scientists because they, too, were taken into custody by the thousands and shipped to the different concentration camps. Through the extermination of intellectuals whose accomplishments they were unable to equal, the so-called Master Race had hoped to rule over the whole world some day and make everyone submissive. As we have seen, they did not succeed.

After the capitulation, it became possible to get hold of and also to arrest some of the chief Nazis. It was not too difficult for former concentration camp inmates to find their former tormentors. Here are a few names of this elite group of S.S. hoodlums:

Loritz, a camp commandant from 1939–1942, was later taken into custody. Höss, a blockleader and later commandant of Concentration Camp Auschwitz, took a job as a field hand in the little village of Gottrupel near Flensburg, where I tracked him down and had him arrested by the Allied military police. At the trial, he admitted having been involved in about four million deaths by gas. In 1947 he was sentenced to death in Warsaw and hanged. Fritz Suhren another supervisor and later commander of the women's concentration camp in Ravensbrück escaped in 1947. While this book was in print (1949) he was recaptured. He had been working under a false name in Bavaria as a brewery worker. Here, too, I had a chance to identify him, which led to his capture. Höpkens, the camp's caretaker of the dress and uniform department, had been shot to death since he had made a good profit selling the clothes of the dead inmates.

The Soviet military tribunal in October 1947, convicted the following criminals to life sentences at hard labor in Siberia: Kaindl, commander from 1942–1945; Körner, a camp leader; Baumkötter, a camp physician; Eccarius, the henchman of the cellblock; Gustav Sorge, nicknamed the Iron Gustav, who was one of the most brutal beasts in human form (It was he who kicked out 17 of my teeth when I fell on the ice one winter morning.); Höhnl, a camp leader; Horst Hempel, who picked out the victims for the gas chamber; labor leader Rehn who gave the order as to who has to be transferred to an extermination camp and gas chamber; Paul Sakowsky, a former inmate who later became a man handler in the crematory, also known as the "heated hallway."

There were still some more of the former camp's supervisors who made life miserable for inmates, like: Fritz Fickert, Fresemann, Knittler, Saathof, and Schubert. Then, there were the criminals by trade, like Paul Saander who worked in the crematory, and Ernst Brennscheidt who was in charge of the "boot-try-out department." These boot runners who were interned in the penal block had to run 40 km a day, carrying baggage around the place just in order to try out the quality and durability of military boots. Brennscheidt and Zander were sentenced to 15 years in Siberia.

Whatever happened to the list of the following sadists? I have not been able to find out by the time this book was in print (i.e. 1948–1949). Here are some names of them: Baierle, nicknamed 'pork jowl' Bugdala, the brutal one; Clausen van Deezen; Dinggräfe; Drechsler; Eilers; Gehring; Grünwald—a camp leader and jewel thief on the side; Hering; Hoffman; Houtjes, a pilferer who took from the inmate's canteens; another camp leader by the name of Jude (Aryan despite his name); Juhren, Janssen, nicknamed "Blaubacke," sergeant and later camp leader of the concentration camp, Natzweiler-Herman Campe; then there were Kaiser, Kessler, Kindervater, Knoop, Köhler, Rönig; camp leader Krämer; Krieber, Kümmerle, Maierhöfer, and a bigshot by the name of Moll, who arranged the mass murders by gas and who drove with two henchmen for assistance from one concentration camp to another. And, still, there are some more like Müller—nicknamed bone breaker; Nägele, Sergeant Nowacki, Pfaff, Pless, Pramann, Prengelmann, who was officer in charge of the inmate's kitchen; a racketeer with the name of Rackers, Ress, camp leader Sauer, the sadist of the cellblock by the name of Siemke; Schanz; Schmuntsch, Schnepper; Thieme; Timmerle, Wiegand, Winnich, Zweyn, Lehmann and Dannel, the chief of the political department.

There are still some more such as: S.S. leader Ballhause, of the special commission that had to pick out victims from among the political inmates in order to have them executed, either by shooting or gas. His assistant was the before-mentioned inmate, Rudolf Haas, alias Kuchan, who was later identified and arrested in Flensburg. Another assistant of this commission was Erdmann, the chief of the criminal department, who also worked in the political department. Troop leader, Böhm, who together with Horst Hempel, picked out the victims for the gas chamber. And before I forget it, there was also the S.S. leader, Ullmann, from the infirmary, who gave injections on a rather large scale, "for research," of course.

There are still more names worth mentioning, like, for instance, several career criminals among the inmates and helpers of the Master Race: Richard Mandel, known as Peronge; Wilhelm Böhm from Worms, known as the hit man in the crematory. Both of their lives came to an end in the concentration camp. Others are the career criminal, Hans Gärtner, who worked in the crematory; Alfred Flegel, helper of the chief of the slave labor department, Rehn; also Wilhelm Jacob, foreman of the boot running and try-out department and also, Wilhelm Thierhoff, the helping hand in the infirmary to Ullmann the poison murderer. This list can go on and on and still remain incomplete. Nevertheless, these names may still be a reminder for the people that survived the pain and agony of Concentration Camp Sachsenhausen.

CHAPTER 20

TALK BETWEEN THE BARRACKS

"Germany has erased the word Pacifism from its dictionary."
   von Papen, Ambassador to Ankara

"Frederic the Great was the first National-Socialist."
   Dr. Hjalmar Horace Greeley Schacht

Every newcomer who lost his freedom for the first time or who had been transferred from a jail or other penal institution was exposed to the same "training methods" and general atmosphere which was so depressing that even men who had been in prison before would say, "Rather 10 years in a prison than one month in a concentration camp." Before the Nazi system came to power, a prisoner was still considered a human being if he obeyed the rules and regulations, taking for granted, of course, that he had to accept some kind of punishment for his wrongdoing. Any one of these arrests and penalties could be endured without being subjected to physical violence. Under no circumstances did anyone have to fear mistreatment, torture—some even with a fatal ending—nothing like that; in fact, there were always ways to gain some favors in return for good behavior. Things like that were impossible in a concentration camp.

In a concentration camp, life and health were constantly threatened. "Protective custody" is what the Nazis called these places of confinement which took away the confidence for a halfway decent way of life. Nobody needed protection from his own people or from his fellow prisoners; instead, in a concentration camp, he had to protect himself against the S.S. brutalities, so that the description "protective custody" was nothing but a joke, especially when the camp's leadership wanted to point out that these inmates were not prisoners at all and that protective custody cannot be called punishment. According to rumors, there was supposed to be a pamphlet in the camp's library with the title, "The Rights of Inmates in Custody." However, upon questioning any of the inmates, one could never find out if any of them had ever seen such a book. Under the rule of Commandant Loritz, the super sadist, the week consisted of seven working days, and if the inmates couldn't manage to catch some sleep in between, then that could mean up to 24 hours of duty. On bitterly cold days and during rainstorms, the noontime meals had to be eaten outside while standing in the plaza. After 10 minutes, at most, the inmates had to be finished eating, still standing at attention or marching back to work.

Making visits to one of the other barracks was prohibited and could mean a beating for the offender. The same was true for providing any kind of entertainment in groups on holidays such as Christmas, New Year, Easter, or Pentecost.

Packages, such as gifts, from relatives for inmates could not be received by them, and the senders would never get a thank you note, nor even an acknowledgement. Incoming packages were opened by the S.S. who kept the contents for themselves. This happened quite often to Polish and Czech inmates who found out about the theft later on why they didn't get anything from home. Even later, after Loritz had been replaced in 1942, the S.S. blockleader who took his place considered it his privilege to steal these packages.

Time and circumstances permitting, it could happen that inmates would have a little conversation among themselves and exchange ideas. Especially the political inmates liked to take any opportunity they could to get in touch with the other inmates, just to get as much information from them as possible. This way, they might be able to give warnings to their fellow inmates or special instructions to make life easier for them. Of course, these conversations had to go on in a low voice. Even some new jokes were told which had been picked up from recently arrived newcomers. These jokes were always a reflection on the Nazis and their followers but, most often, they were about Hitler, Göring, and Goebbels, as the "three wise guys from the East" and then the drunkard, Dr. Ley.

One would hear from different fellow inmates why they had been brought here, from what kind of a family they had come, and what kind of a business or occupation they had had, and, most of all, for what kind of "crime" they were here. For instance, a man from Cologne, by the name of Backhaus, came to this camp because he allegedly tried to marry the same girl a Gestapo man wanted for his own. Upon his arrival, he was placed into a prison cell with the order for extra punishment. A few weeks later, he was found beaten to death. If the Gestapo man finally married the girl remained a mystery.

The mail from home which always had been censured beforehand by S.S. men, was not exactly filled with happy news. On the contrary, these letters were full of sorrow and worries as to how to meet expenses, since their breadwinner had been taken from them and also about the hard times the wives and children and, sometimes, the parents, too, had to go through. If the letter writer happened to be too open-hearted while explaining the hardships experienced by members of his or her family, then the censors would cut out portions of the letter so that the receiver would only get pieces of scrap paper, usually with his name left in place. The remnants were often not large enough for the receiver of the letter to be able to understand what had been written and since both sides of the letter had been written on, there was really not much possibility to get a message out of it. There wasn't much use in answering these letters since the inmate could not know what to write and then he would never be sure his family would ever receive it anyway.

One of the saddest chapters was that which concerned the brutal interference with married inmates by members of the Nazi gang when told in letters how the S.S. tried to break up families by promising the women a much better life if they would divorce their inmate husbands who were now in a concentration camp anyway. This systematic breakup of marriages and even rape of the wives at home led, in many cases, to a divorce which the inmate husband had to accept and, in some cases, he had to take a lawyer to make it legal. Besides the everyday, normal hardships these inmates suffered and endured in camp, many of them also lost their homes and families through the actions of the Gestapo.

Fortunately, the wives of political inmates would almost always stick to their husbands since they, too, had been fighting the Nazi regime for many years.

It has not always been easy to advise a fellow inmate whose wife was suing him for a divorce. Therefore, in most cases, one could only recommend, *"If your wife doesn't want to stay married to you because you are a prisoner in a concentration camp, you might as well forget about her because her intentions of being a true partner could not have been too sincere in the first place. So, let her go. The time will come when she will regret it."* How true these arguments were could later be seen after the Nazi capitulation when many of the divorced wives were very sorry for having left their husbands.

In the evening, we could walk over to the plaza to hear the news. Five loudspeakers had been installed and around 8:00 p.m. the inmates could listen to the radio messages. But actually they didn't think much of these programs as they sounded more like fairy tales. Later, the announcer would say, "This is Hans Fritsche speaking"—more nonsense—after which Joseph Goebbels would generally have something to say. But on Friday evenings his column which appeared in the newspaper *Das Reich* was broadcast to the inmates who really couldn't care less.

Afterward, the people at the concentration camp would comment and, of course, criticize what they had just heard because these radio messages didn't even put a damper on their spirits—not at all! They more or less took these messages as a joke. After looking around and making sure that no one was around who was not supposed to be listening in—the politicals, oh yes, they wanted them around—they made some fun of the so-called important news and then everyone felt more relaxed.

It seemed remarkable that hardly any of the regular criminals and the antisocials among them (the inmates) would come in to listen to the so-called news. The people who came over were mostly political prisoners. After the broadcast was finished, they would go over the events that took place during the day. Some orders were given out and then one would try to make some new friends or at least connections with the new arrivals among the inmates. It was here that some of the new people who had not been active in their way to work against the Nazi system got their training and how to look out for themselves while in the concentration camp and also how to fight for the common cause in the underground movement and against the S.S. organization that brought them to the concentration camp.

At first, newcomers were taken into confidence and got acquainted with the politicals, but only after one was absolutely sure about his personal background and, of course, that he had been imprisoned only for political reasons. First, he had to endure all kinds of torture, while being kept by the Gestapo or in any kind of labor camp like Esterwegen and Lichtenberg, for instance, also a failed attempt to escape which was by a punishment consisting of being tied to a pole and being hit with a bat some 50 times. Afterward, half a year in stockade, then transferred to a quarry or an extermination camp. After he had endured all of this, his will to live must have been strong as it kept him going; he knew he had to hold on and that he would make it. After all, the Nazis would not be in power forever. A time has to come when the sun would shine again; that is, the sun of freedom, not only in Germany but also in other enslaved countries as well.

Like a living skeleton, this political martyr arrived at Sachsenhausen. He was one among many. He needed help and so he got it. Some of the comrades gave him a piece of their daily bread ration, others, a little margarine or a little left-over from their last meal, whatever they could spare. And, later, this starved fellow would really admit that for once he had his stomach filled after so many years of being hungry. But this was not all. From now on, a certain number of inmates would make their daily contributions from their own meager rations so that this starved newcomer would have a better chance to survive and look more like a human being again, instead of skin and bones. After a few weeks, one could notice the difference in his appearance. These newcomers were very thankful and appreciated every little bit of help they could get from their new comrades. For the new ones, it was the friendly spirit in the community. An atmosphere like this would overcome the brutal force that still existed at the concentration camp. However, one could not yet estimate as to how long this tyranny might last.

This way the political inmates worked together for the common benefit of all concerned, as compared with the common criminals who only had their own well-being in mind. Instead of helping others, they would even steal from their own comrades. They may even go so far as to ask, "What can you give me for what I may let you have to eat?" Outside that, the criminals were completely unconcerned if one or more of the inmates would starve to death or not. One could see that these antisocials were enemies of their own kind, too, and that they were only interested in their own benefit and survival. They were completely unconcerned and would denounce their own comrades in order to gain favors from the S.S. And, of course, they would take any opportunity they could to turn in one of the politicals if they could get any benefit or anything worthwhile from their Nazi oppressors. Whenever they had a chance, they would not only turn in any of the political inmates, no, nothing would stop them from denouncing their own kind, too.

Compared to these selfish no-good inmates, the foreigners, and Jehovah's Witnesses, were great people as they helped the common cause whenever they could. We will never forget the inmates from Norway and Denmark who were getting packages regularly from their homeland, through the Red Cross, which they would divide among their fellow inmates. They even gave them parts of their own rations and also never forgot the Russian inmates, as they were worse off than any other group; they didn't have a chance of getting anything from their homeland.

Just like sunshine may change to rain, so it happened, sometimes, that after many bad days, a few good hours could also be enjoyed at this concentration camp. This did not happen very often but then, the inmates did make the best of these happier moments. This way, everything was more endurable for all the people around.

There had been some happy hours but they were so few that we could count them on our fingers. Besides some new jokes, one would also hear about some incidents that had happened in the meantime. And some of them could be funny, especially where members of the Nazis had been involved. A farmer from Hanover just didn't want to join the "party," that is, the Nazi party, and, therefore, he was taken to this concentration camp. His offense can be explained as follows: "*Well, when I said, you can do as you please but I am not going to join the party nor the S.S., and if you want to give me your suit, that will do for a masquerade together with that cheese box on the head to match.*" *They threw me out of the union so that I no longer could buy seeds and fertilizer. And, if nothing is put into the ground as fertilizer, not much will come out of the old seeds as I have only sandy soil. When everyone else's oats were growing nicely, mine could hardly be noticed. Hardly a foot high and only a stalk of oat was here and there. The ground was so bare one could walk on it without disturbing the stalks. Then a spokesman from the farmer's union came and told me I could no longer be a farmer. I didn't say anything but a few days later, I put two boards of wood into the ground on opposite sides of the field so that everyone could see them. Then my son (who happened to be a painter) came and painted a sign in big letters on the boards that read, "Give me four years." After that, I had the laughs all on my side but not the spokesman from the farmer's union. He went to the Gestapo to denounce me and while I was arrested, one of the Gestapo men asked me who wanted the four years. The oats, of course, I said, so they can grow four feet in four years instead of only one foot in one year. This was considered to be making fun of the Führer and I was told that I should know that oats need only one year to grow, not four years after another; every farmer knows that. But when I said that with Adolf Hitler, everything went much faster and that 1,000 years would pass merely like*

Twelve Years of Night | 239

a year, the Gestapo man got hold of my arm and took me to the nearest jail. Finally, I ended up at this concentration camp."

Tales like these provided fun and entertainment and also showed us that even among the people on the farms, some anti-Nazis could entertain their audiences with humor and satire, which came more or less as a surprise. Two villagers were also thrown into this camp for a similar reason, making fun of the system. It happened like this. One of the men was a merchant and the other was a teller at the village bank. They were talking to each other while a nearby customer denounced both of them for being anti-Nazi. The conversation went something like this: the merchant asked the teller, *"If I put 1,000 Marks into my account, who will guarantee that I will get it back?" "The Führer will see to it,"* said the teller. *"But when the Führer dies, what then?"* asked the merchant. *"In this case, Göring will guarantee it,"* was the teller's reply. *"But when he, too, dies?"* was the next question. *"Well, then the whole Nazi party will make sure the deposit has not been lost,"* said the teller. *"O.K., fine, but what happens if the whole Nazi party goes broke. What about my money in that case?"* Hereupon, the teller answered in a whispering voice, *"Wouldn't that be worth 1,000 Marks?"* That was too much. Both of them were waiting here in the concentration camp for the Nazi party to go broke. They would not mind sacrificing another 1,000 Marks to make this happen and maybe still, another 1,000, to have the person who denounced them beaten up really good.

We also got some worthwhile information concerning how he landed in this camp, from a policeman who had been on guard duty near Goebbels. His crime was to give the wrong answer. Upon questioning as to the number of girls attending the so-called bride's school, he answered, "Oh, you mean the Reich's bordello for the Buck of Babelsberg?" (Nickname for Goebbels). Well, that did it! He landed here in this concentration camp. But it was still interesting to find out something more about this bride's school. The policeman had heard that the brides of the S.S. men were trained there to make coffee, clean house, and care for children. Lessons on how to act in bed were given nights by Josef himself, according to the former policeman who was now an inmate.

Then came a day that created quite an uproar. The date was June 22, 1941, "War against Russia!!" The Führer had done it again at the right time as he always liked to do it in previous attacks and invasions. The loudspeaker at the plaza kept on bringing news, overwhelming in fact, so the inmates could listen to the so-called bulletins about victories. For instance: "The fall of Leningrad is expected in just a few hours," and similar broadcasts, could be heard over the radio. The fact that it had to come to a break in diplomatic relations with Russia was certain, and so on.

The politicals, among themselves, were very much involved in some discussions about what was mainly going on in the eastern battlefields. Some of the inmates became quite optimistic, figuring an earlier end of the war could now be expected because the fighting went from one to two fronts. Of course, some of the politicals seemed to be a little worried but most of them were under the impression that the outcome of the war would depend on the Russian strategy.

The victory reports of the Nazi radio could no longer spoil the wishful thinking of the politicals. The war with the Soviets became a deciding factor on who was going to win because the day was sure to come when Hitler's luck on the fighting front will run out; at least this was the general impression the inmates had. Not only among the politicals, but also among other groups, the foreigners, and even among some criminals and the so-called antisocials, one could hear their opinions which sounded rather hopeful. Most of the inmates were optimistic, hoping that the Allies would win the war and put an end to the captivity of inmates in this and other concentration camps. The hope for an early end of the war and a victory for the Allies as well as the release from long-time imprisonment in concentration camps also had an effect on the inmates working outside these buildings: far fewer inmates than before tried to escape. For instance, after the evening roll call was over the 1,000 inmates had to march to the freight yard in Oranienburg only under normal guard by S.S. men, in order to unload the trains and bring the goods in pushcarts in the woods, near Camp Sachsenhausen.

Not a single escape attempt had been reported, although it could have been possible without too much trouble to disappear somewhere into the darkness. Nothing happened. The inmates stayed, with the thought of freedom on their minds, which to them seemed only a matter of time.

Like it used to be in the army where the battle songs were supposed to keep the tired soldiers from falling behind so it was with the compulsive singing in the concentration camps. After the roll call at the plaza, singing took place, not as enjoyment by listening to the men's choir, no, this was mainly done in order to take away more free time from the inmates. It was sickening to be forced to keep on singing over and over again for long periods of time or until, eventually the S.S., themselves, got sick and tired of it, too. If the lyrics did not come out right, extra lessons had to be taken later in the barracks. There was definitely no enthusiasm for this kind of singing. Only songs that the inmates could select themselves—mostly those that were prohibited, of course—could mean some entertainment.

On the march to the railroad station, the older politicals went first, hereby singing freedom songs followed by the other inmates who joined in also. Even the people living in Oranienburg, where they lined the streets, gave us some applause. Some of these songs were not exactly pro-Nazi, but then, the S.S. couldn't figure out what they meant to say. Obviously, they couldn't understand the text. Until one of these fine days the workmen's song by Jacob Audorf was included in the repertoire while marching through the streets of Oranienburg, S.S. leader Nowaki put an end to it: it was not a concentration camp song. But, if he had found out the meaning of this particular song, some kind of collective punishment would surely have been dished out.

However, the next evening after marching long enough that the concentration camp's surrounding wall was no longer in sight, more freedom songs could be heard while marching through Oranienburg. There was no protest this time, not even when the song, *The Internationale* was presented, just for kicks, of course. It seemed obvious the S.S. didn't understand its content anyhow. But finally, any presentation of these songs was prohibited because it was not a Nazi song.

Coming back to the wagons full of goods at the railroad station, these wagons did not contain merchandise delivered by the government for the consumption of the camp's inmates. No, this was actually stolen from the Allies' supply and a lot of it was from private property. Even some farmer's push-carts were among them, no matter what shape they were in. Some of the carts had been taken from among the poorest of farmers and, afterward, they were used as firewood.

Among the regular criminals who were also ordered to bring wagons into the concentration camp, there happened to be also some "businessmen" who went to work on their own by selling the best wagons directly to civilians for as high as 200–300 Marks, and maybe more. Once a case like this had been reported to the camp commander's office. The reason was the "buyer" wanted to exchange the truck for another one. This request didn't do him any good. He, too, was arrested right then and there for buying stolen merchandise and was placed behind bars in this concentration camp, where he had a chance for a talk with the crooked inmate salesman from whom he got the wagon.

Among the inmates, themselves, there always seemed to be some kind of exchange business going on. Money, itself, especially the camp's money, had lost its buying power. Now it was cigarettes, even the cheapest kind that took the place of real cash. For a cigarette, one could get almost anything, even food from the S.S. kitchen. Of course, this was not considered theft; no way, the inmates felt they had the right because the S.S. had taken these food items from them when they received packages from home.

On the other hand, any kind of theft and robbery among the inmates was punished by their own law-abiding comrades, themselves. It just couldn't be tolerated when the criminal element among them would steal from the meager rations the inmates had to get along on. The culprits would get a warning first and if this didn't help, they would get a well-deserved beating which, in most cases, made them think twice before taking any food or other items again.

When it came to criminals by trade, no warning would help. They could break any lock, enter any barracks, and take whatever they wanted in order to exchange it for things they wanted most of all. Anything to smoke, since cigars and cigarettes served as an exchange for other articles, was in demand. By the time when more and more inmates with a criminal background filled this concentration camp, special caution had to be taken by the other inmates. That meant at every roll call, some inmates had to stay behind as watchmen to guard the barracks. Even during the night such security took place. The reason for having so many criminals transferred to Sachsenhausen was simple. Prisons and jails in war zones had to be emptied, therefore, even murderers, rapists, and other hardened criminals were relocated here. The scum of humanity became, therefore, integrated with our regular inmates. By the thousands, these career criminals arrived in concentration camps, as early as 1942. Federal prisons had to make room mainly for the arrested political offenders from Germany as well as from other newly occupied countries.

It seems strange but the majority of these professional criminals did not do very well in a concentration camp. Being used to a more or less regulated way of life, heated cells, and better food, they now became subjected to some inhumane treatment, exposed to the cold, and were fed rather meager rations. Sometimes only after a few days of confinement in a camp, these long-time prisoners could get sick and a few died. It became clear that this kind of "relocation" as ordered by Himmler, had only one purpose in mind, to get rid of these long-term criminals. Actually, the political inmates didn't feel too sorry about them. After all, who would be sympathetic towards people who were nothing but enemies of mankind? Some of them, even the worst of them, were those who would collaborate with the Nazis if this would be to their advantage. Spying for the Nazis and denouncing a political inmate could lead to harsh punishment and even death for the politicals.

Holding together and helping each other was the highest pledge for the politicals. They were building up a moral force for the fight against the oppressors, no matter how difficult the situation used to be in these concentration camps. "Keep your heads up," was the slogan, because somehow and sometimes, the day has to come when all those people that are being kept in these camps will be set free again. No matter how many times the radios would send their messages about so-called irreplaceable losses for the enemy, it was not convincing. No matter how often the issued Nazi paper described the lack of fighting spirit among the enemy, reports like these just couldn't dampen the minds of the political inmates. They never lost confidence or hope that this time of terror had to come to an end eventually.

It didn't matter how many German troops marched deeper and deeper into Soviet Russian territory or how many other countries had been occupied in the Balkan countries or North Africa, the politicals and other comrades on their side did not lose hope, not even the foreigners whose countries the Nazis tried to devastate. It was different with the S.S. leadership, who saw in all these proclaimed victories the certainty that they must be getting closer and closer to the final victory over all the people. In anticipation of this event which to them seemed so certain they even showed some kindness towards the inmates by dropping a few strict rules and letting a more relaxed attitude prevail.

For instance, it was allowed to have some afternoon hours set aside for entertainment and so one could see in Barrack #28—otherwise used for drying clothes—a stage being set up where one could see, at first, some variety shows in which artists of different countries gave their performances as best as they could. It turned out to be a real international kind of show. For instance, some inmates played *The Biberpelz* by Gerhard Hauptmann and a few others gave a presentation of another humorous play, *Der Maulkorb*—muzzle. Setting up this stage and putting all these different wardrobes together was not much of a great problem, and the plays, themselves, were as good as in any other little theater. Even the actors who had to play ladies' roles gave a very good and convincing performance.

It was also permitted for inmates to have musical instruments sent to them by friends or members of their family. It didn't take long until a political inmate by the name of Peter Adam, who used to be a musician and conductor, to put his own orchestra together with some forty to fifty musicians, all picked from among the inmates. These men really had some wonderful programs, among others; they would also play Beethoven's *Ninth Symphony*.

For anybody interested in sports, there was the plaza for the roll calls, which was made available after the end of the day as well as on Sunday afternoons. Here, the men could play soccer. They also wore different uniforms to distinguish between the various countries they represented. Even a stadium was erected for the spectators. This was in front of the bathhouse. Besides that, thousands of inmates were given a chance to be spectators and the Russian prisoners of war could give some performances with their native folk dances and the Balalaika orchestra.

The library was open to the inmates, offering books that even the political inmates liked to read instead of only pro-Nazi propaganda. Books in foreign languages were also made available. For instance, the Danes and Norwegians had a lot of books collected which possibly had been sent to them in packages from home and now they could enjoy reading them. The fact that among these books some left-wing literature could be found may also be mentioned here. This was not surprising as the Nazis in charge were apparently unable to read them. But just the same, as a precaution, any of these books with a critical viewpoint towards the Nazis had to be held in a safe place and only loaned out to inmates trustworthy enough and able to read them.

These few highlights in the entertainment world could make us, at least temporarily, forget the misery we had to live with at this concentration camp. By the next morning, brutal reality was with us again as was the fight for life and health. After the morning roll call, we heard a request for volunteers to search for bombs. Promises for special rewards for those willing to endanger their lives while searching were also made. Berlin and the surrounding countryside had been bombed heavily and the removal and detonating of these bombs, most of which were time bombs, had already caused the death of some of our comrades.

After ten expeditions searching for bombs, the inmates were promised release from concentration camps. That's why, at first, so many inmates volunteered for these dangerous missions. On the other hand, the camp's leaders, of course, were hoping nobody would survive ten of these missions; that's why this promise was made. However, anyone who survived ten of these expeditions—death marches—we may say, was in for a disappointment, because the Nazis, like always, never kept their promises. Instead of freedom, they were allowed to let their hair grow long. No wonder that was the end of applying to be a volunteer and, therefore, from that time on, inmates were picked at random and forced to go on these "Ascension Day" missions, as they were called, from that time on.

Some politicals who were already earmarked by the Nazi leaders as being "ready for liquidation" were among the first to be ordered to search for bombs. Camp leader Kolb—already mentioned before—had made up his mind to have a political offender by the name of Erich Duus (45212) who was held here for being a pacifist, go up in smoke with a bomb. Not less than 32 times did he participate on these rides to hell without any mishap. After that, he was transferred to Buchenwald with the order not to let him work in his own profession as a dentist but to give him the most dangerous bomb-searching jobs available. Duus seemed to be somehow protected by a guardian angel; and, therefore, he was finally shipped to Cologne to work among the rubble where fate finally and, unfortunately, caught up with him. While detonating a bomb he had a serious accident that left him a cripple for the rest of his life.

The camp's leadership could not prevent the inmates from talking about these bomb-searching missions. In most cases, we at camp found out somehow that one or the other of our comrades had been hurt or torn to pieces by these bombs; but at the evening formation, we knew for sure who had not returned. In many cases, we heard the details of what had happened to the victims, who they were, and who came back alive, as well as those who had been killed. We also heard that these bomb-searching squads got a lot of sympathy from the civilians, especially for those who perished during these deadly missions.

By spreading out the labor commandos, more of our inmates came in contact with the civilians who also were able to give us more information about what it looked like on the other side of the fence, how the war was progressing, and how the political and economic situations were. All efforts by the camp's leadership to prevent inmates from talking to civilians were in vain. Even the guards saw themselves outnumbered and could care less whenever an inmate had a conversation with someone from the general public. It can also be mentioned that many of the new S.S. men were on their job more or less against their wills as some of them even admitted. Some of them had been forced into these positions.

The camp's inmates were so used to it that the leadership never delivered on their promises. One misery made room for another, and one sensation followed the next but never has there been something pleasant during their stay at the concentration camp, except some time off for entertainment for the inmates. But again new methods of killing, new tortures were tried out, even though the S.S. men tried their best to hide it from the inmates.

Now the employees in the dental clinic had to work overtime: dental plates from the dead had to be cleaned off. The teeth, well let's say the remnants of them, had to be separated from any gold bridge work in an acid solution. This time the Nazis got hold of fillings that had a silvery shine to it—maybe platinum—well, anyway, this means that the victims must have been Russians. These fillings, as well as the gold salvaged from other dead people, had to be weighed and taken over to the S.S. men in charge. And they sure took care of it, that is, the business end. All these broken-out gold bridges, crowns, and fillings became valuable merchandise for the S.S. Besides these items, they were also looking for strangely formed skulls and curved spines which also turned into a lucrative business. Constantly, these skulls and skeletons had to be boiled off and ready for the S.S. who always had steady buyers for this kind of merchandise. And if among the newcomers to Sachsenhausen happened to be an individual with an odd-shaped skull, the chances were about 100 to one that one of these days this poor victim got the order from above to go to the infirmary for "observation." While there he would get an injection that made him ready for the next transport to the undertaker. A few days later his skull and skeleton were ready for sale. That these events were happening one would hear through the grapevine within the cellblocks.

It was not always possible to walk from one cellblock to another to visit a friend. If, for instance, one of the cellblocks was under quarantine, like in a case of scarlet fever, for example, or any other disease that did occur frequently, all contact with the inmates had to be disrupted. Only during the evening hours was it possible to talk from a distance through open windows in order to find out something that could be interesting. Oh, yes, something worthwhile had to be made public to all the politicals whenever possible. There used to be always some so-called reports in the *Völkischer Beobachter* which we nicknamed the "Rag for Children" because it brought constantly nearly the same news that not even the children could be made to believe or be interested in, never mind the old guys in a concentration camp.
Advertisements and articles were always read with great interest but also with some reservations. Papers were handed down from person to person so that everybody could get a "real picture" of the general situation and the political development. Even something that had not happened before, something new, was published by the Nazi paper, like this announcement where a young girl got married to a dead person:

> "I make it known today that I have been married to Lieutenant Herrman Krause who was killed on February 17, 1944."
> Berlin, May 5, 1944.
> signed: Hannchen Krause (nee Meyer)

Well, after all, during the so-called Thousand-Year Reich of Adolf Hitler, it could be made possible to marry a dead person. Maybe in times to come it could be possible for some of the supermen in the Nazi party to perform miracles like waking up the dead as happened while Jesus Christ was living. Who knows?

The general publications, as well as the war news reports, always gave the impression that victory was not far away. If not all enemy aircraft had been destroyed in the air, then the remaining forces could easily be wiped out on the ground. If the enemy had been successful in overcoming our troops, then, of course, we had to retaliate. Enemy troops had to be surrounded, after that it would not take too long until one could hear: "The enemy is awaiting his doom while the Nazi soldiers are closing in on them." And on and on one could read or hear the same news reports. Well, of course, everyone knew that these so-called news reports were all phony. Yes, even some wisecracks were made by some of the inmates who had some humor left. As, for instance: "Italian war news:" A foreign motorbike had been attacked near Tripoli and with success. The cover of the rear wheel has been struck with a bullet. There is still a fight going on of what to do with the right pedal." Then someone made a joke about Goebbels like this: "Our troops under Rommel in the Sahara are constantly marching forward. Besides lots of sand, there is no resistance. But we do need the sand to throw it into the eyes of the people. We just cannot get enough sand."

Another rumor had it that Goebbels made an urgent request to occupy Greenland. Why? We need Greenland to make it clear to the German people that the winter relief action also had to be applied through the summer, too, because in Greenland there is always winter.

Some more jokes were circulating in the form of a so-called theater program which read like this: Sunday: *Twilight of the Gods*, starring Adolf Hitler; Monday: *A Comedy: Nothing but Lies*, starring Joseph Goebbels; Tuesday: *The Happy Farmer*, starring Chief Darreo, the production manager for turnips, Wednesday: *Fight for the Fat Pig Jolanthe*, starring Hermann Göring, Thursday: *Someone Too Many on Board*, starring Robert Ley. High-priced seats are only available for cognac or brandy as payment. Friday: *The Student Prince*, starring

Hilgendorf, the man in charge of the winter relief action. Saturday: *Schiller's Robbers*, starring all players mentioned before in the program for the last week.

It is not hard to understand that by listening to Goebbel's phony news reports, the people had not much confidence in any of them and that is why sometimes the most unbelievable stories were passed from barrack to barrack, giving the inmates occasionally some fun anyway.

Although the official broadcast had nothing but so-called victory news to report, it seemed that not even the concentration camp's leadership, by watching the measures they took, believed what they heard. Constantly they were looking for volunteers for the army and the S.S. forces and this, by promising the most favorable conditions which, of course, nobody wanted to believe. After an evening formation, some parachute jumpers were sought who could speak with an accent something like London slang. A few of the criminals by trade volunteered, hoping to get into a POW camp by jumping out over England. Upon investigating their knowledge of the English language, especially the London dialect, it became clear that they thought they could get away with the dialect spoken in Hamburg, the Platt-German (Plattdeutsch) speech, which, of course, gave the people at camp something to laugh and talk about.

As time went on, one could see the general change in the atmosphere. Discipline seemed to have vanished. Since sometime during 1943 no more roll calls at noon time and soon after that they also did away with the evening roll calls as well. Despite all the victory news, the inmates were aware that the conditions on the outside were different than those presented in the broadcasts. At camp, food rationing became worse. What was mostly on the menus were soups made from turnips and cabbage. For the inmates, there was hardly any underwear left, the same with shoes and socks. Also, there were not enough zebra suits left for the inmates and, therefore, the camp's high command gave orders to look over the civilian suits left behind and mostly by the dead, especially those that had belonged to foreigners and Jews.

To prevent any inmate from getting lost or running away while working with the outside commandos, they had to wear coats and jackets that had a big colorful cross painted on their front, as well as on their backs. Now one could see inmates dressed in all kinds of suits, including tuxedos, dinner jackets and tails, with painted crosses on them. One could get the impression this was some kind of a masquerade. It certainly was amusing just to see these costumes at camp instead of the striped uniforms.

By the time the summer of 1942 came to an end, an appeal was made according to which the inmates had to inform their relatives and friends that underwear, socks, and shoes were desperately needed by the inmates. This way there may be some underwear left over for those inmates who had no families to depend on and who were nearly out of anything to wear under their suits or whatever they had on.

When, at the same time, the food supplies were getting shorter, inmates were also asked to have packages sent to them by members of their families. To make it look like a nice gesture, they were even encouraged to have as many packages as possible shipped to them from the outside world. This was at a time when most likely all the people were hard off themselves and had nothing to spare anymore. But, despite their own hardship, families made it possible to take from their meager rations in order to send them to their relatives in concentration camps. Unfortunately, the S.S. got hold of these packages first and removed from them items like butter, margarine, and lard, besides articles for smoking, mostly tobacco, before handing the remaining ingredients over to the inmates to whom these packages were addressed. While being among ourselves, we heard of quite a few of these incidents where this had happened and felt sorry for the inmates who had been deprived of part of their gifts.

Whenever it came to collective punishment, the foreman and blockleader were the first ones to feel it. Like on a day set for searching for bombs. The date happened to be March 28, 1941. Blockleader Otto Fleischhauer (a member of Parliament in Thuringia) refused to go along with his comrades. For that reason, he had to stand outside the gate for 11 hours in all kinds of weather without anything to eat. Despite that, he could call himself fortunate; all he got was pneumonia while his comrades, all five of them, perished in a bomb blast, among them his assistant, Heinrich Krützer, from Hamburg. The rest of this group were severely injured. One of the fellows had been disfigured a great deal in his face with many bluish scars all over. But, despite such an injury he was not set free as had been promised.

We had to get used to these kinds of bad news; we were powerless and unable to interfere. Day after day, we were threatened to lose our lives and death was always lurking around us. Without having the slightest notion, a comrade may be sitting at his table in his barracks. Then all of a sudden a courier may come into the room, calling: "Go to the main office right away!" Many had been called this way, but not everyone came back: liquidated!

Sometimes, those who had been called did return. This happened to me also. A courier came running towards me in the political department with the command to go at once to the leader of the concentration camp. Having to go there is always serious; however, an order is an order and anyone who does not obey this call will be taken by the S.S. On my way to the commandant, I had to stop first at the office of the blockleader in order to find out if he knew something about why I had to appear before Commandant Loritz, and in such a hurry. Harry Naujock, the man I talked to, only knew that I was supposed to act as an interpreter for the "Iron Gustav." Well, at least this time the order didn't have anything to do with myself, only with my job. What a relief. This made my walk to the commandant's office a whole lot easier.

While introducing myself to the "Iron Gustav," I saw Comrade Seip from Oslo standing there like a victim near the door and he looked worried all right. Now, the commandant ordered me to tell my comrade, in his own language, that he had been caught smuggling letters in and out and, therefore, he had to face some kind of punishment. However, this time he would only go on probation, but after a repeat performance, he could expect to be beaten up severely, maybe even shot or hanged on the gallows or something similar in the line of punishment. He tried to impress this on him by using words like hoodlum, beast, pig, or whatever came to his mind. Comrade Seip, as rector of the University of Oslo, certainly did know the German language but the "Iron Gustav" was not aware of it.

Since Gustav—Sorge was his real name—was not familiar with foreign languages, I took the liberty myself of explaining to the defendant that this time he would go free but if he did it again, well, listen to me: "What I have to tell you is this, should it ever happen again then this hoodlum sitting behind the desk and happens to be in command will see to it that you could get shot, hanged, or severely beaten, or he may find any other kind of punishment." Obviously shaken, the rector from Oslo, Norway, acted very scared and frightened. This even gave Gustav a cause to smile; after all, he happened to be the authority. Then he asked us to leave.

Never before did we run down the stairs so fast and disappear between the barracks like after this "conference." Upon asking Comrade Seip why he had been so scared, he said he was under the impression the "Iron Gustav" might understand enough Norwegian in order to notice the fun I was making about him. If that had been the case then, of course, I would have been more careful; otherwise, I myself could have been marked for "liquidation." But I happened to know guys like this one, well-known for their brutality, and also that he was not too smart. Foreign languages were unknown to him, so why shouldn't we take a little advantage in a case like this?

CHAPTER 21

DANCE OF THE DEAD

"Adolf Hitler is really the Holy Ghost."
            Kerrl, Reichsminister of Church Affairs

"Only once did history come up with a man like Adolf Hitler. — Hitler is lonesome, God is lonesome; Hitler is like God himself."
            Dr. Frank, Supreme Court Justice.

Some of us may have seen an old famous painting called *Dance of the Dead* where we see skeletons dancing around like live people, a gruesome sight to look at. Actually, this was a symbol, meaning death's victory over life. Just thinking about it gave me an idea and a reason to compare the conditions at Sachsenhausen with death. Most of the people here had to suffer from maltreatment and sickness and finally had to die; oftentimes, they didn't even have the strength or willpower to keep on living under these miserable circumstances.

Then one day during the summer of 1943, we thought we had a vision: What we saw was a group of half-naked people looking more like living skeletons with skulls on top and limbs shaking slowly. This way they were moving through the gate towards the hospital section. Just the sight of this spectacle reminded me of that painting mentioned before, only now the scenery was real. By taking a closer look one could make out that these white skulls were the bald heads of people who were still alive but walking their last mile, according to the diagnosis of the doctor in charge. Actually, they were Russians, overcome by hunger, as we found out later. These Russian prisoners had to dismantle weapons and while doing this they found some greasy-looking substances within the weapons which were toxic. However, they were so hungry that they ate from it. This way, they hoped they might get rid of that awful hungry feeling. The heads of these unfortunate people were in a very bad shape, mainly the skin. They had already been treated with some kind of ointment and had been wrapped in white paper bandages. In some cases, one could only see the eyes, nose, and mouth, topped with a bald skull.

It happened on a wintry day around 1939–1940, in front of the closed gate of a hospital building. More than a hundred patients had been waiting in the bitter cold to be let inside. They kept moving from one foot to the other, some even collapsed because of the freezing temperature. Then they tried to get up but couldn't make it, and they died on the ground. Meanwhile, some of the other patients cried out for help, while others were barefooted and had frozen limbs. Just the same they tried to shake the gate, pulling on the iron bars, but nobody opened it up. The commandant wanted to admit only a small number of patients for treatment.

One might as well say that the dying patients were better off dead, after all, they didn't need any more beds and, therefore, they could be transported into the morgue down in the cellar. Jewish patients, whose life expectancies could be estimated as no more than half a day, could not be reported as being sick. Only when it was absolutely certain that a patient had died and had been checked out by the caretaker of the cellblock, then he was brought to the hospital. If he happened to be dead on arrival, as in most cases, he was taken directly into the morgue, undressed, and his body was thrown upon a big heap. At the time when the cellar that was used for the morgue was located under Barracks II, one could see the dead bodies lying around in all kinds of grotesque positions, like sitting or leaning against something with horrible-looking faces that could scare anybody away who had to enter this dungeon. No painter had yet been able to create such a gruesome sight. No S.S. man would dare to enter this place of horror;

only the carriers who had to handle these corpses came in to pull the bodies apart in order to place them into transport boxes that were wheeled to the crematories. Nothing was done to the corpses, they were just pulled from the big heap and thrown, mostly two at a time, into boxes; well, they were dead anyway.

From among a group of outside labor commandos a Russian, looking for freedom, had climbed into a tree. Camp leader Grünwald saw and shot him down as if he were hunting for apes. The critically shot victim tried to hold on to a branch but soon fell to the ground, still moving, and a second bullet ended his life right then and there. Another inmate who accidentally came against a chain used to confine a working area also got a bullet in his back from an S.S. watchman. He, too, stumbled a few times until he collapsed near a ditch.

As long as the labor commando troop, known as "Klinker" returned to camp in the evening, there were always some bodies taken back besides those who were almost worked to death. They just looked like skeletons, held up by two comrades as they were walked to the infirmary, right upon arrival. One could see by their shaky movement that they, too, were on their last mile. Those who were dead on arrival were taken to the morgue directly, thrown on a cart, and taken down to the cellar for the dead. Later in the evening, a special van would bring more dead, or near dead, from the "Klinker." This place took its toll.

An inspection walk through the barracks for patients with dysentery presented, to those brave enough to come into this place of horror, a gruesome sight. There were always some patients who tried to get out of their bed in order to go to the toilet, by holding onto the nearest bedpost, door knob, wall, or whatever. Some made it, others collapsed to the floor, moved maybe a little, trying to get up again but couldn't make it—they, too, were dead a short time later.

One look into the ward for dysentery patients who were lying close together, five in a row on two bunk beds pushed close together, resembling some kind of drawers containing dying patients. It was an awful sight; they looked more dead than alive. These bunk beds stood three, sometimes four, on top filled with death candidates.

Hardly anybody could move, never mind get out of bed in order to go to the bathroom. Everything went into the bunks and leaked through to those underneath and so on. Oh, what a mess! It was nauseating. Continuously, the push-carts for the dead made their trips from here to the morgue. The sight was so gruesome that it never had been shown in a film.

Conditions were hardly any better where patients dying from disease were kept where the whole body was covered with sores and puss running out and all over the bunk beds and on the floor. It was a gruesome sight just to take a look into this barrack. Even paper bandages were no longer available, also no more cardboard rolls that used to be inside toilet paper rolls. Toilet paper had to be used as bandages.

The next place in line for dying on a grand scale was the barracks for TB patients. These three barracks that have just been mentioned, supplied the highest number of patients for the gas chamber. This was saving time by bringing them into the morgue which was located under the department for pathology, which was also getting more and more insufficient due to the ever-rising number of dead people.

The room for pathology and dismembering the bodies also gave a horrible picture of what took place here. The number of dead bodies that were brought here was always very high. What they tried to do with them was mainly salvaging the skeletons which were later sold by some S.S. men. In fact, this was one of their most profitable sources of income. Besides complete skeletons, the S.S. would also pick out some odd-formed skulls which they could sell for a much higher price to individuals or groups of curiosity seekers and not necessarily to scientific institutions. All these abnormally formed skulls and skeletons did not remain for sale for a long time but sold quickly and, therefore, in order to keep up with the demand, it happened from time to time that inmates with an odd or unusual shape were earmarked for extinction and ordered to come to the hospital for an "examination." This means they got an injection which very shortly afterward ended their misery in this world. They ended up in the morgue instead.

Here is one example: On January 24, 1942, a man with a deformed spine, whose name was Heinrich Kuhne, was taken to this concentration camp. On the death notice for March 8, 1942—already several weeks later—we noticed his name in it. According to his death certificate, he had died of pneumonia and malfunction of the circulatory system. His relatives had been informed that his body had been cremated. End of the story? No, not quite. In April, hardly 14 days later, the deformed skeleton of H. Kuhne was on exhibition in the glass case at the office of a doctor working in pathology. There was a small note on the inside of the window pane which read, "Born November 21, 1898, died March 8, 1942." While checking these dates with the death notices for March 8, as well as this identification paper, it became obvious that this was the spine of the former H. Kuhne.

From time to time, the employees in the political department would take a look through the files of identification cards belonging to inmates who had been marked with tattoos. Sometimes, inmates with extraordinary or strange-looking tattoos were ordered to go to the hospital and some unknown experts in the art of tattooing would take a good look at them. Inmates with especially weird-looking patterns had to stay in the hospital where they were given some kind of drug. A few days later, they complained of being sick whereupon they would receive some medication. Eventually, they would get an injection or they had to go for a special examination of their "sickness" in which case they were transferred to another concentration camp or to some unknown location. They never came back but reports came in that these inmates had been sold for their skin. After being put to death, their tattooed skins were treated like leather and used for lampshades, handbags, or something: just another way to end up.

The real purpose of a hospital is supposed to be a place where sick people are helped back to their health through medical treatment by the doctors as well as good care and adequate nutrition. However, in a concentration camp, the hospital station or infirmary was merely a transfer station for the dead or those on their way out. The S.S. was not in the least interested in getting these sick inmates back on their feet; they aimed to get rid of all the ailing ones and those who otherwise needed care or could become a burden.

As has been mentioned before, the "Klinker" was the most notorious supplier of murdered inmates who had been put out of their misery in many different ways. One can only give some examples since it would be impossible to print out all the names of inmates who had been killed here. From the beginning of July until August 18, 1942, 89 inmates had been put to death after being held captive, following an accusation of being gay. (Against penal code #175.)

And now some statistics: Take the date of January 31, 1940: number of inmates at a concentration camp, 12,187, of these 702 died during January. Among 2,935 who died between December 1939 and May 1940, there were 16% Jewish inmates. According to age levels, 1% are under 20 years of age; 11% between 20 and 30 years; 25% between 30 and 40 years; 27% between 40 and 50 years; 24% between 50 and 60 years; and 11% over 60. In May 1942, there were 96 Jewish inmates among the 256 people who died.

For medical experiments, Jewish inmates were taken, preferably. In Building R II (for internal diseases) there used to be eleven Jews, mostly teenagers, who were given different kinds of injections, more or less poisonous, in order to find out the results. Mostly every other day these boys would get an injection which was often very painful besides causing fever so the victims had to stay in bed after that. Until the capitalization, there were still some of these victims in the infirmary. They carried the registration numbers from about 70,000 and up.

Of those inmates who came with the March 1940 transport, 53 men died, some after being only a few days at the concentration camp. Most of the remaining inmates died during the next 14 days. The number of those who had been shot or who ended up at the gallows between August 1, 1940, and March 17, 1941, came to 58. Included in this number were 33 Polish prisoners who had been shot on September 11, 1940, at the command of the chief of the security police, also known as the "Heydrich-revenge-action." Those who had to die at the gallows were marched before along the mortuary of the hospital, while those who were to be shot were taken directly to the shooting stand in the industrial yard.

Two well-known criminals, brothers by the name of Sass, were taken around the concentration camp and then directly to the stand in order to be shot. Another well-known figure, politically, was Leo Sklarek. He was shot after the roll call on May 22, 1942. On October 20, 1942, 30 Ukrainian civilian workers were put to death because they were no longer able to work. They were just too weak to do anything. On the same day, a member of the Socialist party, Otto Schmidt, by name (13514) ended at the gallows after being kept in a dark cell for three years. His name had been mentioned in a previous chapter as a person who somehow could predict the future, such as a clairvoyant.

The number of inmates who died as a result of mistreatment was tremendous. Some of these victims committed suicide by hanging or by drowning in the channel around the "Klinker." There were quite a few who tried to reach the high-tension wires. If they did not die right away they would be killed by bullets from the guard tower. In one case an inmate killed himself in the S.S. garage with a bullet from a service revolver. That happened on February 11, 1942. Here the bullet went right through his head and then through the wooden wall into the adjoining barracks where it hit an S.S. man in the heart while he was sitting at his desk. Of course, he died, too.

The hospital had to serve two functions for the S.S.; it had to look presentable as such in front of visitors from the outside who made their rounds of inspections, and it had to serve as a place for the liquidation of inmates who were too ill and presumably no longer useful. Like it had been outlined before, the Barracks #1 and #2 had always been kept immaculately clean and in perfect order. Even the treatment of the patients who needed operations and care afterward was excellent thanks to the staff of male nurses and orderlies as well as the assistant physicians; many of whom were former inmates. Some of these were already very capable surgeons, specialists, and internists. Here I would like to mention the name of a Norwegian physician, Sven Oftedal, who had been in charge of the hospital block for months. He also helped out with medications purchased from Norway, just to be able to help his fellow inmates as best as he could. For the hospital section with TB patients there used to be a Dr. Jahn, a specialist from Holland in charge.

The other purpose of the hospital, however, was horrible. With more and more patients being taken in, many of whom were already victims of malnutrition, hunger, cold, and mistreatment, the quarters were by far not large enough to take care of all the patients. Therefore four barracks previously used as living quarters were converted into sick rooms because people staying here were already more or less on their way out. But soon afterward, another barracks was converted, too, into a place for sick people. Besides that, within the isolation block for the Russians, another section was converted to hold the sick people. So, at least, whenever some outside visitors were coming on an inspection tour, one could show them that even prisoners of war were being well taken care of. With a crew of 15,600 inmates on average during the months of September and until the middle of December 1942, there used to be around 1,000 sick cases a day in the hospital. Besides that, more sick inmates died. According to statistics, 1,229 passed away as the result of different diseases like dysentery, pneumonia, TB, infectious diseases, heart ailments, lung diseases, malnutrition, poisoning, suicides, and being shot while trying to escape

Here it may be said that the death certificates in most cases did not give the real cause of how death had occurred; and this had been done on purpose so it did not become evident that the dead inmate had been the victim of savage beatings, drowning, poisoning, and so on. Well, finally, one found a name for all these violent cases that ended in death. They were classified as a malfunction of the circulatory system. This was not unusual because it was the cause of death no matter what the circumstances. Anyway, this sounded so much better; after all, the surviving family members had to be notified when one of their relatives had passed away.

After several thousand invalids had been transferred from Sachsenhausen to larger extermination camps like Dachau, Gross-Rosen, and Auschwitz during the spring of 1942, the number of inmates kept at Sachsenhausen went down to 9,503 of whom one has to classify 329 as total invalids. Besides that, there was another group consisting of halfway invalids, sickly and old people, and those who could no longer perform some kind of work. During the years from 1940 until 1942, 395 inmates marked as "gay" died here under strange circumstances which means with some kind of outside help, of course. Added to this number, all the other "gays" who had their lives cut short while working at the "Klinker" the total figure of this particular group came to over 600. How many sick and disabled inmates were still left at Sachsenhausen at the time of the capitulation is hard to say; perhaps only a few since gay people were marked for extinction anyway.

At the time when Sachsenhausen was not yet the big human slaughterhouse with four crematories, the sickly and feeble and the half-dead ones who could hardly move were shipped to the extermination camps, as they used to be larger. According to an inspection during 1940, as many as 4,000 of these ailing inmates were transported to Dachau in exchange for 2600–3000 able-bodied workers who, unfortunately, sometime later and after being put to work at hard labor, eventually resembled those sickly ones they were supposed to replace.

For all those who died of malnutrition or more or less starvation, one could read in the death certificate the same stereotypical statement: *"The autopsy revealed that the deceased had been in a very poor physical condition. Despite ample doses of digitalis and other medications, the heartbeat went down constantly and death occurred at one o'clock or whatever."* In reality, it can be said that any kind of physical examination had hardly ever been made upon their arrival. Instead, the physician in charge, or his replacement, mostly an S.S. man serving as an orderly, would walk along the lined-up death candidates in rather fast-moving steps either through the infirmary or through the hallway leading to the barrack marked II, while hardly noticing the deplorable looking figures. Many of them were already lying on the floor or they just dropped down and stayed there.

The Russian POWs who came to Sachsenhausen in September 1941, were also in some kind of starving condition. According to their own statements, they had been chased into the woods which were sealed off with barbed wire fences. Since they did not get any kind of food, they tried to get along with plants, roots, and even the bark of trees. Many of them did not survive. It is hard to estimate how many died this way. More than half of the prisoners who came with a transport had already swollen body parts and faces, even the eyes seemed to be closed with puss running out. Anyway, it was an awful sight for the inmates at the concentration camp. Hardly any of these starved prisoners of war lived longer than two days. Not able to see, just like blind people, they fell over each other and down to the floor while still crying for help, but many of them died right away.

Another horrible picture dealing with death can also be seen here. In Barrack #7 in which during the first years the belongings of the inmates were kept, a break-in and entry took place, and the thief was presumably still inside. The S.S. finally found him in an air duct and fired several shots into it. After the duct was removed the critically wounded man crept out and stumbled along for some steps before a few more shots were fired into him and after that, the S.S. men threw him down from the roof to the ground. While being pulled along on the roadway, he died on his way to the infirmary. Meanwhile, other inmates on their way to the roll call where they had to be every so often, still could see some faint movement in the legs before his troubles were all over.

The very sick, including those with contagious diseases, were also pulled along the way and across the exercise place to the hospital. In case they died on the way, the corpses were dropped right then and there on the ground upon the command of S.S. men until the cart for the dead bodies would be brought in later to pick them up.

Dying people were being treated the same way as dying animals which were taken to the dumping ground. Any deathly sick person who arrived at the registration office but whose end seemed to be near was put together with patients in the barrack for contagious diseases. This is the reason the number of dying cases was so high. New poisons have been tried out for their effectiveness on TB patients, mostly Russians and other POWs from the Balkan states. The victims had to wait in the ambulance named R I and were then taken to the sanitation station in R II one by one, even some patients infected with syphilis were among them, as we understand.

In R II, a S.S. man, Ullman, was in charge of what went on together with a former criminal by the name of Thierhoff; both of whom were ready and eager to use the poison-containing injection needles. The victim would just shake a little, turn his eyes around and that was the end: instant death. The cart to pick up the dead bodies was already standing at the door to take the victims to the morgue in the cellar. Between the room where the poison murders took place and the morgue was a walkway. It took about 5 minutes each way to walk back and forth. Well-equipped with poisons and needles, these murderers went from barrack to barrack, often for days, to pick up their victims for experimentation. Whenever the sick and ailing patients became aware of these killers and saw them walking around with the poisoned needles, they tried to escape in time, even those who were hardly able to stand on their legs. This flight could mean the difference between a crummy life and a certain death.

Here is a statistic to show how many sick inmates were among the total number of inmates at the concentration camp. There seemed to be between 100 and 1500 sick cases daily. On February 22, 1942, the number came to 1250; on April 17, 1942, there were only 889 sick cases left. The total number of inmates on this particular day was 9034 of whom 2118 men were stationed outside the camp's territory. The difference, that is 6916, were still inside the concentration camp but some 1285 were in the infirmary. But then on March 18, 1943, the number of sick cases went up to around 1500. Besides that, there were quite a few outside patients who had to be placed in barracks originally planned for living quarters since there was not enough room in the infirmary and the hospital barracks. During the typhoid epidemic in 1941–42, 51 of the 200 Russian POWs died of typhoid fever and also of spotted fever.

Due to overcrowded and unsanitary conditions, many patients were infected with lice. According to statistics, there were 1628 cases where inmates were covered with lice and 1384 others infected with some other kind of vermin. This happened in January 1941. A year later, in 1942, it was much worse: 3461 cases in January; 2410 in February; and 7355 in August, but then in October, it went down to 5888. New infections went from about 50 to over 500 in a short time. These were for scabs. Here the number of infections went up and down. It was very difficult to keep track of. But, it can be mentioned that of the Russian laborers who had been taken into this camp, about 90% were full of lice and other vermin. Afraid of being contaminated themselves, the camp's commandant had this section of the concentration camp exterminated with a new kind of chemical called "Kupres" at a total expense of some 75,000 RM. This came to about 4.80 RM per liter.

Medical treatment for female inmates, who came from the surrounding camps like, for instance, Oranienburg and Auer during the last years, also took place in the infirmary because there were no facilities available elsewhere. These patients presented about the same picture as their male counterparts: faded worn-out dresses, barefooted in wooden sandals, many of them helped along by some nurse's aides. This way they came along the place for the roll call toward the hospital. Many of them looked already more dead than alive.

Those who could not walk anymore were put on a cart with two wheels, no cushions or blankets in it, of course. Then some other female inmates who were still able to walk and had only minor problems, like having their eyes examined or their ears or who needed another dressing, or who may have to go to a dentist, well, these women had to be the caretakers who pushed the carts to the infirmary.

It didn't matter how the weather was. These transports came in storm or rain or during the winter with no blankets or any kind of covering provided as protection against the elements. Soaking wet and shivering from the cold, these sick women, many of them already feverish, arrived at the hospital. The fact that quite a few of these patients were dead on arrival may also be mentioned. Just to think that cases with pneumonia and high fever were being transported in open push-carts without covers, dressed only in thin and worn-out clothing at temperatures that could go to -10°F or even more. No wonder many of them died while being transported. But that's the way the camp's commandant wanted it.

The constantly overcrowded hospital facilities made it necessary for the patients to move back into their cellblocks long before their recovery. And so one could see these pitiful figures who looked more like skeletons trying to walk along while holding onto the walls with some ill-fitting and torn clothing. With quite some effort, they tried to move forward. If they couldn't make it they collapsed wherever they were, even if they were supposed to be on their way to recovery. Far from it! In fact, several patients died this way. It didn't make much difference which concentration camp they died in, death came in many different ways. All told, one would see people from the concentration camps dying in all kinds of positions or situations which looked so much more real than the famous painting exhibiting the infamous *Dance of Death* which one could see in city museums like Strasbourg, Bonn, Constance, Lucerne, Dresden, Luebeck, Basel, Freiburg, and others.

CHAPTER 22

CHAOS

"In case the German people should perish under these circumstances, I shall waste no tears; they deserve the fate that is coming to them."

Hitler, Christmas 1944,
foreseeing the doomsday that lay ahead.

Day and night one could hear the sirens, signaling death and destruction. Even the inmates of the concentration camp understood the warning sirens which could be heard from Oranienburg and places even farther away. We could see the bombers, dozens of them, flying overhead, destination: Berlin to unload their deadly cargo over the city. One could see in the sky the fireballs coming down, followed by explosions on the ground, causing heavy casualties.

Protection against air assaults went into effect at the concentration camp at once with the inmates handling the necessary machinery. There was no special excitement. What else could happen to them, to these people who were constantly threatened by deadly incidents, caused by the S.S. criminals? In fact, the inmates were not as much afraid of these air raids as were the camp's high commanding officers. These "brave" officers in charge, who never seemed to get enough protection, always were worrying because these bombs could miss their targets and land here instead. They fled with their girlfriends or mistresses into safer territory within the inmate's compound, wherever there were some kind of fortification.

Why? These concentration camps were not considered enemy

territory by the Allies and were not supposed to be bombed, since they housed victims of many countries and nations, imprisoned by the S.S. criminals. In fact, the inmates were protected by the Allies and, therefore, not to be bombed. There were some reconnaissance planes that would fly ahead, dropping some flares near the camp's surroundings so that the bombers could see the camp's triangle, to avoid dropping their deadly cargo on it.

With the worsening of the general conditions, due to the war, the uneasiness among the camp's commanding officers and S.S. troops became more widespread. It seemed as if even the Nazis in charge at camp lost their confidence in the daily broadcasts by Goebbels, who assured them every night that the final victory was close at hand, due to the newest and most dependable weapons at their command. Of course, while having a conversation with the inmates, they tried their best to convince them that Germany would win the war in no time flat.

The conditions at camp changed drastically, as the Nazis used to say, when during the evening broadcast of June 6, 1944—more or less on the sidelines—an announcement was made that sounded rather important, and according to which the Allied forces had landed at the Seine estuary. Well, they would say over the radio, this was only a small part they got ahold of, the Atlantic was so big, impossible for big armies to come across and their "Führer" would soon put an end to this kind of nonsense. But for us being in so-called protective custody and who, anyhow, took every bit of news on the radio with a grain of salt, we recognized the news about of what was supposed to be the successes of Hitler's war. In fact, we were more and more sure that the tide had turned and that the day that would bring us freedom may not be too far away. From now on, one had to be patient and keep their eyes and ears open.

The German, as well as the foreign, prisoners were from now on following the news with more interest than before. They were also wondering how long Hitler's armies could hold out. Like a bombshell, we heard the news on July 20, 1944, concerning the assassination attempt against Hitler that failed, unfortunately. What is going to happen to the camp's inmates, especially the political ones whom the Nazis liked to get rid of anyhow? Could this mean another blood bath? Every one of us was very tense, very anxious to figure out what might happen now. Could there be another massacre? By all means, we had to count on being taken out of our beds during one of the next nights and being marched to the industrial yard, to be shot, at least a part of the politicals, Germans as well as foreign ones.

So far nothing happened. However, more action took place within the country surrounding the camp, a "thunderstorm" as we used to call it. For instance, more older people were being taken prisoner and brought into this camp and, as we found out, members of the Socialist and Communist parties, some of them people in important positions. It happened that among others, the former president of Silesia, Hermann Lüdemann, arrived here but, unfortunately, in such a deplorable physical shape that we had to fear he would never survive this ordeal. For many years he had been transferred from one concentration camp or jail to another, and here I had to meet him as a human wreck. Karl Vollmerhaus from the workmen's organization came with him to me. Like with all political friends he, too, was being taken care of in the best possible way so that by the time of the evacuation he would be able to leave this place together with us, too.

Meanwhile, the latest political newcomers, called "thunderstorm" people were considered by the Nazis as being somehow or somewhere connected with the assassination attempt on Hitler. They filled the concentration camps to the seams, so to speak. Not only members of left-wing parties were thrown into this camp, members of all other parties as well as those without any specific political background were taken into custody. The reason was that they may have remarked, according to which they seemed to feel sorry, that the attempt against Hitler didn't turn out the way it was supposed to.

But not only had the concentration camp buildings become more and more crowded with prisoners after July 20, 1944, even the industry buildings were filling up. Here people were taken into custody day and night, sometimes hundreds of them. In fact, anybody who was under suspicion to know something of the assassination attempt or who might have made a remark of approval for the assassins was arrested. These were very busy days for the S.S. criminals; by the hundreds, these unlucky and innocent people were shot without having their names registered beforehand. The chimneys of the crematories produced a lot of black smoke those days, around the clock, while consuming the bodies of the murdered victims.

The concentration camp, which was already so overcrowded for a long time got even more inmates through the continuous input of new arrivals. In the barracks, four cots had to stand on each other and each of these was occupied by two men. Even the day rooms and working quarters had to serve as sleeping quarters. Alongside the overcrowding, the available food rations had to be stretched to meet the demand.

Soups made from carrots, cabbage, or turnips that were already low in calories, had to be diluted with so much more water; bread rations, too, had to be decreased, same with oleo, marmalade, sausage, and cheese. The general standard of living went downhill fast as did the health of the inmates. Kidney diseases and swollen limbs became more and more commonplace, as well as other signs of malnutrition.

The people in cities like, for instance, Berlin, also got less food and other necessities and, therefore, it didn't take long until more thefts and robberies took place. Maybe nothing unusual, but people plagued with hunger for a long time may get desperate enough to steal whatever they could get hold of or get involved in crimes they would never have thought of under normal circumstances. The police force was powerless, after all, the odds were against them; they had enough worries themselves. So why arrest and fight the hungry mob? They were hungry enough themselves. Soon so-called special actions took place which meant large-scale arrests of those individuals who were fighting the regime that caused the lack of food and other necessities.

Columns of hungry people were driven into this camp, mostly younger men, some hardly out of school. They came in rags and poor physical condition, but they were called "terrorists" just the same.

Marked with a black cross on their foreheads, they were herded into the already overcrowded isolation barracks, just like animals. There was hardly any standing room left, never mind room for sitting or even sleeping. Anyone who could not fit inside anymore had to stay outside, but not for long. The S.S. came and took them in groups of fifty to the human slaughterhouse where they found a quick end to their miseries by inhaling poison gas. Sometimes these "terrorists" didn't even stay in Sachsenhausen for one hour, because as soon as the gas chambers had been emptied of the previous victims, new ones were taken inside. For weeks, this mass slaughter of desperate and hungry young men took place which was described to the outside world as an "action against terrorists." Only a few of us had some ways and means of finding out what was really going on.

The clothes for the inmates were in bad shape and getting worse. Sometimes for weeks, they would not get any clean underwear because none was available. Infestation with vermin was rampant; lice were abundant in record numbers. Garbage pails and thrown-out waste materials were searched by a growing number of hungry inmates. Consumption of spoiled food caused more illness and even death among the inmates. Nothing was done by the camp's supervisor or people in charge to alleviate these conditions or to bring in more food. However, in contrast to this, at the headquarters of the Nazi leaders, there was plenty of food and drink; they could indulge themselves in plenty of delicacies including wines and liqueurs, besides the company of women.

As we have seen, inmates did not only succumb to hunger and cold but also to poison gas, the noose, bullets, or the result of torture. Within the compound, but separated from the buildings by barbed wire, the construction of a stand of machine guns and flame throwers took place, which were operated mostly by S.S. troops who could talk foreign languages, in this case preferably Romanian. One could get the impression that one of these days, this whole concentration camp complex might be taken over by enemy troops and liquidated.

Among the political inmates, the general belief was that this could mean the S.S., themselves, were going to bomb the whole place and, afterward, make-believe through radio and the press that Allied bombers had committed this mass murder. Nothing happened but just the same a feeling of uncertainty and unrest persisted among the inmates. "What is going to happen to us? Are we coming out alive?" These were the general thoughts. Despite all this, we were not desperate. Wait and see what happens; the inmates had the willpower to fight for themselves at any given opportunity. They certainly didn't want to die for nothing but rather put on a defense instead.

It was not too difficult to rip the electric wire to pieces with some chunks of wood thrown repeatedly against it and after that to push a hole through the fence along the concentration camp. The guards in the towers could be smoked out of their headquarters with some ignited straw mattresses. Besides that, we had access to some burnable material as well as corrosive chemicals. All these items had been taken from the industrial section long beforehand.

Hunger became more widespread. Besides the grown-ups, one could also see some little children, maybe between 3 and 5 years of age, running around asking the inmates for some food. Out of their meager rations, they would give some bread or whatever to the little ones. Clothing for women and children was in very poor condition and there was hardly anything useable left in the clothes department that would fit anybody. During the winter months, many of these youngsters froze to death which left the officers in command quite unconcerned.

It was close to Christmas, 1944. The inmates kept wondering if they would maybe see freedom again before the holidays. No, this was only wishful thinking. They were not let free, even though the Allied forces were closing in on the German Army, which sustained losses in catastrophic proportions. With great interest, the inmates would keep track of the positions of the Allies on the war maps, in the west as well as in the east. They made great progress and according to the inmate's point of view, it was good news; one could see smiles on their faces.

The Russian front which had come to a standstill for some time made new advances. The Nazi press remained cheerful and tried to console the people that the German reserve forces would soon push the Russians back again. Nothing could go wrong because in East Prussia, the National Guard, consisting of men between teenagers and the real old, had dig ditches along the borders for the Russian tanks to drop in and sink. Leadership of this regiment was in the hands of men holding garden tools and many of these men were professors of the University of Konigsberg. After all, what could go wrong?

Then in January 1945, the Russians broke through towards the west with some forces and through the German lines, hereby surrounding whole sections of the army. Then we heard rumors that, due to the advancing Russian troops, the so-called enemy of the country itself, in this case, Russian POWs and political prisoners, mainly the prominent ones among them, had to be eliminated and, if possible, in large numbers. Anxiety increased daily among the inmates.

A new bulletin and order was introduced. Every invalid inmate as well as all others who were unable to march long distances, had to be registered in order to be transported by train the next day, to one of the larger concentration camps in the west where the general care was supposed to be "excellent" or so we heard. The name of this concentration camp was not mentioned. Inmates who took care of the clothes bins had to pack whatever was left together for the trip, load them on the train, and finally, they too, had to get on the train. However, this way they found out that the destination of this train was Belsen-Bergen, near Celle in the province of Hanover. Nobody knew this camp, but blockleaders of the S.S. got orders from above to describe the conditions over there as "very good." The trip was supposed to take between 2 and 3 days. Everyone would get some bread with margarine, cold cuts to eat on the way, and a little container as well as two woolen blankets. All this sounded really good.

But the old guys here at camp knew only too well what was behind all this and that all those who were supposed to be taken by train would, in all possibility, meet the same fate as the victims before them when they were being taken to the so-called "health resorts" but, instead, ended their lives in the gas chambers. More than 21,000 made the trip to Belsen-Bergen, among them also some people who had been advised beforehand to avoid this kind of transportation, if humanly possible. They just could not believe that they would meet the same horrible fate at Belsen-Bergen.

Professor Johs Verweyen from Bonn, a language teacher, thought he might be useful and be of service and, therefore, went along on one of these transports. Unfortunately, he, too, was killed. But then by force, some of our best comrades were carted off to Belsen. One of them was the Norwegian Carsten Ösebö and Klemens Högg from Augsburg, both politicals. Outside of these people, quite a few of our best comrades were forced into these deadly journeys.

Other transports went to Mauthausen and Flossenburg. One had to make room in these overfilled concentration camps because more and more inmates from concentration camps in the east were transported to this camp and these men were really in a very deplorable condition. Thousands of them may have died already from hunger or the bitter cold and it is possible some of their bodies were eaten by hungry wolves, which followed their tracks.

One transport arrived from Hungary had 1800 men to start. But they had to march about 800 km through snow and ice, many of them with hardly any footwear. Less than 200 arrived at Sachsenhausen. No wonder they arrived in a terrible condition; one can easily understand. For over two months, they had been on their feet, always driven forward like cattle by the S.S. bullies who would push anyone down on the ground who could no longer walk. And of those who finally did arrive at Sachsenhausen, only very few could be kept alive; they just died like flies. Many had to have their hands and feet amputated and for the dead, autopsies revealed, in most cases, death through starvation and the bitter cold. They arrived too late in order to get some warm food or soup at this camp. Those who made it halfway alive were too weak to eat. These were really terrible conditions. It was a gruesome sight, these dying people. The first of February 1945, came to an end. Outside the usual alarm that was sounded at 11 p.m., nothing had happened. But then, after midnight, the sleeping inmates were awakened by the screams and voices of commanding officers in charge, and shots were fired outside. The murderous crew among the S.S. was already picking out some victims they had earmarked on a special list for one reason or another and pulled or kicked these sleeping inmates from their cots and outside to the roll call. However, these victims could see that their lives were in danger and some of them tried to flee or put up resistance. Too late. The S.S. bullets cut them down. Like cattle being driven to the slaughterhouse, so were these inmates kicked forward towards the industrial section where, again, some tried to escape before being gunned down.

At dawn the block elder came to the barracks they were in charge of to find out who was missing. 178 of our best comrades were lost—dead—which was recorded as no longer belonging to the camp's labor force; the S.S. had murdered these defenseless victims in cold blood. The chimneys of the crematories gave evidence of another busy day by belching a lot of black smoke; it was the end of our good comrades. The worst hit of all was the penal section where more than 30 victims were captured and killed, most of these were foreigners like men from Luxembourg, France, Poland, and Russia, and of these, quite a few happened to be in the ranks of officers. Here are the names of some of the victims from Luxembourg: Jacques Pixius, a police officer, Nicolas Schaack, Francois Spautz, Ferdinand Nepper, Jean Boever, Mich, Marc Bormann, Jean Gaasch, Marcel Brimeyer, Jean-Marc Herschbach, Norbert Kaues, Anton Robert Lamboray, Jean Ney, Victor Reuland, Emile Reding, Math Pierre Reisen, Nic. Ed. Schmitz, Antoine Schleich, Camille Schaeler, and Paul Weidert.

Of these men from Luxembourg, three very brave ones besides their leader, Victor Reuland, were able to take the guns away from the S.S. and even shoot at them. Unfortunately, they were overpowered in the end. Then some members of the British Marines put up some resistance while being taken to the gas chambers. Two of them were shot out in the yard while a third one escaped through a window of a workshop, where he was gunned down by some S.S. Some comrades who were on the night shift, among them Wilhelm Thomsen from Flensburg (40317), gave us a report in the morning about this night of terror. Besides that, the pools of blood and dug-out floors gave evidence enough of what had gone on there.

Of those seven members of the British Marines, only Sergeant Alfred Roy stayed alive because he went on sick leave just in time. But all the others, five British POWs and their commander, Goodwin, were killed. They belonged to a speedboat crew that ran aground against a rock in the Norwegian fjord. On their flight, they were caught in Esbjerg (Denmark) by the Nazis and taken to Sachsenhausen, despite the protest of their commanding officer, who argued that they were protected by the laws of the Geneva Convention. Their protest that they were POWs and, therefore, belonged in a special facility for these people was answered by the camp leader, Kolb, who referred them to his helper in charge of the penal station. The order to "Jacob" was to treat the British as cruel and as inhumane as possible. Jacob was known for his miserable treatments.

The ringleaders of this gruesome night, February 1 through February 2, were S.S. men Höhn, Rehn, Böhm, and Hempel. In the morning of February 2, one could still see them walking around in their blood-stained uniforms. Now they were entitled to a "day off" which they celebrated by eating and, mainly, drinking in the commandant's headquarters, hereby bragging about their heroic deeds during the last night.

The next day appeared to be calm. One would, however, take this merely as the quiet before the storm. When is the next action due? How long will it take until the next group of men will be taken from their cots during the night to be murdered? Evidently, this was it. It seemed that the foreign broadcast had spread some special news already because even during the 2nd of February, the secret transmitter belonging to one of the inmates, gave an account of the terrible things that went on to the next one outside the walls from which these news were transferred to the nearest foreign transmitter. And so it did not take long until the Nazi leaders in their quarters heard all this bad news too, as well as every S.S. man who listened to the radio. They tried their best to find out how these reports about the recent mass murders could have leaked out, despite all the precautions that had been taken. They thought that perhaps someone among their men had committed treason. They tried to turn the stations, but neither the sender nor the crew working there could be at fault. Nobody came upon the idea that one or more of the inmates had their own receiver and transmitter.

Soon after this news came in that the Norwegians and Danes—about 2400 inmates—were supposed to be picked up by cars from the Swedish Red Cross. We were somewhat concerned because good news like this may have an ugly background. But not this time. It was for real. One morning about ten Red Cross cars complete with a Swedish crew arrived at Sachsenhausen. It was under the leadership of Count Folke Bernadotte, the president of the Swedish Red Cross. They picked up their Scandinavian comrades on the street right in front of the entrance to the concentration camp, after they had been given a warm meal, before going on the trip. One saw these cars drive away with some mixed feelings. In one way, we were glad to see these comrades leave the hell of Sachsenhausen behind; on the other hand, we missed them. It happened to be just these comrades who helped the hungry ones among all the others with food packages received through the Red Cross. Maybe hundreds, or even thousands, among them owed their survival or even their lives, to these Scandinavian comrades. This was something no one could ever forget. After the last cars drove away in a northerly direction, everything seemed to be calm again. However, a time of rest and relaxation did not exist here at camp; the uncertainty among the political prisoners could always be felt. Everyone lived in fear that something could happen to him, the question was, when and what. One had the feeling that any of us could be picked up at random to be deposed of by one method or another. Then our names would appear once more on the ever-growing list of former comrades, saying: "No longer an inmate at S.H."

The selection of inmates marked for the gas chamber continued almost daily, even though it was not noticed by most people at this concentration camp. But the evidence was there. One could see the big clouds of black smoke rising from the crematory chimneys, not to mention the stench in the air, which took place for hours and one knew that the mass murders continued without noticeable interruption. On the other hand, no special precaution was taken while enemy aircraft flew overhead, sometimes twice a day. By now, the inmates were used to it and hardly took any notice. They were sure that the Allied flyers would never intentionally drop their bombs on a concentration camp's ground.

However, some changes took place. One didn't have much confidence in the S.S. anymore, or their leadership. One was under the impression that they would rather try to get away on time instead of defending the concentration camp. If Allied troops would take over Sachsenhausen, the inmates themselves would have to deal with them. And so a new kind of formation took place, a police force consisting only of inmates. Of course, these people had to be selected. Under no circumstances could an inmate with a criminal record be chosen. Everyone had to be a volunteer and had to be from the political section. About 500 men were taken and transferred to Barracks #1 and 2, near the place for the roll call. Many of these men had been soldiers before, like in World War I, and some were from the foreign legion, some had been hunters, but they had to be reliable and know how to handle a rifle. Even some uniforms were somehow found, but there were no weapons and ammunition. But, they finally got that too. As the leader of the inmate police force, an old political inmate was picked out; his name was Arthur V. Lankisch-Hoernitz, a former officer in World War I, and an able and reliable comrade. I, myself, got a job in the office as his assistant or representative.

Among the S.S. guards, one could see new faces almost daily. According to rumors, many of the former guards who had criminal records, like being cruel and inhumane towards the inmates, had been transferred to other concentration camps—for safety's sake—where nobody knew them. After all, one could well imagine the hatred the inmates held for their former tormentors and that they might be waiting for an opportunity to get revenge. This could be an opportunity in case a turnover could take place. The Allied forces were already coming closer and closer. Of course, somebody like the camp leader, Kolb, who had been one of the meanest supervisors, had the nerve to tell the inmates that they, the Nazis, were still in command, hereby stressing the word "still." However, one could hear already the uncertainty in his voice, which was due to the devastating conditions of the military situation, in general, as far as the Nazis were concerned. Under no circumstances would the Nazi leadership admit the poor outlook of which we, the inmates, were very well aware of. No, not at all; instead, they kept on shouting, "*Today Germany belongs to us, tomorrow the whole world.*" On the other hand, we were quite sure that the slogan would soon be, that is from the Allied point of view, "*Tomorrow Germany, and after that, the whole world belongs to us!*"

Eventually, according to the latest news, we found out that a big part of the Nazi leadership had been drafted to the front lines. We even heard the names announced of the S.S. leaders who had been killed while on duty. The reaction was an honest confession with remarks like, "Thank goodness he, or even they, are dead and out of our way." More and more S.S. guards were taken to the front: gun fodder which was very much in demand. After no more S.S. men could be spared, new policies at camp went into effect. The camp's commandant was looking for volunteers who might join the army, but nobody was ready to be gun fodder at the front lines. Therefore, a draft became mandatory. First in line were the criminals among the inmates, followed by the so-called unsociables. Next, came the Gypsies and, after that, the big game hunters, of which there were quite a few at camp. Austria had a lot of game hunters among their inmates and they would talk about the game they used to shoot which also made a delicious meal. Added to these outdoor men were inmates who used to like going fishing. The fact that these men might have never seen a rifle didn't matter. They were programmed and trained to handle a gun, thus emphasizing that the "final victory was close at hand."

The demand for soldiers who had to save the Hitler state, already lying in agony, became bigger and bigger. Finally, other inmates among them, also politicals, were forced into military service, which meant those people who regarded it as their highest duty to fight the Nazi system, now had to fight against the Allies, their liberators. However, with the entry of the politicals into the Nazi Army, the Germans had no satisfaction, because until they would have been trained well enough for combat duty, there might not have been a fighting front left.

The camp's commanding officers still tried to appear unworried and undisturbed; however, one could never trust them. Years of experience had shown us that they were more or less like Jekyll-Hyde characters. There was enough reason to mistrust them because some positions formerly held by political inmates were now handed over to regular criminals and so-called antisocials, who were still among the inmates. And so, a criminal with the name of "Flegel"—the German word for being "rude" got an important position. Another crook by the name of Maschke had to watch out for air raids. He also was a yes-man for the camp's officers in charge. The position of caretaker for the block was handed over to an outcast, named Kuhnke, who had nothing better to do than to denounce the prominent men among the politicals, thereby falling back into his old habit of helping himself to the food supply and also taking some of the inmate's belongings. But, after some time, the Nazis, too, got sick and tired of him as he was involved in a scandal in which even the Master Race was shortchanged. It didn't take long until Kuhnke was transferred to another concentration camp.

His successor was another criminal—Kurt Beyer—the last blockleader in Sachsenhausen. He had the same game as the one before him who also was caught stealing and taken to the penal station where his former colleagues made it clear to him what self-justice was. He got a beating so bad that, afterward, he could hardly be recognized. There was no mercy this time. This was supposed to be a warning for many of his kind but, unfortunately, not for too long; after all, a criminal remains a criminal. Back to Kurt Beyer who happened to be the last caretaker of the blocks. While in office, he replaced the reliable politicals with his own kind, the common criminals, to serve under him which, of course, caused quite some uproar among the politicals. The Nazi leaders could care less. This way they didn't have to take revenge against the politicals. Eventually, this troublemaker ran out of luck. It was easier to teach him a lesson than the S.S. At no time did the word sabotage have such an important meaning than at this crucial moment when there was a chance to strike against the common enemy. The resistance was broken. Beyer showed a low profile because he, too, noticed the gunfire in the not-too-far distance coming closer and closer, especially during the night. The Russians were on their way towards Sachsenhausen and this gave Beyer something to think about. He became very passive.

The Allied Air Force was very busy dropping leaflets with news bulletins which were also dropped on camp grounds. Although it was forbidden under strict penalty—even death in repeated cases—to pick up these informative papers, some inmates, mostly politicals, collected all they could get hold of. The fact that in Yalta on the Crimean Peninsula, the political leaders of the United States, Great Britain, and Soviet Russia had an important conference was great news for the inmates. Of course, it was a guess about what kind of resolutions were in the making.

Then, one day in March 1945, a somewhat colorful piece of paper landed on the roof of a barracks belonging to the hospital and then dropped to the ground. I picked up this piece, thinking this could be an advertisement of some sort, and decided to take a look. I was very much surprised that this was real news. This was a very important piece of information when I saw the headlines which read: Declaration made by the leaders of the three Allied nations: United States, Great Britain, and Soviet Russia (Fig. 16).

Fig. 16. Three powers flags. Label of the declaration made by the leaders of the three Allied nations: United States, Great Britain, and Soviet Russia.

The contents were as follows: "During the first half of February, a conference of the three leading powers took place on the Crimean Peninsula which lasted for eight days, consisting of Prime Minister Churchill of Great Britain, President Roosevelt of the United States, and Premier Stalin of the Soviet Union, besides their foreign ministers and advisors."

The results are as follows:

1. *"We, the three powers, have agreed to work at the destruction of the common enemy. Conferences between our staff members have been held daily. The deliberations have been very successful in every way and have led to closer coordination of the military efforts of the three Allies than it ever has been. Exchange of very important information took place. The arranged schedule, and the extent of the coordination for newer and more powerful weapons that our combined armies and the air force are going to use from the east, the west as well as the south, and the north against the heart of Germany had been fully discussed and agreed upon. The very close operation of our three Allies which had been established during the conference will lead to a quicker end of the war. Nazi Germany is doomed. If the German people should try to continue their hopeless resistance they will have to pay for their defeat ever harder."*

2. Concerning the war aims of the Allies: "Our definite goal is the destruction of German militarism and the Nazi system, as well as having the guarantee that Germany will never be in a position again to disturb the peace of the whole world. We are determined to disarm and dissolve all German forces and to destroy once and for all the German general staff which continuously contributed to a repeated rise of militarism and we also want to confiscate or destroy all German military equipment as well as the whole German war industry or at least have it under control. All war criminals are going to be tried and punished as quickly as possible and the German people are going to be held responsible for all the damage they have caused. They will also have to make restitution. The Nazi party, the Nazi laws, their organizations, and institutions will have to be liquidated, any influence by the Nazis or their military or their bureaucracy has to be eradicated, and places of culture, commerce, and industry of the German people have to be eliminated. Together, the Allies will take measures in dealing with Germany until the following peace and security for the whole world has been secured."

"Our conference on the Crimean Peninsula has confirmed our determination to keep and enforce our goals and actions which during this war has made the victory for the United Nations possible and undisputable. Only with continuing and increasing collaboration and mutual understanding among our three countries and among all peace-loving people can the greatest struggle of mankind become a reality and a steady and lasting peace with the guarantee that all people in every country can spend their lives free of fear and want."

3. Concern for the German people.

> "The destruction of the German people is not one of our goals. Only after the Nazi system and its militarism have been eliminated will there be some hope for the German people to lead a life of dignity and a chance to find a place to live among the other nations. The conference on the Crimean Peninsula which was held by the leaders of the three great powers destroyed the last hope for the Nazi system to cause a split among the Allies. There is no way out for the Nazi war criminals. Nazi Germany is doomed. The Crimean Conference is showing the German people the only way out: Break away from the doomed criminal Hitler block and work for an end to the hopeless continuation of a lost war. German officers and soldiers: put up resistance, capitulate, or go into captivity. Any other way is only leading to your destruction."

Only a few of my comrades found out about this pamphlet. But those few of us knew by now that the end of the Nazi terror was coming closer by leaps and bounds. We followed the news bulletins with close attention; we heard that the military situation for the Nazis was getting worse and more hopeless by the hour. Maybe it would take only a few more days until the Russians from the east and the British and American forces from the west would unite and divide Germany into a northern and a southern part. Even Hitler saw these developments and ordered that a capital city be selected for each part of Germany. For the south the city of Villach was taken and for the north, Flensburg.

It was springtime again. But, oh, how many springtimes had we already spent in this concentration camp, always hoping that one of them would bring us freedom from the Nazi terror and a place in the sun away from the barbed wires and grey prison walls. How close were we? Would we be able to get out in time or could it be that our lives might be lost just in the nick of time? Spring was here all right, and the ever-rising sun gave us hope that our dreams might be fulfilled. Hardly anywhere else has the desire for a German defeat been so great as here in the concentration camp, especially during this time, which seemed to promise an end to all our miseries.

However, with the approach of warmer days ahead, a new enemy became evident, the danger of diseases and epidemics. During the last bombings, the sewer system at Oranienburg had been damaged which also collected the waste water from the concentration camp complex. The pipelines for fresh water were also hardly working at all. Due to the overpopulation at camp, the danger of pestilence became real. All water toilets had to be closed at once and ditches had to be dug behind the barracks for latrines. From then on a terrible stench was in the air to make life miserable in a different way.

Group leaders from the political inmates went to the camp's commanding officer, explaining the danger of contamination, not only to everyone at this camp, but also to the people of the surrounding villages, including Oranienburg. Right away, because the S.S. were afraid and worried about their own health, chemicals like calcium chloride were brought in for disinfection. The three-foot-deep ditches were filled with human waste in no time and had to be covered up as fast as possible. New ditches were made all around the barracks, which became a real menace to the health of the camp's population and got worse day by day. It could also happen that during the dark hours, some inmates on their way home, often times older ones who either could not see too well or were not-too-strong on their feet, would stumble and fall into these ditches from which they had to be rescued and, afterward, sprayed off with a water hose. There have been cases where some of the not so strong and able-bodied inmates fell unnoticed into these cesspools and were unable to get out by themselves, and died in this terrible manner. And, finally, they were not even noticed anymore; even the bodies stayed where they were until they were covered with some dirt. What does a human life mean at Sachsenhausen? And a dead one? Even less.

April 10, 1945, happened to be a rather sunny day. As early as 10 in the morning, the sirens went off over the camp and Oranienburg.

Like swarms of insects, bomber squadrons were flying from the west and northwest and above the camp. One could see that they meant business and that some mass bombing was in progress. From far away, one could hear the explosions, followed by columns of smoke and fire, indicating that mass destruction of human lives and property had just taken place.

Some of the bombs dropped nearby and set fire to a part of the industrial section and, soon after, the shoe factory went up in flames. Here at camp, it looked as if a panic would break out but it was finally calmed down through the disciplinary action of the political inmates. It seemed as if Sachsenhausen was selected for destruction. Luckily, no inmates lost their lives. It also became evident that the bombs that were dropped nearby were harmless ones. After a few hours, everything was quiet again. There was the usual alarm in the evening, but no more bombs were being dropped on Sachsenhausen.

During the following days, the nervous tension among the commanding officers and the S.S. increased noticeably. It gave the impression as if the S.S. was possibly ready to quit, because they were afraid of the Russian troops stationed not-too-far from the camp's complex. From that moment on, the Nazi blockleaders could be seen moving casually among the inmates as if they were one of them, asking for cigarettes and even discussing the latest developments. They didn't mention anymore that they were so sure of a final victory.

The evening news broadcast on the loudspeakers from the exercise plaza indicated that the general military situation during the last few days had gone from bad to worse. After the usual army bulletin, a new kind of attraction had been put into effect, the so-called "werewolf," obviously put together in order to confuse the public. In scrambled words, one could hear something like, "Caesar 6 over 11 north" and other similar unintelligible words.

After darkness had set in, the ladies from the red light district would show up at the exercise plaza; Henny, Gretchen, Margret, or whoever their names were, would be walking arm in arm with some inmates between the barracks. Compulsory prostitution no longer existed. Camp leader Höhn happened to be among this kind of congregation one evening when suddenly he was pushed around by one of the inmates. However, he did not put up any resistance or complaint. Before long, this inmate would have been arrested and possibly taken to a bunker. The will and enthusiasm to work decreased perceptibly; in fact, it didn't even seem to matter if only half of the labor force marched toward their place of employment. There was less restriction all over from day to day. Now the date was April 20, 1945, Adolf Hitler's birthday. What was going to happen? One could hardly think of dismissal for some inmates of whom we had not heard anymore except those unfortunate one who still went up in smoke through the chimneys of the crematories. But still, we had the feeling as if something unusual was going to happen.

Some kind of bombing action, even if not here at camp, could be expected. Certainly, the Allies would give us some kind of ovation in the form of glowing metal fragments, bouquets of fire flowers in extra big numbers, the way they used to display it on his birthday during the last few years. Sure enough, one didn't have to wait too long. At 11 a.m., all hell broke loose. All around the camp's complex, the bombs came down. The working quarters were empty; in awareness of things to come, the labor force did not report for work.

Without interruption, the bombs came down and caused the barracks to shake, even the stoves started to come loose. However, the inmates had to stay inside their quarters, which was not easy; otherwise panic might have broken out. Fortunately, everyone remained calm and, after one hour or so, the alarm was called off. The question was: When was the next bombing raid due? Maybe in the afternoon at five o'clock tea? Nothing happened. At eight o'clock in the evening, we heard the usual news and Josef Goebbels spoke in honor of the "Führer" and so on, like we are going to win, we have to win, and we will have to win because we have our Führer.

Somewhere along the line, there was a disconnection, maybe due to some bombing. Well, anyway, the camp didn't get the latest news about the so-called final victory during this evening's broadcast. Even what they called werewolf news did not come through and so one had to get along without any further news. We had to make our own conclusions, but our thoughts were always concerned with what could happen during the next few hours. At 11 p.m., there was always an air raid, according to the program or schedule, but on this so important day, one could count on an extra heavy air raid.

By now it was time to retire. Everything was quiet all around. I had been on guard duty but a younger comrade came to take my post, put an Italian steel helmet over his head, and went out into the dark. It was way past midnight and nothing seemed to move. Then, around two o'clock in the morning, a blockleader came running across the roll call plaza towards his superior who was in charge of the barracks. "Go at once to the commanding officer." he was told. Ten minutes later he came back and informed the blockleaders of the nearest barracks that this concentration camp had to be evacuated by six o'clock in the morning. Involuntarily, the question came up: "Where to?" From all sides, the Allies came closer. Forty-two thousand people, men, women, and some children had to be moved; an army in a state of near starvation had to make a march of some 80 km within four days in a north-westerly direction where the city of Wittstock was indicated as a possible goal. As a food ration for these four days, something had to be figured out, like: 1500 g bread for four inmates with a 1000 g can of blood sausage, called sore-looking eyes by the inmates, or liverwurst, called mud-paste. Yes, the inmates had to spoil the appetite, too by giving some food items funny names. Even before the alarm went off, there was life at camp, because a news bulletin like this one went like wildfire from one barrack to the next. The call "freedom" was heard all over. The day had come for which everyone had been waiting, and during the sleeping hours did this important day finally became a reality. Even before the farewell drinks were handed out, a great mix-up of all kinds of people took place on the roll call plaza; it was a big crowd. Women inmates who had been interned, were mixed among the male inmates, and soon these paired-off people came to an agreement on how to celebrate or at least spend the day.

The S.S. could only be seen near the gate; they didn't seem to have any desire to mix with the inmates. From the camp leader's room above the gate, some representatives of the defeated Master Race took a last long look across the territory that used to be the playground of their sadistic and cruel activities. I saw the commanding officer and some of the other leaders, including one called Hoess who used to be in charge of the Auschwitz extermination camp, looking out of the windows with their girlfriends beside them.

At six o'clock in the morning, the first inmate formation was assembled—500 men forming one column—marching out through the gate from where the armed S.S. and inmate's police had to accompany them. It was a cold and wet April morning and the sun didn't even come out by noon time through the clouds. Next to follow were some women, but what a pitiful sight! Dressed in worn-out and insufficient clothes, barefoot in wooden sandals with crying children on their hands or maybe dying babies in their arms. In this condition, they, too, walked through the gate. Next to follow were Polish and other foreign inmates.

This was the exodus from Sachsenhausen, the date was April 21, 1945, a very important day, the day for the march to freedom, although nobody really knew if this was already a time to celebrate. After getting outside and on the road, most of the people would turn around once more to have a long last look at the gatehouse that still carried the inscription: "Protective custody." Soon this dreaded place of confinement appeared smaller and dimmer in the background until it could no longer be seen. The country road, the free nature with woods and meadows around them became the surroundings for those who were freed. However, quite a few frightened inhabitants were standing near the railroad station of Sachsenhausen where a bomb had caused some ruins, possibly on account of the "Führer's" birthday on April 20. Well, one had to keep on going. At least one was in the fresh air that was supposed to be the air of freedom and something to be thankful for.

CHAPTER 23

HUNGER MARCH ON THE STREETS OF ADOLF HITLER

"Nobody is going to be hungry or cold."

Hitler

"We have to be victorious; otherwise history wouldn't make any sense."

Goebbels

Hitler had big ideas with his followers. As a remaining souvenir, the streets had to last so that they could remind anyone stepping on them in years to come of the "great Führer." He had the streets of the old Roman Empire in mind; streets that lasted more than 2000 years. Well, anyway, his "Reich" had been scheduled to last for 1000 years, and, therefore, it had to have streets that would surpass the Roman ways of transportation. And so he created the highways built for cars which were supposed to be praised by everyone as the streets of Adolf Hitler. Just like the Romans of long ago who had built their roads to serve for quicker and easier troop movement, so were Hitler's roads constructed for fast advancement of motor vehicles like cars, trucks, tanks, etc. for the coming war he had in mind. They were excellent highways, macadamized, and the Nazis were very proud of them.

However, we looked at these roads differently. We saw them with the never-ending stream of people moving from the east, the fugitives by wagons or on foot, the fleeing soldiers of a defeated army with and without horses, and then the freed inmates of the concentration camps. It was a picture of distress. The old-time inmates used several roads leading in a northwesterly direction, where they made slow progress in groups. After marching for less than half an hour, one could no longer see the concentration camp. The landscape around looked peaceful. Some curious villagers took a look at the marching men, women, and even children that were among them. Everyone had a number attached to his chest and a colored triangle. What kind of people could they be, these starving-looking ones, the villages asked themselves. Some of them asked the newcomers what kind of people they were and where they came from. "Out of the concentration camp" was the answer. But many of the onlookers had no idea what that meant. Therefore, it took some effort to explain the situation and that these wandering people had been released from a concentration camp after suffering hunger, injustice, and often painful, treatment by their oppressors. They sometimes had to endure a life worse than the slaves had years ago.

Slowly darkness set in and the former inmates became very tired. Since they were not used to long marches during their long captivity or even before, they sat down on the curb of the road. Anyone who had something like a tin can with him would look for the nearest well to get some drinking water. Others found some straw, little pieces of wood, or twigs to start a fire on which to heat some edible kind of food they had taken along. As it was near a village, some barns and sheds were made available to some of the refugees to stay overnight. Others had to find a place under trees, bushes, or a ditch near the road. Nearly frozen and with stiff arms and legs they woke up the next morning which was rather damp and cold.

A group of mothers with babies and little children had spent the night under some bushes in the woods. No wonder some of these babies had died during the night from cold and hunger. These mothers, however, did not have much time for mourning; instead, they had to find a place where they could dig a grave, in order to bury the little ones as best they could. After that, it was necessary to keep on marching and to save all their strength to get forward and not to stay behind or sit down. Weakness could mean death either by fatigue or by a bullet from an S.S. guard who followed the caravan of people.

These people were getting hungry after being on the march for hours. Just as there was very little provision made for shelter, so it was for food. In order to stay alive, the former inmates had to look for some kind of edible foodstuff like raw potatoes, for instance, which they could find in the barns to satisfy their hunger. Cows and horses which refugees from the east had been taking along were hardly better off than people. Many of them succumbed on the roads and the remaining skeletons gave evidence that some hungry travelers had already made use of their flesh for food. The few rest periods were mostly used to search for wild berries, roots, edible weeds, or even some bark of trees. A bonfire was made to cook or roast anything that might be edible, but most of the foodstuff was not done at all, just warmed up. People had to get along on these "nutritious" meals because there was not much time left. The march had to go on.

The morning of the second day of marching presented a gruesome sight. Near the gutter and on the grass, we saw several corpses of former inmates. A close look gave evidence that they had been shot in the neck. It was clear that they had been too weak and, therefore, unable to keep on marching. S.S. henchmen shot them to take them out of their misery. Just like wolves looking for the weaker ones among the prey, so were the S.S. men.

The number of murdered people grew from day to day. Just to give you an example: On the road between the villages of Klosterheide and Zechlin, I counted 218 murdered former inmates who belonged to a previous group from the concentration camp. On other roads that were used in the same general direction, either left or right, the number of dead was about the same as we found out in the evening, upon arriving in Zechlin, from our comrades who had followed those roads. In fact, it had been their gruesome task to bury these victims in shallow graves along the roads so that the civilian population would not find out about these horrible crimes that had taken place. But just the same, it didn't hinder the S.S. men from murdering former inmates in the villages, too, in the towns of Lindows and Linow near Rheinsberg, as we found out later. Here, the murdered victims of the previous column of marchers were still lying on the streets and in the marketplace.

As much as it was humanly possible to put former inmates who were no longer able to walk on some available carts, it was done, just to save them from the henchmen's deadly bullets. However, not even the stronger comrades were able to take care of everyone. And so, unfortunately, these poor people had to be left behind for the S.S. men, in case they were not able to hide behind some bushes. Some of these people were able to get away and walk over to the nearest inhabitants who had enough sympathy to hide them and care for them until the danger of being discovered had passed.

While passing through the little villages, even the smallest ones, the people noticed that everyone had been blocked with cut-down trees to prevent traffic from passing through. This, of course, was an order of the "high command" and was supposed to keep the Russian Army trucks from entering this territory, something that could be expected any day. However, the refugees who were able to escape a few days ago now had a chance to make contact with the forerunners of the Russian troops that were following the columns of the former concentration camp inmates and members of the German Army. Not only were the roads blocked but also the bridges were mined with explosives to keep the Russians from advancing. Occasionally, we, the former inmates, had the opportunity to warn the peasants and villagers about these dangerous methods, and so it happened that the mayor of a little town named Berlinchen decided not to do it because of the useless effort of keeping the Russians from getting through.

In the township of Zechlin, a rest period of several days took place because several barns and tool sheds could be made available as somewhat dry living quarters. Meanwhile, the pitiful-looking columns of concentration camp refugees and others were passing a crossroads leading to the village of Schweinrich. It was a strange sight, like in a film where, from early in the morning until late at night, the picture is changing, like soldiers marching on foot to the refugees with all kinds of wagons, carts, and such, loaded down with the most necessary household articles, including dogs and cats accompanied by horses, cows, calves, goats, and sheep. An old grandfather in a wheelchair was being pushed along by his grandchildren, holding onto his meager belongings on his lap. Next to him, the grandmother, still able to walk, holding on to a basket containing a cooking pot filled with some leftover meal. After that, came a troop of concentration camp officers who had to follow in a different direction, followed by armored trucks occupied by some soldiers and some refugees, both men and women and even some children were among them. Everything that we saw at these crossroads looked so unreal, that even people with strong nerves would be shocked by such a display. This went on for weeks when the columns of refugees had to pass through these roads, but it would still take a few more days until the last ones had passed and meanwhile, the Russians were coming closer.

On April 24, 1945, during the three-day stay in Zechlin, several cars from the International Red Cross arrived with packages that were at first accepted by the S.S. before they were handed over to the former concentration camp inmates. Here, I had a chance to talk to the transport leader, explaining that the previous packages had been confiscated by the S.S. men and we, the inmates, got hardly anything. Furthermore, I told him about the mass murders that took place all along the route of those inmates who were no longer able to walk, thus pleading that he give this information to his officer in charge. This he promised to do.

After leaving Zechlin, the next stop was made in the village of Dranse where the S.S. men gave us a part of the Red Cross packages. Ten men received one package, although one package was intended for only two men. Whoever could not find quarters in Dranse, took up shelter in a barn near this village where they found plenty of potatoes, which these hungry people roasted over an open fire, later in the evening.

From some separated columns of inmates with whom we had constant communication just the same, we found out that on the way to the village of Grabow, specifically near the woodland at a forest house belonging to the village of Below, typhoid fever from hunger had broken out, and that already hundreds of former inmates had died because they couldn't get anything to eat or drink. They were not even allowed to use the wells; they were turned off. Nothing had been done to take care of these people, no food, no water, and no shelter. They had to lay under brushes or branches as well as they could.

Several days later, on our way to Berlinchen, we, too, arrived at this infected territory where we could see for ourselves that the information about these pitiful conditions was indeed very true. In fact, we also noticed while taking a close look at the hallways that the buried corpses of our former inmates had indeed died from starvation. The trees and bushes that had been stripped of their bark showed what they had eaten for their last meal. Here and there we saw a dead man's bony hand reaching up from the ground until the troop of workers in charge of burying the dead, finished the burials.

Our troop walked a little way off the main road until we came to Gravow. Here we saw only a few bodies of inmates who had been shot. While coming together later in the village, we did notice the loss among our comrades that had taken place. Evidently, these men had to stay behind, lying on the roads somewhere after they were no longer able to walk and get away in time, so the S.S. hyenas shot them. In the village, some examinations took place. Anyone who was no longer able to walk was supposed to be transported by the German Red Cross cars that had arrived in the meantime. It was with quite some hesitation that some comrades came forward because they were afraid and suspected that these vehicles might take them to the nearest gas chambers and crematories. This shows what kind of a bad reputation the German Red Cross had at that time.

Meanwhile, one of our political friends and the man in charge of the infirmary of Sachsenhausen, George Wieben, as well as several nurse's aides, had arrived at Grabow. They told us that at the time of leaving the concentration camp, several thousand sick inmates had stayed behind as they had been unable to walk. By that time, the S.S. men had deserted the camp, leaving care and administration up to the political inmates.

It was early in the morning of April 22, 1945, when the Russian troops arrived and, subsequently, freed the remaining inmates. One of these men came with the news that the S.S. men had fled in cars, leaving the gate open and without a guard. Soon after, a Russian soldier arrived and rang the bell on the exercise plaza. Anybody still able to move or walk came out of the infirmary and stationed themselves around the soldier in a rather happy mood. It didn't take long until a troop of Cossacks on horseback arrived. After the Russians took over the command of the concentration camp, the first thing they did was to look for the food supply, especially, in the depots belonging to the commanding officers of the camp, so that everybody could get something to eat. All invalids were promptly taken care of. It happened that some of the undernourished people got a little sick from so much food because they were not used to such a rich diet all of a sudden. It also happened that some of the severe cases couldn't take it and quite a few of them even died as they were not used to all this good food.

Meanwhile, the hungry inmates who had arrived at Grabow kept on moving through sandy roads without finding something edible, until they came to the little village of Freyenstein where they made a stop along the road. Here in the barns they found some potato bins, ate some of their contents, and kept their hunger down somewhat for the next few hours. Later in the evening, a stop was made near Meyenburg where some farmers offered them several barns to stay there overnight. Here the leader of the troop by the name of Koerner was asked by his fellow inmates for some bread which, unfortunately, he couldn't provide. All they could do was help themselves to some water from wells which were located nearby. He didn't even know when the next rationing of bread might take place.

The next morning the troop had to keep on marching and came through Meyenburg which was crowded with refugees from the east who were lined up on the streets waiting for any kind of transportation going west in the direction of Parchim. The former inmates in the meantime, miserable as they felt, kept on trotting through the sandy roads towards the village of Klein Pankow, which was supposed to be the next stop. Just before entering the village, the whole crew took a rest because a delivery truck from the International Red Cross had arrived and all the men received a parcel with foodstuffs from the Americans, which was handed to them by the truck drivers. The contents were delicacies that the former inmates had not seen in years, never mind been eating.

The date was May 1, 1945, a day nobody will forget. The officer in charge and his assistants supervised the distribution of these gift packages themselves and did not let any of the S.S. men get near them. With a good deal of satisfaction, I could see that my messages of April 24, 1945, to the transport leader of the International Red Cross had been successful. It did not take long until other International Red Cross vehicles arrived in order to take as many of the invalid inmates along as they could. Here, people were trying eagerly to get a place on the international vehicles while avoiding the German Red Cross cars for fear this could mean another one-way trip to the gas chambers. The contents of these gift packages made it possible for the receiver to feel like a human being again and to satisfy his hunger. One could also exchange luxury items like tea and coffee for some bread from the farmers as this was always scarce.

A day later, on May 2, the march had to go on via Siggelkow towards Parchim where the men were allowed to make just another stop before entering the village. Here we could have a picnic, thanks to the help of the Allies, whose food transports had been able to pass through enemy lines without interference. Walking through Parchim in bright sunlight did not give us any impression that some shooting or even bombing had taken place. It was a peaceful landscape until after leaving this village. Here, on the main road to Criwitz, we noticed several smaller roads running into this one. Soon, we saw lines of refugees, as well as deserting troops of the German military that were still on the march.

There always seemed to be a stop ahead as the roads were covered with broken-down military cars, tanks, trucks, and other kinds of vehicles, that had been demolished by low-flying bombers during the last few days. The roads and nearby fields presented a picture of terror like we had hardly seen before. Former inmates and citizens, most of them refugees, had been shot and were lying all over. The S.S. murder gang had done a complete job: victims were lying in rows on the ground; all of them had been shot through their heads. Among them were the bodies of victims killed directly by low-flying bombers, and in the trees, there were parts of human and animal bodies still hanging and swinging in the air.

The dead children of refugees were lying at the sides of the roads or had been thrown into a ditch. Dead women, who had given birth, were lying there, too, together with their infants who may have been born dead already. Here and there, some of the following people tried their best to cover the victims up with some burlap bags or similar material in order to spare any onlookers who may pass through, this gruesome sight. This was the way Hitler's roads shocked any passerby. In fact, these happened to be the same ones on which World War II had taken place in such a horrible way.

Now we came to a stop near the woods. Trying to get into it seemed to be impossible as the military had already blocked the whole place off. Besides that, anybody who would come near enough to pick up some old pieces of wood to make a fire was threatened with a gun. The reason for being so strict remained unanswered until these guards received some cigarettes. Then they started to talk. The reason why nobody was allowed to get into these woods was not for protection against some kind of a robber gang who might be hiding there, oh no, in this case, it happened to be an arm of the government itself, under the leadership of Admiral Dönitz, who had used this territory as a place of escape and had moved on already in a northwesterly direction with members of his so-called government. To avoid any kind of inconvenience for this outspoken guard, we promised secrecy and only marked this incident in our notebook.

Shortly before arriving in the town of Criwitz, after a march of some 50 km, Camp Commander Koerner was asked by one of the troop leaders if they could make a stop for an overnight stay, as the men could hardly stand on their feet any longer. Koerner therefore suggested that they stop at a sand pit for the night. The men refused this suggestion because they had heard through the grapevine that a few nights ago a troop of marching people had been killed by flame throwers while staying in a sand pit. Thereupon Koerner's answer was to keep on walking until we keeled over. We kept on marching slowly because, with so many men on the go, the narrow streets of Criwitz soon became pretty crowded and too tight for fast movement. From far away, one could hear the thunder of guns and see the bright glare in the sky, whenever a storage depot of ammunition was detonated by fleeing German Army or S.S. troops.

After some difficulty, we finally succeeded in getting through the village and found our way in the direction of Schwerin, where we had to make a stop on the highway, as it was pitch dark by now. The marching troop of former inmates tried to disband already because the gang of S.S. guards who were in charge had already thrown their weapons away and were disappearing into the nearby woodlands. They were also bold enough to steal from the belongings of the inmates who still had some care packages leftovers with them. This way, I also found myself without my knapsack because one of the fleeing S.S. men had grabbed it in the darkness. The overnight stay lasted until the early morning hours and after getting a little warmed up near a campfire, we continued marching towards Schwerin. The progress was slow due to fatigue and lack of food. Around nine o'clock in the morning bread had arrived, one slice for each inmate, for as long as the supply lasted. One couldn't see too many of the S.S. guards around anymore and, therefore, the policing was done by inmates, who took care of law and order.

Camp leader Koerner gave the impression that things were not the way he would like them to be, so he walked among the inmates, his head dropping until he finally found the courage to ask five of the inmate police, mostly the older ones, to make the following announcement: "Tell your comrades that they have until 10 o'clock to take a break and finish their bread. I have sent some of the inmate police over to the Americans who are located several kilometers from here, in order to find out if we will have to march in individual groups or all together in a single troop column."

What was that? It was unheard of for an S.S. leader to talk to the inmates in such a casual and almost friendly manner. After all, inmates were more or less being taken for criminals, individuals who had to take orders and who could expect physical punishment at any time. We knew already on account of the maps we had with us, that we were only about 6 kilometers away from the American demarcation line. Besides that, we got news through some couriers that on May 2, the American forces had marched into Schwerin and occupied the city around noontime.

What we had to do now was to try to get in touch with the Americans as soon as possible without waiting for the return of the alleged inmate police to give us an answer. Behind the long lines of slow-moving wagons filled with refugees, military vehicles, and tanks, the inmates found themselves together in bigger and smaller groups, each of which had a political group leader with knowledge of the English language.

As soon as the overtired comrades heard the news that they may be free after only walking just a few more kilometers, they all of a sudden seemed to be strong enough to finish the march. The will to live was there again. They had been waiting so long for this moment and now the time had come to make the final move. They pulled themselves together to finish the last few miles to their destination. Not even hunger pains could dampen their spirits, no; it even gave them an incentive to get it over with.

It was about 3 o'clock in the afternoon of May 3, 1945, when the first troops of former concentration camp inmates arrived at the American demarcation line—a bridge south of Schwerin. After a short speech of orientation between the American officer and some interpreters among the political inmates, the enemies of the Hitler regime were back in their own country where they could move around again as free people.

From now on they could feel free and didn't have to worry anymore that the S.S. would be after them again. The tables had turned around. At the same place where the former inmates had been set free, the S.S. guards who came along were arrested by the Allies. Even those S.S. bandits who had been able to dress themselves in civilian clothes, just in time, or who were hiding in uniforms belonging to deceased inmates, were soon picked out by observant inmates and turned over to the Allied military police.

Without interruption, the evacuees with their wagons or on foot moved over this bridge. After that, they, too, could take it easy. Anything that had not yet been thrown away in the line of weapons by the fleeing armed forces or the S.S. had to be turned over to the Allied officers in charge, who dumped everything on a big heap.

It was like a migration of nations, as if a real invasion took place, something that had never happened before in the city of Schwerin. Everything was being thrown around. Horses without owners were feeding on grass-covered places or near ditches. Discarded articles used during the war were piling up everywhere. Law and order had turned into chaos. These used to be the streets of Adolf Hitler. The former officers of Hitler's Army didn't like to hear it anymore when the inmates called over to them, saying: *"Look at the streets now. You can see for yourself what became of them, thanks to the Hitler regime."* But now they didn't want to be reminded anymore of their former *"Führer"*; they wanted to keep on going, hoping to find or be taken into an American POW camp. It took days for the stream of people, refugees mixed with members of the former German armed forces to cross over the demarcation line. The former Nazis really had it; they were fed up with the way the streets were looking now.

About 42,000 inmates, men, women, and children, had left Sachsenhausen fourteen days ago. Hardly 28,000 made it to the demarcation line in Schwerin. The remaining 14,000 had either died from hunger, cold, or exhaustion, or they had been killed in one way or another during their long walk. Only a small fraction of the original number of people had been able to get lost or escape and hide someplace until they could get in touch with the following troops of the Soviet Union where they may have received some help or at least something to eat for the time being. At least this way they didn't fall into the hands of the dreadful Gestapo anymore.

Now it was up to the city of Schwerin to find temporary shelter and food for the incoming masses of people, which was done rather successfully. Since all inmates arrived without any papers of identification because the S.S. men had everything destroyed beforehand, the employees at City Hall got very busy making out temporary identification cards for everyone in need of it, so that these people were able to line up for rationing cards. Besides that, they were given 100 Marks each so that they could buy themselves something to eat for the next few days.

After only several days, however, it became evident that the freed criminals by trade, among the inmates, had registered as "political prisoners." Even S.S. men wearing the uniforms of murdered inmates had the nerve to declare themselves as politicals. They were not only satisfied with one identification card, but some had two or more with different names, of course, which had been handed to them without any suspicion by the city's employees. This was the way these criminals and S.S. men took advantage of the city's taxpayers who, after all, were holding the bag.

During my daily reports I had to make at the Justice Department in Schwerin, where the American military police was located, I gave notice of what these two criminally inclined groups were doing. Consequently, a special unit was organized by the military police together with some political inmates in order to catch, at first, the former S.S. men who were hiding someplace around and to arrest them. But since these hoodlums changed their quarters from one military barrack to another, while also changing their names, it became, at first, a difficult task. Eventually, however, they were caught. Of course, it was also in our own interest to stay away from these criminally inclined elements with whom we had been together in the concentration camp for all these years.

The cells of the Schwerin jail were filling up like years ago the barracks of the concentration camps did. The number of S.S. men held captive was bigger than we thought. Now they had a chance to find out for themselves how it is to be stuck in a small cell and be rationed with watery soups. Now the regular criminal inmates took advantage of the situation. They were back in their own business again, by trading soup and bread for liquor and tobacco, as they did before, in the concentration camp with jewelry and cash, like one crook cheating on another.

Several days after the occupation of Western Mecklenburg by American troops, the inhabitants were asked to take part in a funeral ceremony. On a campsite near Hagenow, around 200 bodies of starved former inmates had been found and had to be taken to a cemetery near Schwerin for burial. The people were asked to pass by the graves that were still open after the American minister delivered the sermon in the English and German languages, on behalf of these deceased inmates. The ceremony made a big impression with the attending bystanders and they left the place of mass burial in a rather pensive mood.

Already on the day of arrival in Schwerin, some men who came from about the same territory as I did, talked to me about the possibility for us to keep on moving in the direction of Flensburg, near the Danish border. There were no connections anymore via telegraph, telephone, and mail service. The post office did not operate anymore. Also, there were no more railroads and busses in operation, but maybe it could be possible to get hold of a couple of ownerless military horses and a wagon, for transportation, in order to get home. Fortunately, we didn't have to worry about our homecoming much longer. The military police provided us with bicycles and a generous selection of lunches.

On a sunny morning, our journey started in the direction of the city of Gadebusch, while passing the temporary camps for German POWs. Everything went fine until we came to the village of Rhena. Here at the entrance to the town, our group was stopped by the American Military Police. After a short interview with the officer in charge, to whom we introduced ourselves as former concentration camp political prisoners, we were provided with some papers that we could use as our passport so that we didn't have to worry anymore about any obstacles that could cause unnecessary delay. Our friend, Willy Meyer, from Eckernförde, was very lucky when he was reunited in this town with his wife, whom he had not seen in nine years. Both of them had to spend all these years in different concentration camps and their son, who in the meantime, had reached military age, had to fight in the army for the Hitler regime. Their apartment had been cleaned out by the Nazis long ago.

Until we reached the town of Schlutup, we did not notice any kind of destruction or devastation. Not before we reached the highway to Eutin, looking in the direction of Lübeck, could we see what the bombs had done to the country. Besides one destroyed farmhouse in the village of Techau, where we could sleep overnight in a clean cow barn provided with some meals from the owner, we did not see any more damage by bombs on the way toward the cities of Eutin and Plön. From there, the trip home continued via the towns of Preetz and Elmschenhagen, a suburb of Kiel—that is, the mountain of debris that used to be Kiel. We had to drag and carry our bikes through the ruins and rubble, walking in the direction of what used to be the highway toward Eckernförde. We finally found it and kept on riding our bikes until we reached the bridge of Lebensau, which was blocked by the British Military Police. Long columns of people were lining up on the highway leading to the bridge. Thanks to our passports, we had no trouble getting over the bridge. From here, it was less than 80 kilometers to Flensburg on the Danish border.

In Eckernförde, where one of our comrades found his family again, we had a chance to stay overnight. To my relatives who lived in this city, I must have looked like someone who came back from the dead as they had lost every hope of seeing me alive again. The whole landscape from here until Schleswig looked very peaceful. Also, the Kiel Canal did not look damaged. After passing through Schleswig, we met some German soldiers who took their belongings with them on pushcarts, bikes, even baby carriages. They came from Denmark and were now on their way home in a southerly direction, to wherever they used to live. It was shortly after noontime when we saw the familiar first steeples and buildings of Flensburg, after having been away so long. Only little damage had been done to the city. It was the Saturday before Pentecost when I arrived unexpectedly at my wife's apartment; the same one that the Gestapo had taken me away from six years ago and into the concentration camp.

CHAPTER 24

FLENSBURG—THE END OF THE THOUSAND-YEAR REICH

> "The time when a country is ready to collapse is determined by the predominating activities of the worst elements."
>
> Hitler, *Mein Kampf*, Chapter 9.

The German broadcast on May 1, 1945, gave out the following bulletin for the German people: *"From the "Führer's" headquarters comes the announcement that our Führer, Adolf Hitler, this afternoon as commander-in-chief has died in combat in the Reich's chancery while fighting to the end for Germany against Bolshevism. On April 30, the Führer nominated Grand Admiral Dönitz to be his successor. The Grand Admiral and successor of the Führer has made the following proclamation to the German people, and so on…"*

In this proclamation, a challenge was made for the last time to keep on resisting, hereby always hinting at the make-believe final victory which supposedly was not far away. And, therefore, Dönitz was the Führer from here on. However, since he was unable to rule at the head of the government, which was supposed to be in Berlin, his "reign" took place on his escape route in the back seat of a car until he got a foothold in Flensburg. One could say this so-called government was more like an ambulatory undertaking.

Besides, the "Dönitz government" there was also Himmler and his gang on his flight, towards Flensburg, because from here on there was still the possibility of crossing the border into Denmark. In this race towards Flensburg, Himmler and his gang were the first ones to arrive; the date was May 2, 1945. Some of his people were given quarters in the museum which became, after some time, quite a bit messed up and unsightly. Himmler lived for several days in room #59 of the police station. During the day he stayed mostly in the school for firemen at Harrisleefeld in the northern part of Flensburg where some of the vehicles in which he and his men arrived were parked. Among them was a large truck which had been converted into a cow barn. In it stood a cow for the convenience of Himmler, of course.

In Harrislee, also north of Flensburg, some noisy S.S. parties took place. Everything was available such as a choice assortment of food and also luxury items like canned ham, cold cuts, chocolate, cigars, and cigarettes, in fact, everything the common people had not been able to buy for many years.

Himmler's flight to Flensburg was quite an adventure as he wanted to escape the fast-approaching British troops who wanted to arrest him. He had in mind to have a conference with the Count Folke Bernadotte, whom he tried to meet either in Hohenlychen or Lübeck. Bernadotte used to be the president of the Swedish Red Cross at that time and Himmler had in mind to get some personal favors from him until he finally could see for himself that this option was lost already. There was no chance anymore for negotiations. All of a sudden, the once powerful "Reichs Heinrich" had to leave behind quite a few of his original vehicles. That was between the village of Techau on the road towards the Timmendorfer Strand, where I could see these cars either standing or tipped over lying on the road.

While on my way, I found out from the farmers that the British Army was looking for Himmler. They didn't only question the farmers and inhabitants; they also searched through the buildings and barns. Somewhere between Eutin and Plön, the trace had been lost somehow. Himmler had already made his escape to the northern part of Schleswig-Holstein ahead of the advancing occupation troops.

Commandant Lüth, still wearing his diamonds, was willing to

either defend the city of Flensburg or to have it demolished. Until this ultimatum could be finalized, the inhabitants of Flensburg were very worried and waited hour after hour for the British troops, who were still south of the Kiel Canal, to move in and bombard their city which could mean the end of them and Flensburg.

During these fateful hours, a turn of events took place when a simple German sailor showed a daring act of heroism. He shot and killed Commandant Lüth, thereby saving the lives of maybe thousands of people who might have perished during the total bombardment of their city. After this someone from the naval command made a phone call to the city of Neumünster, which was by now occupied by British troops, to declare Flensburg an open city. At the same time—on May 3, 1945—the Kiel police department took the initiative by surrendering with a white flag and sending out interpreters in the direction of Neumünster. On their way towards Bordesholm, they met with advancing British troops who were informed that Kiel, too, offered no resistance. On May 4, at 4 o'clock in the afternoon, a British military group in armored trucks arrived at Kiel City Hall where the surrender of this city took place.

The Gestapo in Flensburg evacuated the police department and drove with several truckloads, filled with official papers and documents, to a building called Boreas Mühle, where they burned most of the papers that had to do with political offenders. From then on the empty offices of the police department were taken over by members of the Berlin Gestapo who ransacked through anything that was left. They didn't even leave one typewriter in the building when they finally left the place. Himmler not only took the Gestapo along, he also rescued the Reich's military tribunal and brought it to Flensburg where he found quarters for it in an elementary school serving otherwise as a shelter for young people. The location was on Apenraderstrasse. On the courtyard of the post office building a truck represented the "Reich's" radio communications although the regular station at Jürgensby—a part of Flensburg—was still in use. Himmler took precaution by reserving this new broadcasting station in a truck for himself only since he had to take it for granted that the official transmitter for the "Reich" at Jürgensby had been taken over by Dönitz. Himmler just couldn't take a chance as he did not even have a single Gestapo man nor anyone from the S.S. at his disposal. Now Dönitz had the power in his hand to have even Himmler, the once so powerful Reichsleader of the S.S., arrested. With this possibility on his mind, Himmler also avoided the vicinity of the Kriegsmarine station in Mürwik.

On May 5, 1945, Himmler gave the order for a meeting at the Flensburg Police Station from where he wanted to declare a so-called "Untouchable Germany" from Flensburg down to the Eider River. Beforehand, always having his own safety in mind, he had made contact with an innkeeper in Flensburg who showed him quite a few possible hide-away corners in his establishment. Even he didn't have too much confidence in this new "untouchable" Germany. Not a man of great courage himself, he fled into an air raid shelter of an apartment building near the Reichsbank when on May 3, he heard the sirens screaming. Here, finally, the apartment dwellers could see for themselves what kind of a miserable coward he really was after having been once one of the most powerful men in Germany, a dictator who used to rule over millions of people.

During the first few days of his stay in Flensburg, he could still be seen in the full uniform of a former warlord, while walking on the streets as well as in the "Bahnhof Hotel." But when the general conditions became too unpleasant for him, he moved back to Harrislee, a little town near the Danish border where he stayed in the training school for firemen, while also selecting a uniform for himself which he later exchanged again for a civilian suit. Dressed like a civilian, Himmler remained for several days in Flensburg where he took up quarters in the inn with the name "Schwarzer Walfisch." In this establishment, a guest could still allow himself to get drunk for about three days or until he would drop under the table and lay there like a stiff broom handle. Himmler, however, couldn't do that anymore; time was marching on and he had to leave from a rather unpleasant situation. Getting across the border to Denmark was impossible, and, therefore, he moved temporarily in with a farmer in the little village of Ausacker from where he fled soon afterward like a hunted deer in a southern direction. He made it across the Kiel Canal and finally ended up near Bremen where he committed suicide by taking poison (Fig. 17).

Fig. 17. Himmler's last stop in Ausacker-Hüholz, Kreis, Flensburg.

The so-called untouchable Germany from Flensburg south to the Eider River as Himmler had declared it, unofficially, of course, may also have been a dream Hitler had when he thought that the northern part of Germany was disconnected. If he had known that in the vicinity of the city of Glücksstadt some several hundred years ago, a fortified wall had been in existence with the name "Hitler-Schanze", then quite likely he would have used this old relic as a last stand for the defense. But in those days this little fortification had only been used to lock up thieves and other criminals. But since Hitler revealed himself as one of the worst criminals the world had ever known, well, in that case, this little bulwark would have been desecrated by his name.

North of the Eider River, there was another bulwark by the name of Dannewerk which had been built during the reign of the Danish Queen Thyra. It was located between the old Viking village of Haitabu near Schleswig and not-too-far from Hollingstedt. Only a genius in the science of warfare like Adolf Hitler could have chosen this bulwark as a last stronghold against the oncoming Allied troops and armored vehicles. How the oppressed Germans reacted under the regime of their war hero, Adolf Hitler, has been described by a Danish journalist, Bo Bojesen, in a little newspaper article "Rummelpot." A funny picture showed Queen Thyra on one side and Adolf directing toy-size war machinery on the other while talking to a passersby (Fig. 18).

Fig. 18. *The Last Chance* caricature (in Danish).

During the last few days of Nazi domination when the end seemed to be in sight for the normal observer the Gestapo thought they were still very powerful. They came upon a bookstore where the owner had put a sign in the window saying: "Start learning English." Some books in English were also on display. One of the Gestapo men didn't like that and asked the owner to take that sign out and replace it with another saying: "Start learning German before it is too late." Instead of the English books, German literature had to be put on display. However, this kind of advertisement could also be taken as a joke and the Gestapo men decided to tell the store owner to take the books and sign out of the window and replace them with life-size pictures of Hitler and Mussolini side by side. The owner put a large book of *Les Misérables* in front of the pictures. Of course, the store owner went into hiding before the Gestapo found out about it and did not reappear until the rest of the Nazi Army had left Denmark.

Into the country north of the Kiel Canal that was already overfilled with refugees from the eastern countries of Europe, more and more people kept moving in because they were afraid of the advancing Russian troops. Among these refugees who had been on the road for months, happened to be also a few prominent members of the Nazi party and their families. They had packed their suitcases just in time and arrived in cars, calling themselves "Guests of the Führer," while being overbearing and arrogant to the general public. It had not come to their minds yet that this was the end station and that the end of the Third Reich was well in sight.

It so happened that Flensburg gave shelter to Alfred Rosenberg and his wife and daughter. At that moment, he was not exactly worried about the "Twentieth Century Myth" as he was more interested in finding out how to get out of this net that seemed to be getting smaller and smaller. Escape into Denmark was the question. Well, yes, but some minor incidents caused some delay. His only pair of brown shoes needed new soles but the shoemaker took his time and time was very important for Rosenberg, so he had to find another way to disappear. Hitler's personal physician gave him a cast—feigning a broken leg—this way he was taken into the infirmary. However, after a few days, it was already discovered that this was nothing but deceit. He was arrested along with his participating physician, Dr. Brandt, as well as the hospital attendants. This was the end of his dream to escape into a foreign country.

Dönitz did have a chance to talk to Himmler in Lübeck during his flight on the night of April 30 until May 1. He crossed the Kiel Canal soon after in Holtenau where he had a conference with Admiral von Friedeburg, which concerned the inevitable capitulation of Germany. After he arrival in Flensburg, on May 2, he settled on the *Patria* which was anchored at the pier of the Marine Academy in Mürwik (Fig. 19). His staff had already been taken to nearby barracks. The conference of the so-called Dönitz cabinet started on May 3, at 10 a.m., in the building for the high command. Participants besides Dönitz were Minister of the Exterior von Krosigk of Schwerin, Minister Seldte and—last but not least—the tolerated Himmler. The big question was, "Will there be another battle?" The decisions that had to be made now may have given this final cabinet quite some headache because these gentlemen had been watched getting in and out of the building, always taking in a fresh deep breath of air from the sea before returning inside. This puppet government in the newly established "Wilhelmstrasse" got more worries added on to the ones they already had. The government officials of the Allies arrived in Mürwik on May 5 and confined the so-called "Dönitz government" to an enclave, which nobody was allowed to leave.

Fig. 19. Patria, the last place for the Dönitz Government (Reichsregierung) in Flensburg-Mürwik. Dönitz was arrested here.

Several hours before the members of the Allied government arrived, Dönitz made an announcement over the Flensburg broadcasting station saying that Germany would not capitulate. Instead, they were going to fight to the very end—the same words the Germans were used to hearing for years while listening to the speeches of Hitler and Goebbels. How they intended to keep on fighting, they did not mention. Whatever transpired in the building that Dönitz occupied for his own purposes and on the *Patria* and the space in between was more like an operetta. Armed sailors of the Kriegsmarine guarded the bridge of the ship. Groups of men in uniform, decorated with all kinds of medals and ribbons were mingling around, dozens of generals, admirals, and other higher-ranking officials were passing each other, trying to give out orders or say "hello" to each other. Some of the men divided up the rooms to be used either as a conference hall or a waiting room. Soldiers who didn't have any medals were taken into arrest but for a few hours.

Already, during the night of May 5 to May 6, British military forces moved into Flensburg and occupied the main post office building. More British troops arrived on May 6, around noon time. They came over to Schleswig and took up quarters at the airport. On Tuesday, May 8, the new Foreign Minister Krosigk from Schwerin, announced over the Flensburg radio station the unconditional surrender of all German forces on land, at sea, and in the air.

General Jodl and Admiral Friedeburg, as representatives of the German forces, signed the surrender document at Eisenhower's headquarters in Reims, France on May 7, at 2:41 a.m., hereby declaring that the German people, as well as the German forces, had surrendered to the victorious Allied forces. The ratification of this unconditional surrender took place in Berlin on May 8, where Field Marshall Keitel, signed the document of surrender in front of Zhukov and Tedder, as representatives of the Allies. On May 8, one minute after midnight, the command went out to all the armies, declaring hereby to stop fighting immediately. This was the end of World War II in Europe.

In Flensburg-Mürwik, it was Dönitz who kept up with his regime as if the capitulation was none of his concern. He tried to stay in command or at least he thought so. This kind of spectacle continued, thanks to the new arrival of some military personnel, who had tried to escape but instead landed here and joined the show.

A similar spectacle took place in the outer part of the Flensburg fjord, near the coast at the Danish town of Swendborg. It was a final act when it was certain that nothing could be saved anymore and that the capitulation had taken place already. It was clear that Dönitz was no longer in command of the German Army, Navy, or Air Force. Every officer who had been in command of men tried to continue, according to his own decisions, and was ready to continue the war if it was at all possible.

After Adolf Hitler's death was announced, an uproar took place among all the German military forces on land, at sea, and in the air. For the soldiers the war was over; they wanted to go home, or at least avoid becoming a POW. It was different with many officers who wanted to keep on fighting in order to save their positions and some did not even hesitate to shoot and kill, just to hold on to their so-called discipline. It so happened in the Danish city of Sønderborg during the early part of May, fourteen members of the Kriegsmarine had been shot, execution-style, all on account of this so-called discipline.

The fast-advancing British troops, under General Montgomery's command, made it possible that on May 5, a partial capitulation of the German Army took place. After that, the ships also were no longer allowed to leave their present position in the ports or wherever they were anchored. Captain Sander of Sønderborg had his own ideas to keep on fighting. He wanted to put together a battalion with which to save Berlin, after it had already fallen and then continue to fight the Russians.

To keep up the spirit and the desire to continue the war, Sander arranged for a social evening on May 5, where he tried to convince his guests of the importance of continuing the war, otherwise imprisonment, and, by all means, the discipline has to be kept up. His explanations were expressed in these words: *"Reconstruction can only be done through the policies of the National-Socialist movement!"*

The fact that the ambition to keep the war alive was completely gone was very visible. Wehrmann, a member of the Kriegsmarine, and three of his comrades did not want to keep on fighting; all they wanted was to go home. After all, they had had their share of the war, prison camps, and barbed wires. Unfortunately, they did not have any success. A group of Danish resistance fighters picked them up and returned all four of them to Sander's battalion where they were put, at first, into a cell on the speedboat *Buea*.

During the same night of May 6 several speedboats, including the *Buea* left the port of Sønderborg (in Denmark) and anchored in the Geltinger Bucht (part of the southwestern Baltic), although it was against Montgomery's orders to move ships from their present location or to sink them. Sander, a fanatical Nazi, ignored any orders that would lead to an armistice.

May 6 passed without any incidents. Everybody waited for a command until May 7, when there were rumors early in the morning that these speedboats were supposed to be sent against Russia. Around 7 o'clock in the evening it was announced on the *Buea* that the capitulation with all the enemy powers had taken place and that at 12 midnight all acts of war had come to a standstill. On May 8, the surrender should take place in the Geltinger Bucht. In the hours before noon, the ships were at anchor next to each other, the flags were taken down, and then the National Anthem was sung. The next day, on May 9, a boat returned from Kurland and took position in line with the other speedboats.

The continuation of the war as Sander had in his mind was over, but just the same, he wanted to show everybody that he was still in command over the whole manpower. The sailors who were now under arrest had to be punished severely because they disregarded his discipline. And, besides that, they were also deserters in his opinion, even if it happened at a time when the war was over and chaos had set in.

Finally, the gruesome spectacle took place. Sander, as POW of the Allies, on the morning of May 9, the day after the capitulation, called together a court-martial, which had to pass a verdict upon the four sailors as deserters. This court-martial took place on board the *Buea* with Captain and Counsellor Faustian, as a witness. The flag which had been taken down the day before, served as cover on the judge's bench in front of which the four sailors had to stand as defendants.

Getting a defense attorney for these men was not considered necessary, according to Judge Holwig.

The trial, itself, should be nothing more than a formality. Therefore, it took hardly 20 minutes until a verdict was passed. Three of the sailors got the death sentence; the fourth one, Schwalenberg, got three years in prison. Now the verdicts had to be confirmed. Dönitz, who happened to be in Flensburg, was far away from the Geltinger Bucht. Therefore, Sander presented the verdict to Commodore Rudolf Petersen, son of a pastor from the island of Alsen (Als in Danish). But Petersen did not want to put his signature on this document. Finally, after Sander had put pressure on him for hours, he confirmed the three death sentences which were executed two days after the end of the war, on the deck of the speedboat, *Buea*. It was May 10, 1945. The whole crew had to be present and witness the gruesome act of shooting their comrades to death. Captain Merkel who was in charge of the execution fired the shots. The day after, he was still proud of his accomplishment and expressed himself with these words, *"These pigs don't deserve anything better than being bumped off."*

After the shooting, the papers of the protocol for this trial disappeared and no record was made about the execution. This "court-martial" after the capitulation was done, according to a passage in the military penal code where it says, "It is the judge's duty to make his decisions in the spirit of the new law enforcement by the National-Socialists." Anyway, this new justice system went hand in hand with the ideologies of the National-Socialists. It is not known if Dönitz had been informed of the massacre in the Geltinger Bucht; but in case he did, it is doubtful if someone would carry them out.

A high-ranking employee from the broadcasting system who had himself transferred from Jüterbog to Flensburg via Plön had made it possible to set up his own broadcasting station: "Reich's Newscast" that is, with the help of some craftsmen he had picked up along the road. Plön, by the way, was the town where Ribbentrop got his daily half-can of meat ration which he divided with his own chauffeur, while at the same time, thousands of soldiers were kept marching in the opposite direction to fight the "war for Berlin" with not much to eat, I suppose. The purpose was to keep communication open with the German staff who, under the direction of Zhukov, Montgomery, and Eisenhower were disbanding the German military troops.

In the township of Twedterholz (now Twedter Holz), and on the roads around the fjord, some vehicles that did the broadcasting kept moving around. The broadcasters put on their earphones, not exactly with pleasure, but they would rather stay in their wagons from where they could send messages than go into some kind of a camp from which there may be no escape. Broadcasting people had been organized to inform who was supposed to move on to Eisenhower in Krefeld, to Montgomery in Lunenburg, and Zhukow in Berlin. One major, who had also been a communications officer at the Führer's headquarters, spoke of discipline, and unkempt hair and suggested jail sentences. "Freedom corps for Germany" said one First Lieutenant and stuck out his chin, but about half an hour later, he threw his pistol into the fjord. But, eventually, a communication system could be established.

One general from the west complained that the Allies had given him a low-class position while ordering the march in reverse for his troops and the surrender of weapons. Jodl answered on the radio: *"Calm down. You too are only a chicken who tries to lay an egg before ending up in the soup."*

At the Dönitz episode on the *Patria*, Himmler played his role only during the first part of the first act. After that, he thought it would be wiser to disappear behind the scenes and take care of his own safety first of all. Instead of him, another player showed up to keep the spectacle going. When, on May 5, members of the parliament arrived in Mürwik, Himmler had already left and was going on a tour all by himself. Not quite as active in his role, was the chief quartermaster by the name of Toppe, who at a later trial by the officers of the Allies, only had to make statements concerning the value and contents of the warehouses belonging to the German Army.

The number of "players" on the *Patria* since the capitulation had grown by a few more. These were high-ranking officers of the Allies who had been engaged for observation but who let Dönitz keep going on with his own "administration" by giving orders without interference. It was not even difficult for me to get on board the *Patria*, thanks to my nephew, Harald Wichelmann, who, in the uniform of an ensign, served as an interpreter for the British officers. On the sidelines, I also heard that on May 17, a lieutenant commander had been shot to death on Dönitz's order. If this happened to be true I do not know, but because the Nazis committed mass murders of millions of innocent people, it is very likely to be the case.

There was one thing on board the *Patria* that was typical. The former Nazi officers tried to keep on going the way they were used to. Dönitz and his crew could not forgive the British officers because they had them interrogated by an ensign only. Besides that, they were not respected according to their rank. No difference had been made by the ensign interpreter as to what kind of rank they used to have. Even the admiral had to answer all the questions and give the ensign the information he asked for. Not only that, they also had to accept criticism and, in some cases, they were even reprimanded.

Very interesting was the interrogation of former administration officer Seldte (Reichminister for Labor), who had to answer questions concerning his political background. He tried his best to describe himself as a completely unimportant person and being under the dominance of Dr. Ley (head of the German Labor Front), he sounded almost convincing in the way he acted. As a rule, during these trials, one had the impression that nobody seemed to have much of an influence on the outcome. This goes for the so-called high-ranking individuals, as well as those with less importance, a tendency one could later notice during the war crime trials, also.

It was very hard for the officers around Dönitz to give up their high-ranking titles as well as the fact that the subordinates no longer had to salute them with their titles. However, there were some two-faced individuals among them, who applied a double standard.

Lt. Kap. Walkerling was one of them who would salute every Allied officer and orderly in an obsequious manner while saying "good morning" or whatever; while at the same time, he would drop the titles for the German officers, but rather rudely address them, even before the repeal was in effect.

On May 13, large numbers of Allied troops came to Flensburg and marched through the streets. The school for naval cadets in Mürwik was not occupied by the Allies. Members of the so-called Dönitz staff could move around as freely as the lions and tigers in the Hagenbeck Zoo.

There was a little change in the program on May 18, 1945. A Russian military delegation arrived in Flensburg and boarded the *Patria* where good relationships seem to exist. Allied and German officers moved around easily as if a surrender had not taken place. Even I could move through the rooms on board without being challenged; no one asked what my purpose was. Overall I received any desired information asked for and so I assumed that I was accepted as a high-ranking civilian official.

In the meantime, the Dönitz-opera reached the third act, which in the last scene was very different from what one expects to see in an opera. The calendar showed May 23, 1945. A tank brigade occupied a dozen street crossings at the Flensburg fjord. A few hundred soldiers with red cap coverings jumped from their vehicles and surrounded the Mürwik Naval Academy like a chain. British tank soldiers then moved through the barracks and surroundings looking for billeting. Several dozen Wehrmacht generals awoke from a comfortable slumber. The opera was now over.

Suddenly, in the middle of the day on May 23, the British troops occupied the area. The dream of staying in the barracks for weeks or maybe months was now over for the Dönitz staff. The generals had to leave their quarters with the same tempo as the soldiers. Machine guns persuaded the German troops to leave their trucks, and even the panzer troops from the "Grossdeutschland" division, who had made themselves well-known in combat, were made to feel humble. The German officers protested because they thought that their enclave was guaranteed by the Allied high command. "Shut up and go on," said the Tommy police with the red hats.

It happened to be the SHAEF (Supreme Headquarters Allied Expeditionary Forces), a commission of American, British, and Russian officers who all of a sudden interrupted the comfortable lifestyle of the Dönitz puppet government. Everything changed. What did happen and what is going to be? It never had a cabinet meeting, government press conference, or provided civil laws. Now it meant the government had to accept orders.

Admiral Dönitz, the so-called head of government, was asked to board the *Patria*. He went and understood that this invitation meant the same as being arrested. Admiral von Friedeburg did not accept this invitation. He chose to commit suicide in the washroom of the headquarters building

Dr. Thierack, the Reich's Justice Minister who first fled to Flensburg, took a similar end. He did not participate in the cabinet meetings but rather stayed by himself. He had taken up quarters with his daughter in Flensburg's courthouse, which was located right next to the prison. He took the suite that belonged to the highest official, Justice Stiemke, and hid there for 14 days until the military police brought him into custody. Dr. Thierack, who was well aware of Hitler's justice system, had an idea of what was in store for him. That was reason enough for him to avoid the judgment of an earthly judge. His suicide was not given much publicity.

Of all the Nazi leaders who had escaped to Flensburg, no one had the courage to take the consequences and "face the music." Not one of them was brave enough to get out of their misery by taking a bullet or something similar to end their lives. They also could not bring themselves to swallow a potassium cyanide pill although they were well supplied with poisons like that when they arrived in Flensburg.

And now the finish of the story in a few lines. It was early in the morning of May 25, 1945. On the meadow columns of soldiers formed, with the officers separated from the enlisted men. One could see Dönitz walking towards a waiting car that was to bring him to the next airport. All the remaining members of the armed forces—about 2000 men—that once belonged to Hitler's Army were put in motion and marched through Flensburg. After that, they had to continue marching towards the internment camps in the county of Eiderstedt, which had served as a receiving station. Only two military vehicles were used to guard the camps.

In the meantime Dönitz went to stand trial with the other Nazis at Nuremberg. The last bastion of the Nazis government ended in Flensburg-Mürwik. Millions of soldiers from the eastern front as well as from the west overran the north German territory of Schleswig-Holstein. These German forces were made to stay where they were because of the lack of transportation to intern them somewhere else.

The official capitulation of the Nazi regime had been announced from Berlin on May 8, 1945, yet the Dönitz regime had hung on for a little longer. Members of the S.S. dressed like ordinary Wehrmacht soldiers to avoid punishment. They also moved around the villages near the Danish border posing as postal and utility workers. This was the end of the fun and games for the S.S. men.

Only in Mürwik were the players in a dream world until May 23, 1945. This day marked the end of the career of the little man with the Mickey Mouse face, who back in 1939 entered the navy as a simple captain and whose ambition was to rise up through the ranks until he became the successor to the Führer. Instead, he played the last act of the Thousand-Year Reich of which Flensburg was supposed to be the capital as (if) selected by Adolf Hitler himself. As a symbol of such a success, it had a graveyard of sunken ships on a large scale. There were hundreds of torpedoed vessels and sunken ships, of which more than fifty submarines with their crew members lay at the bottom of the inner and outer fjords of the Baltic Sea. This was also a symbol of the end of a sea power, which Dönitz served and later commanded, that sank with the Third Reich.

The End

EPILOG

My grandfather had never been to the United States and after WWII he communicated with my mother by frequent letters. Although he could have come to the United States, he and my parents thought it would be better for his grandchildren to come to Germany for several months during the 1952 school summer vacation. And so my sister Dotty and I took a voyage on the Greek ship SS *Neptunia* where he met us at a Bremerhaven pier. On the way back by car to Flensburg where he lived with our grandmother we stopped in Hamburg to visit relatives. I was shocked by the several bombed out buildings I saw and the occasional man missing a leg and walking with crutches.

Opa Lienau was in the seaweed-to-bread business and was still looking for Nazi criminals. I talked in bad German with him but we had no trouble understanding each other. Occasionally he would meet people and he would switch speaking from High German to Platt-German to Danish, depending on who the other person was. He received an unusual amount of respect that I had never seen before or since. He took Dotty and myself to many places in Schleswig-Holstein and Denmark. We saw many things too numerous to describe here and I am very grateful for this experience.

I next, and last, saw him between 1955 and 1957 when I was stationed with the United States Army in Kaiserslautern. After returning to the United States we would correspond by letters in German. He lived long enough to learn that he was two times a great grandfather (Fig. 20).

Fig. 20. Lienau after the war, somewhat recovered.

About the Author's Grandson

Ted Simonsen grew up in a German-American household during WWII when Germany was the enemy of the United States. He could understand German but not speak it until the 10th grade when he learned it in school. In 1952 he and his sister went by ship to visit their grandparents for the first time. They spent four months in their Flensburg home getting to know each other, visiting friends, places, and relatives. After high school graduation, he joined the U.S. Army and after Basic Training went to Fort Belvoir Engineer School. Next he was sent to the 984th Engineer Co. in Kaiserslautern, Germany. Here he worked on the maintenance and repair of tractors and graders, etc. During annual leaves he was able to visit his grandparents again and learn more and more about them. Next, he studied mechanical and electrical engineering at NCE (Newark College of Engineering) receiving a BSEE degree in 1961. Lastly, he worked for GE (General Electric Co.) in several departments, ending up as Senior Design Engineer at GE Ordnance Systems, located in Pittsfield, MA. He retired in 1992 and has become an amateur water color painter. Ted currently lives in Panama City Beach, FL.

Ted Simonsen.

Ted Simonsen and his Great Grandson.